THE FIREBOX

THE FIREBOX

Poetry in Britain and Ireland after 1945

Edited by Sean O'Brien

PICADOR

First published 1998 by Picador

an imprint of Macmillan Publishers Ltd
25 Eccleston Place, London SW1W 9NF
and Basingstoke

Associated companies throughout the world

ISBN 0 330 37255 6 (hardback)
ISBN 0 330 36918 0 (trade paperback)

5 7 9 8 6 4

A CIP catalogue record for this book is available from
the British Library.

Typeset by SetSystems Ltd, Saffron Walden, Essex
Printed and bound in Great Britain by
Mackays of Chatham plc, Chatham, Kent

Contents

Contents – ix

Contents – xiii

Contents – xxiii

A Note on Principles of Selection

It is the purpose of this anthology to reveal the strength and diversity of its chosen period, concentrating on poetry which thinks of itself as resident in the post-war world even when it harks back beyond the great divide of 1939–45. To have included work by poets who became established in the years before 1945 would have meant producing a very different kind of book, in which the arguments suggested by this one, and the relationships of the poems included, would have been obscured. At the other end of the scale, it seemed unwise to include younger poets whose reputation does not yet rest on a substantial body of work. As a result, and with regret, a number of writers with only one book to their names have had to be excluded. It is likely that future editions will be able to represent them. Some latitude has been permitted, however, in the earlier pages of the book. For example, Basil Bunting was publishing his poems and being anthologized by Ezra Pound in the pre-war years, but it is to *Briggflatts* (1966) that present-day readers owe their initial awareness of his work. Patrick Kavanagh was at work in the 1930s and *The Great Hunger* appeared during wartime. Gavin Ewart (like some older Scots poets) was published before the war but ceased publication for many years, while Roy Fuller, though beginning as a disciple of Auden in the late 1930s, wrote prolifically for the next half-century, undefined by any school or tendency. In the case of Keith Douglas (1920–44), no comprehensive edition of his work was available until after 1945.

Even taking into account the exclusions mentioned above, an editor is always aware that this or that handful of poems would give a fuller picture and do justice to a poet undeserving of neglect.

Introduction

From the perspective of the late 1990s it might seem presumptuous or anachronistic to offer an anthology of post-war poetry from Britain and Ireland. For one thing, some ideas of nation and nationality no longer seem as respectable or secure as they might have done even a generation ago. In the aftermath of the Thatcherite assault on the post-war consensus, and while the death-struggle of Englishness is waged in the counsels of Europe, the term 'British' continues to irk the Scots and the Welsh, who sometimes read it as a synonym for 'English', and whose developing political independence (like that of Northern Ireland) derives in no small part from a cultural assurance which their English neighbours may in fact envy. Further, to include the work of Irish poets – from North or South – as if it were part of the same enterprise as English poetry may suggest arrogance, or compensation for the mediocrity of the domestic product. Given this minefield of implication, the reason for the contents of this anthology had better be made clear at the outset. Like a number of poets of my generation, born in the 1950s, I am of mixed Irish and English parentage, born, brought up and educated in England, but still at some level attached to Ireland. Irish poetry forms part of the imaginative community to which we feel we belong; and this residual fidelity is accompanied by an openness to other literary cultures – Scots, Welsh, Caribbean – with which we share a language (there are also poets represented here from America, Australia and New Zealand). This inclusive pleasure has also been the experience of many of our contemporaries and successors from rather different backgrounds. As the various literatures have revealed their contours more clearly, so they have gained in attraction. Politically distinct, they retain an imaginative intimacy which the English reader would be wise to acknowledge.

For an art form often consigned to a quiet corner by those who never read it, poetry displays a vigour verging on ferocity. It re-creates and renews itself, replenishing the fire which by tradition Prometheus stole from the gods – the fire of creation, understanding and language itself. The title of this anthology, *The Firebox*, is intended to suggest that intense and sustained energy, the transforming fire of the imagination. This has been a period as poetically rich as any since the Romantics. It has seen the melting of familiar categories and the establishment of unexpected connections, the emergence of new poetries from formerly unsuspected sources. It is this richness, durability and surprise that *The Firebox* seeks to celebrate and commend.

The range of this anthology raises a difficult question for the editor. How can such a variety of work, extending across half a century and arising from several cultures, be introduced in such a way that the interested non-specialist reader has some sense of the shape of the period, its major features, schools, debates, lines of development and so on? In the end, of course, the poems should speak for themselves, and in any case the most important aim of this book is to give pleasure – but it may help the poems to be heard, and assist the reader's enjoyment and understanding, if they are accompanied by a sketch of the context from which they emerge. Needless to say, much that is of importance cannot even be touched on in these few pages.

In a famous introductory essay to an earlier anthology, *The New Poetry*, written nearly forty years ago, A. Alvarez proposed that in English poetry a series of 'negative feedbacks' had taken place, the effect of which was to turn poets away from the lessons of the modernists (such as T. S. Eliot) and towards traditional practices (as embodied by Thomas Hardy). The effect, he suggested, was to encourage a poetry of modest intentions and means, easily outgunned by Americans such as Robert Lowell and Sylvia Plath, the so-called Confessional poets, inheritors of modernist ambition. It seems to be the nature of literary movements to evade the grasp (Romanticism is a famous earlier example), and so we should be grateful to J. A. Cuddon for an admirably clear description of modernism:

As far as literature is concerned modernism reveals a breaking away from established rules, traditions and conventions, fresh ways of looking at man's position and function in the universe and many (in some cases remarkable) experiments in form and style. It is particularly concerned with language and how to use it (representationally or otherwise) and with *writing itself*.

> – *The Penguin Dictionary of Literary Terms and Literary Theory*, 1992, p. 551

Forty years on, Alvarez's American exemplars seem if anything in some ways less curious about language and writing than some poets from this side of the Atlantic (one or two of whom Alvarez was able to include in his anthology). The currents of modernism, it is now clear, have run strongly and variously through the post-war period, for example in the work of Basil Bunting, W. S. Graham (who enquires directly: 'What is the Language Using Us For?'), Edwin Morgan, Christopher Middleton, Charles Tomlinson and Roy Fisher among the older poets represented here – all of whom have an internationalist dimension on their work – and Peter Didsbury, John Ash and even Paul Muldoon among their successors. This is a very varied list in itself, suggesting that any description of modernism will need to include the diversity of its exponents.

When Alvarez was assembling *The New Poetry* there appeared to be two dominant strands in English poetry – the Movement, represented by Philip Larkin, and the renewal of nature poetry spearheaded by Ted Hughes. Alvarez makes his preferences clear. Hughes has energy and confidence. He seems equal to the brutalities of the age of Auschwitz and the H-bomb, while the Movement enshrines a peculiarly English inhibition – 'negative feedback' writ large, attuned to the social and economic austerity of the early 1950s. The Movement's own anthologist, Robert Conquest, summed up the mood of sombre discretion by describing the contributors to *New Lines* (1956, including Larkin, Donald Davie, Thom Gunn and Elizabeth Jennings) as united by 'a negative determination to avoid bad principles'. The critic John Press went a little further:

> The most one can say is that ... contributors to the
> anthology shared a common tone, a suspicion of large
> rhetorical gestures, a belief that intellect and the moral
> judgement must play a part in shaping a poem. The
> addiction to defensive irony and the fear of unregulated,
> unscrutinized emotion were sometimes elevated into
> moral principles.
>
> – *A Map of Modern English Verse*, 1969, p. 253

This reserve, it may be inferred, owed much to the experience of the Second World War, when large political gestures and the exploitation of emotive language had been put in the service of barbarism. Although we can trace the influence of Auden on the formality of much Movement poetry, the attitudes of the 1930s seemed to belong to a remote and hardly comprehensible past, as Donald Davie shows in 'Remembering the Thirties'. As well as exhibiting political caution, the Movement also saw itself in reaction against the poetic excesses of the 1940s, exemplified by the hysterical irrationalism of the New Apocalypse School which brought brief fame to such poets as Henry Treece and J. F. Hendry. But if Press's description appears fair when applied to a kind of Mean Average Movement poem, the best works of Movement poets exceed the terms of the description. Larkin's 'The Whitsun Weddings', for example, 'lifts off', as the poet put it, into a visionary celebration of human potential and fertility:

> ... We slowed again,
> And as the tightened brakes took hold, there swelled
> A sense of falling, like an arrow-shower
> Sent out of sight, somewhere becoming rain.

And in the work of Thom Gunn the academic tendency of Movement practice is subverted by what we now see as gay love poems, and by a fascination with violent self-dramatization which runs quite counter to alleged Movement principles. The aimless journeying of the motorcycle gang in 'On the Move', for example, has to serve as its own existential justification: 'One is always nearer by not keeping still.' If this demonstrates that a good poet will always evade definition, it also suggests the fragility of the Movement as a critical term. The name itself no longer describes the defining presence in the post-war period (as it seemed to do even fifteen years ago), and the best poems, as Gunn says, stand 'apart, winnowed from failures'. A later generation of highly individual poets associated with the Group initiated by Philip Hobsbaum – including Peter Porter, Peter Redgrove, Alan Brownjohn and Fleur Adcock – seems to have comparable claims to attention.

Philip Larkin doubted the value of the 'myth-kitty' into which the poets the Movement opposed were fond of dipping, but common sense alone could hardly be expected to satisfy all tastes. The major alternative to the Movement was Ted Hughes, who from mid-career has gradually disclosed an eclectic personal mythology ranging from the scorched psychic earth of *Crow* by way of *Gaudete* to the House of Windsor. What has maintained Hughes's readability for those sceptical about his myth-making is the matter-of-fact splendour and precision of his re-creations of the natural world. If he owes much to D. H. Lawrence, he also has an indirect connection with modernist concerns: like Gunn's (the work of the two was at one time read and published in tandem) Hughes's early language had a strongly Shakespearean-Jacobean cast, which may be seen in part as an inheritance from T. S. Eliot's influential critical writings on that period.

Two contemporaries of Hughes have also been acclaimed in different quarters for work with mythopoeic inclinations. Peter Redgrove's natural-scientific mysticism draws the poison from Hughes's world in favour of celebration and perpetual metamorphosis. The sombre and scholarly Geoffrey Hill has used the past – the Wars of the Roses in 'Funeral Music', as well as the half-legendary King Offa of Mercia in *Mercian Hymns* – to find dramatic correlatives for his fascination with religious belief, political violence and the nature of Englishness. Hill matches Cuddon's description of modernism very well, in that questions about writing and truthfulness are often in the forefront of his poetry: 'The Songbook of Sebastian Arrurruz', for example, is a 'classically' modernist text in its employment of an imaginary poet-narrator (cf. Pound's 'Hugh Selwyn Mauberley' and the multiple poet-selves created by Fernando Pessoa).

If there was a good deal in post-war English poetry that felt itself to be in reaction against modernism, there was, then, also much work written in the light of its example. The student of literature at the turn of the 1970s could be forgiven for feeling trapped between the battalions of pre-war modernism and post-war reaction. Several things happened to change this state of affairs.

In Northern Ireland from the 1960s onwards a number of important poets emerged – a first wave of Seamus Heaney, Derek Mahon and Michael Longley, and a younger generation including Ciaran Carson, Tom Paulin, Mebdh McGuckian and Paul Muldoon. In no sense do these poets form a school or movement (though a later version of the Group, again prompted by Philip Hobsbaum, had an effect on poets in Belfast.) Some have addressed works to each other and they make a formidable, and many would say exemplary, presence in contemporary poetry. Among their concerns, inevitably, have been history, politics, sectarianism and violence: the flowering of poetry in Northern Ireland coincides with the Civil Rights Movement, which in turn owes much to the 1947 Education Act (the equivalent of the 1944 Butler Act in England). The enormous popularity of Heaney's work has – apart from its quality as writing – much to do with a sense among English readers (and educators in particular) that he could be assimilated as part of the tradition of English nature poetry running from Wordsworth through to Hardy and Edward Thomas. More than any Irish poet since Yeats, Heaney has created a readership for himself beyond Ireland. In his poetry from *Wintering Out* onwards and in his vivid and accomplished critical writings, he has been careful to show the complexity of his inheritance – yes to the English Romantic tradition, but yes, too, to the farmer-poet Patrick Kavanagh, and to poetry in Irish (see his translation, *Sweeney Astray*). His prominence invites a fresh look at some of his immediate predecessors. He has also written as an advocate of Eastern European poetry (Czeslaw Milosz, Zbigniew Herbert) and of the St Lucian Derek Walcott. Such internationalism also characterizes his contemporaries from the North of Ireland – see, for example, Derek Mahon's insistently *European* reading of the world – and is a practical rejoinder to the element of philistinism and xenophobia present in some Movement poets and in English culture at large. Another feature uniting some of these poets is their establishment of a new benchmark for stylishness. Mahon and Muldoon in particular have had marked effects on the attitudes of younger poets towards form.

Among near-contemporaries of Heaney in England and Scotland, political themes also begged questions of method. Where sectarianism and imperialism pressed into Heaney's work, Tony Harrison addressed the issues of language, class and power 'from below', in his ongoing sonnet sequence, *The School of Eloquence*. In this rawly autobiographical but subtly managed project, the most aristocratic of verse forms is adapted to the conflict of 'Them & [uz]', made to speak with a working-class Leeds accent, to smash 'the looms of owned language', and to dream of how the hitherto speechless or tongue-tied might take control of the means of literary production. The working-class scholarship boy sets about taking his revenge:

> So right, yer buggers, then. We'll occupy
> Your lousy leasehold poetry!

Similar concerns emerge in a more fictive and historically elaborate way in the work of the Scots poet Douglas Dunn. In *Barbarians* he employs a number of traditional models in a series of 'Pastorals', which move from an eighteenth-century farm-labourers' revolt to consider the position of the artist in a class-divided society, the nature of English imperialism and the possibility (now partly fulfilled) of Scottish nationhood. Between them, Harrison and Dunn have created the possibility of renovating an explicitly political dimension largely lost from poetry in Britain after the Second World War. They differ from their 1930s predecessors (W. H. Auden, Stephen Spender) by coming from the class whose concerns they speak for. Another important work in this field, showing the importance this poetic generation accorded E. P. Thompson's *The Making of the English Working Class*, is Jeffrey

Wainwright's '1815', which juxtaposes industrialism ('the English miracle') with the battle of Waterloo, in a series of brief tableaux of enormous pathos and force.

There have always been women poets writing in English. Their difficulty has been in getting the fact acknowledged – and then ensuring that it is remembered. The work of women poets has had several eloquent advocates in recent years, among them contributors to this anthology, such as Fleur Adcock and Carol Rumens. From the standpoint of the present it looks as if a scaffolding of assumptions about women's writing has recently been removed – for example, that the woman poet is in some sense peculiar or a special case – and the power and range of women poets has been made plain. (One sign of the confidence of women poets is the debate over the value and effectiveness of women-only anthologies.) While senior figures such as U. A. Fanthorpe and Elma Mitchell are firmly established in the affections of readers, the pivotal writer in this period was an American, Sylvia Plath. Plath's personal tragedy has sometimes seemed to displace her poems in public discussion, but her work from 1960 onwards amounts to a major achievement, a charting of emotional and psychological extremes as precise as it is harrowing. It is harder to say what she has meant to her successors: her legacy has been complex and indirect, and little of value has been written in emulation of her; but she provides a marker for those who come after, while her individuality is an encouragement to the very varied work done by poets such as Rumens, Medbh McGuckian, Jo Shapcott, Carol Ann Duffy and Kathleen Jamie, all of whom have ignored the victim's role into which Plath seems to have been put. Any discussion of contemporary poetry will have to take account of these and other names. Among feminism's greatest successes is the prominence it has gained for women writers. The position of women poets has never been stronger, and the range of their work, from Rumens's political realism, to McGuckian's interiorized *écriture feminine*, from Duffy's highly theatrical monologues to Jamie's lyric directness, defies any ready categorization. As the poems here show, one constant strain is sensual and erotic.

If the strength of women's poetry has produced a widening of the frame of reference, black poetry has required a further and perhaps more radical adjustment, since for many black writers poetry seems to be most fully alive as *an event*, in performance, maintaining an unbroken link with oral tradition. This can make its strengths hard to represent adequately on the page: Linton Kwesi Johnson's densely scored rhythms ask to be heard amid the heat and fire of a reggae band, while Grace Nichols speaks on behalf of a communal history and experience in a way rarely available to poets trained in English traditions. It is to state the obvious to say that black poetry is often political – see the scorching anger with which Jackie Kay confronts institutional racism, or Fred D'Aguiar's wry meditation on belonging and outsiderdom. What black writers have also offered readers in Britain has been a sense of international possibility present in poetry of the Caribbean and the post-war diaspora.

In a variety of ways, both obvious and less so, all these developments have been affected by postmodernism. Postmodernism differs from modernism in that it might be described as a condition rather than an intention: it reflects endurance rather than, like Eliot, depicting catastrophe. But as Cuddon says, postmodernism 'is no easier to define than many other -isms. Like them, it is amorphous by nature.' And as he also points out, 'postmodernism is still happening. When something else develops from it, it will, perhaps, be easier to identify, describe and classify.' Of postmodernism's numerous features, the most relevant and prominent include a renewed interest in the use of narrative; a sceptical view of the fixity of meaning; and the tendency to use various historical literary forms as an ironic pattern-book, so that a postmodernist poem may often seem partly a parody and writing is often construed as rewriting. Some of these features were noted by Blake Morrison and Andrew Motion in the introduction to the important 1982 anthology *The Penguin Book of Contemporary British Poetry* and seen as evidence of a new spirit of adventure. Clearly these are not wholly novel practices, but their conjunction can, for instance, lend poems a playful aspect even when the theme is grave, with the intention of estranging the readers so that we look afresh at familiar matters. A seeming mismatch of tone and context has become the stock-in-trade of discourse far beyond the confines of poetry, and indeed now seems to be widely taken as the proper definition of irony.

The most visible employment of postmodernist techniques is to be found in the Martian poetry (so christened by James Fenton) which emerged in the late 1970s, written by Craig Raine and Christopher Reid. Raine's 'A Martian Sends a Postcard Home' is in a sense the Martian manifesto. It consists of a series of suggestive misunderstandings of life on earth, represented largely by ingenious use of visual simile and metaphor:

> Caxtons are mechanical birds with many wings
> and some are treasured for their markings –
>
> they cause the eyes to melt
> and the body to shriek without pain.

This approach was anticipated by the Scots poet Norman MacCaig (see 'Summer Farm'), as well as by the American Elizabeth Bishop. Bishop's little masterpiece 'The Bight' might seem the last word on the subject, while Martianism in England has not spread and plays an increasingly subordinate role in the work of its leading exponents. The narrative form of postmodernist poetry in England can be represented by Andrew Motion himself, whose 'Secret Narratives' read like cross-sections through novels, richly atmospheric but in some sense unresolved, as – we are to infer – life is felt to be. Philip Larkin's declared inability to understand his young friend's poem 'The Letter' seems to mark a significant division in attitudes. Rather more radical is the handful of poems by James Fenton in which postmodernism in English poetry is most fully tested. Fenton, too, under the influence of John Fuller, incorporates narrative or pseudo-narrative elements into exploded, labyrinthine readings of the class system or the English art of murder, but in addition the whole ground of the poem's (and the reader's) enquiry is thrown into doubt. The strange, celebratory excursions of Peter

Didsbury offer a counterbalance both to Fenton's pessimism and to the shellshocked ironies of Michael Hofmann.

For the most confident and expansive postmodernist poetry, however, we should look again to Ireland. Paul Muldoon has taken narrative, for example, blending ancient literary myth with a Chandleresque modernity ('Immram') and a protean shifting of identity, and propelled the mixture sidelong though several increasingly ambitious poems by means of an extremely fertile ear for varieties of rhyme. The phantasmal lightness of Muldoon's touch, his elusive tone and *faux-naif* charm have attracted many admirers both at home and in England. A related, equally impressive but formally rather different approach has been that of Ciaran Carson, whose long, unspooling lines make strange and poignant 'narratives' from a storyteller's habitual digressions. To this repertoire Carson has added an absorbing re-examination of some nineteenth-century French Symbolist poems of Baudelaire and Rimbaud. The slightly older and more overtly comic Paul Durcan has confronted the repressiveness of life in the Republic of Ireland in a series of wilful fantasies, featuring pregnant nuns and bans on colour photography:

> Colour pictures showed reality to be rich and various
> Whereas reality in point of fact was the opposite . . .
> – 'Irish Hierarchy Bans Colour Photography'

A more complex utopian strain in Durcan's poetry operates on a similar principle, acting *as if the world were otherwise.*

Postmodernism as it occurs in the work of women poets has much to do with the rendering of facets of consciousness and identity for which poetry has not found room before. Selima Hill's crazed erotic monologues, headlong but exact, and Jo Shapcott's comically vertiginous projections (see 'Goat') promise the opening up of whole new territories which criticism has not yet entirely caught up with.

The work of a number of poets born since 1960 suggests that poetry continues to renew itself and to do so from many sources. Simon Armitage's poems reveal an interesting mixture of influences, from the self-consciously hip and playful work of the New York poet Frank O'Hara to Armitage's fellow Yorkshireman, Ted Hughes, together with an admixture of sound-play *à la* Muldoon, which Armitage can shift in the direction of comic patter. An ambitious and prolific poet, he is habitually paired with his southern counterpart, Glyn Maxwell, a writer of similar facility and ingenuity who had made an unmistakable style (acclaimed and derided with equal conviction) from wanton obliquity of meaning and syntax, as well as from a capacity for an air of Audensque judgement and gravitas. Both poets have been prominent participants in the various campaigns to connect poetry with the larger audience which has in recent years been felt to be waiting just out of reach. If nothing else, the pair's capacity and readiness to combine an element of populism with artistic integrity will provide useful evidence about our immediate period.

Among Armitage and Maxwell's contemporaries, several of the most impressive are Scots. W. N. Herbert, Kathleen Jamie, Don Paterson and Robert Crawford show that the vitality of contemporary Scottish fiction is matched by its poets. In different ways, Herbert, Crawford and Jamie offer us maps of a diverse, exciting nation as it approaches independence. As Crawford, also a significant critic, has remarked, homogeneity is the enemy – something evident in these poets' ready transition between English and Scots and back. Herbert's encyclopedic labours make present the resources of a Scots language which he feels is capable of criticizing and extending English, while Jamie's work has gained an enviable lyrical authority. A salutary effect of the current confidence of Scots poetry is to invite the reader back through what recent years have shown to be a most distinguished century of writing. As it closes, it seems clear that W. S. Graham, Edwin Morgan and Douglas Dunn are major figures. Even as we study it, the map changes and discloses a larger world.

A Note of Thanks

Thanks are due to several people without whose help and advice this project would have been a good deal less enjoyable to work on. They include Michael Donaghy, Douglas Houston, Mary Mount, Peg Osterman, Don Paterson, Jo Shapcott and Bill Swainson. My debt to the enormous practical assistance, the good sense, tolerant support and unfailing encouragement of Gerry Wardle has long ceased to be calculable.

Basil Bunting, 1900–85

Born to a Quaker family in Northumberland, Bunting served a prison term as a conscientious objector in 1918. He spent much of his life abroad, in Paris, Rapallo, the United States, the Canary Islands and Persia (and was appointed vice consul in Isfahan in 1945). He also worked as a sailor and a journalist, and, on returning to the North East of England, was sub-editor on a local paper. The young poet Tom Pickard encouraged Bunting to resume writing after a long silence. The result was *Briggflatts* (1966), a major poem of love, time and loss, followed by the gathering of his earlier work. Bunting had known and worked with Ezra Pound (who included his poems in his 1933 *Activist Anthology*) as well as the Objectivist Louis Zukofsky. His work stands boldly outside the mainstream of English poetry, retaining a modernist purity of intent and range of reference, while offering an engraved, uncluttered musicality (he called his long poems sonatas) which is felt by many readers to be distinctively northern in spirit. See *Complete Poems*, associate editor Richard Caddel (1994). Victoria Forde's *The Poetry of Basil Bunting* (1991) is a detailed study.

from Briggflatts

I

Brag, sweet tenor bull,
descant on Rawthey's madrigal,
each pebble its part
for the fells' late spring.
Dance tiptoe, bull,
black against may.
Ridiculous and lovely
chase hurdling shadows
morning into noon.
May on the bull's hide
and through the dale
furrows fill with may,
paving the slowworm's way.

A mason times his mallet
to a lark's twitter,
listening while the marble rests,
lays his rule
at a letter's edge,
fingertips checking,
till the stone spells a name
naming none,
a man abolished.
Painful lark, labouring to rise!
The solemn mallet says:
In the grave's slot
he lies. We rot.

Decay thrusts the blade,
wheat stands in excrement
trembling. Rawthey trembles.
Tongue stumbles, ears err

for fear of spring.
Rub the stone with sand,
wet sandstone rending
roughness away. Fingers
ache on the rubbing stone.
The mason says: Rocks
happen by chance.
No one here bolts the door,
love is so sore.

Stone smooth as skin,
cold as the dead they load
on a low lorry by night.
The moon sits on the fell
but it will rain.
Under sacks on the stone
two children lie,
hear the horse stale,
the mason whistle,
harness mutter to shaft,
felloe to axle squeak,
rut thud the rim,
crushed grit.

Stocking to stocking, jersey to jersey,
head to a hard arm,
they kiss under the rain,
bruised by their marble bed.
In Garsdale, dawn;
at Hawes, tea from the can.
Rain stops, sacks
steam in the sun, they sit up.
Copper-wire moustache,
sea-reflecting eyes
and Baltic plainsong speech
declare: By such rocks
men killed Bloodaxe.

Fierce blood throbs in his tongue,
lean words.
Skulls cropped for steel caps
huddle round Stainmore.
Their becks ring on limestone,
whisper to peat.
The clogged cart pushes the horse downhill.
In such soft air
they trudge and sing,
laying the tune frankly on the air.
All sounds fall still,
fellside bleat,
hide-and-seek peewit.

Her pulse their pace,
palm countering palm,
till a trench is filled,
stone white as cheese
jeers at the dale.
Knotty wood, hard to rive,
smoulders to ash;
smell of October apples.
The road again,
at a trot.
Wetter, warmed, they watch
the mason meditate
on name and date.

Rain rinses the road,
the bull streams and laments.
Sour rye porridge from the hob
with cream and black tea,
meat, crust and crumb.
Her parents in bed
the children dry their clothes.
He has untied the tape
of her striped flannel drawers

4 – Basil Bunting

before the range. Naked
on the pricked rag mat
his fingers comb
thatch of his manhood's home.

Gentle generous voices weave
over bare night
words to confirm and delight
till bird dawn.
Rainwater from the butt
she fetches and flannel
to wash him inch by inch,
kissing the pebbles.
Shining slowworm part of the marvel.
The mason stirs:
Words!
Pens are too light.
Take a chisel to write.

Every birth a crime,
every sentence life.
Wiped of mould and mites
would the ball run true?
No hope of going back.
Hounds falter and stray,
shame deflects the pen.
Love murdered neither bleeds nor stifles
but jogs the draftsman's elbow.
What can he, changed, tell
her, changed, perhaps dead?
Delight dwindles. Blame
stays the same.

Brief words are hard to find,
shapes to carve and discard:
Bloodaxe, king of York,
king of Dublin, king of Orkney.

Take no notice of tears;
letter the stone to stand
over love laid aside lest
insufferable happiness impede
flight to Stainmore,
to trace
lark, mallet,
becks, flocks
and axe knocks.

Dung will not soil the slowworm's
mosaic. Breathless lark
drops to nest in sodden trash;
Rawthey truculent, dingy.
Drudge at the mallet, the may is down,
fog on fells. Guilty of spring
and spring's ending
amputated years ache after
the bull is beef, love a convenience.
It is easier to die than to remember.
Name and date
split in soft slate
a few months obliterate.

Patrick Kavanagh, 1904–67

Patrick Kavanagh was born in Inniskeen, Co. Monaghan, and like his father was a farmer and a cobbler. *The Great Hunger* (1942) secured his eventual reputation. Long, impassioned, vivid and sombre, at once earthbound and visionary, it debunks romanticized versions of rural life, depicting farming as hard labour and the bachelor male condition as sexually frustrated. The early work of Seamus Heaney owes something to Kavanagh's confident realism. Kavanagh was also a controversialist: in Dublin in the 1950s he waged war on the narrowness of politics and the literary establishment in his short-lived paper, *Kavanagh's Weekly*, and lost a libel action. He developed lung cancer in 1953 but recovered to produce some of his finest lyrics. See *Selected Poems*, edited by Antoinette Quinn (1996). For a grimly amusing account of literary life in Kavanagh's Dublin, see Anthony Cronin's *Dead as Doornails* (1976).

from The Great Hunger

III

Poor Paddy Maguire, a fourteen-hour day
He worked for years. It was he that lit the fire
And boiled the kettle and gave the cows their hay.
His mother tall hard as a Protestant spire
Came down the stairs bare-foot at the kettle-call
And talked to her son sharply: 'Did you let
The hens out, you?' She had a venomous drawl
And a wizened face like moth-eaten leatherette.
Two black cats peeped between the banisters
And gloated over the bacon-fizzling pan.
Outside the window showed tin canisters.
The snipe of Dawn fell like a whirring noise
And Patrick on a headland stood alone.

The pull is on the traces, it is March
And a cold old black wind is blowing from Dundalk.
The twisting sod rolls over on her back –
The virgin screams before the irresistible sock.
No worry on Maguire's mind this day
Except that he forgot to bring his matches.
'Hop back there Polly, hoy back, woa, wae,'
From every second hill a neighbour watches
With all the sharpened interest of rivalry.
Yet sometimes when the sun comes through a gap
These men know God the Father in a tree:
The Holy Spirit is the rising sap,
And Christ will be the green leaves that will come
At Easter from the sealed and guarded tomb.

Primroses and the unearthly start of ferns
Among the blackthorn shadows in the ditch,
A dead sparrow and an old waistcoat. Maguire learns

As the horses turn slowly round the which is which
Of love and fear and things half born to mind.
He stands between the plough-handles and he sees
At the end of a long furrow his name signed
Among the poets, prostitute's. With all miseries
He is one. Here with the unfortunate
Who for half moments of paradise
Pay out good days and wait and wait
For sunlight-woven cloaks. O to be wise
As Respectability that knows the price of all things
And marks God's truth in pounds and pence and farthings.

Norman Cameron, 1905–53

Cameron grew up in Edinburgh and studied at Oxford. He worked as an education officer in Nigeria and as an advertising copywriter. During the war he made propaganda films. He wrote only about seventy poems. 'Green, Green is El Aghir' typifies his uncategorizable blend of urbane elegance and zest. *Collected Poems and Translations*, edited by Warren Hope and Jonathan Barker, appeared in 1990.

Green, Green is El Aghir

Sprawled on the crates and sacks in the rear of the truck,
I was gummy-mouthed from the sun and the dust of the
                                                    track
And the two Arab soldiers I'd taken on as hitch-hikers
At a torrid petrol-dump, had been there on their hunkers
Since early morning. I said, in a kind of French
'On ma'a dit, qu'il y a une belle source d'eau fraîche.
Plus loin, à El Aghir' . . .

                    It was eighty more kilometres
Until round a corner we heard a splashing of waters,
And there, in a green, dark street, was a fountain with
                                                    two faces
Discharging both ways, from full-throated faucets
Into basins, thence into troughs and thence into brooks.
Our negro corporal driver slammed his brakes,
And we yelped and leapt from the truck and went at the
                                                    double
To fill our bidons and bottles and drink and dabble.
Then, swollen with water, we went to an inn for wine.
The Arabs came, too, though their faith might have
                                        stood between.
'After all,' they said, 'it's a boisson,' without contrition.

Green, green is El Aghir. It has a railway-station,
And the wealth of its soil has borne many another fruit,
A mairie, a school and an elegant Salle de Fêtes.
Such blessings, as I remarked, in effect, to the waiter,
Are added unto them that have plenty of water.

John Hewitt, 1907–87

John Hewitt was born in Belfast into a nonconformist Protestant family. His working life was spent in the museum service, in Coventry and latterly in Belfast. He was a socialist, seeking an enlightened nonsectarian meeting of Northern Ireland's twin communities; at the same time, he was proud of his identity as Protestant, Irish, British and European. Hewitt was a traditional, even anachronistic poet, drawn to romantic diction but patiently accurate rather than linguistically spectacular. He was an exemplary figure for younger poets in the North of Ireland, one of whom, Frank Ormsby, edited his *Collected Poems* (1991).

Because I Paced My Thought

Because I paced my thought by the natural world,
the earth organic, renewed with the palpable seasons,
rather than the city falling ruinous, slowly
by weather and use, swiftly by bomb and argument,

I found myself alone who had hoped for attention.
If one listened a moment he murmured his dissent:
this is an idle game for a cowardly mind.
The day is urgent. The sun is not on the agenda.

And some who hated the city and man's unreasoning acts
remarked: He is no ally. He does not say that
Power and Hate are the engines of human treason.
There is no answering love in the yellowing leaf.

I should have made it plain that I stake my future
on birds flying in and out of the schoolroom-window,
on the council of sunburnt comrades in the sun,
and the picture carried with singing into the temple.

Robert Garioch, 1909–81

Robert Garioch was born in Edinburgh and educated at Edinburgh University. He spent much of the Second World War in a German prison camp – an experience which provoked his grim poem 'The Wire'. Though he also wrote in English, Garioch's distinction lies in Scots. Especially drawn to Robert Fergusson, Burns's predecessor, he wrote in the Burns stanza (or 'Standard Habbie') and idiom which his contemporary the Scots modernist Hugh McDiarmid had consciously avoided. Garioch's characteristic work is wry, pithy and economical, memorable in its precision. See *Complete Poetical Works* (1983), edited by Robin Fulton.

Elegy

They are lang deid, folk that I used to ken,
their firm-set lips aa mowdert and agley,
sherp-tempert een rusty amang the cley:
they are baith deid, thae wycelike, bienlie men,

heidmaisters, that had been in pouer for ten
or twenty year afore fate's taiglie wey
brocht me, a young, weill-harnit, blate and fey
new-cleckit dominie, intill their den.

Ane tellt me it was time I learnt to write –
round-haund, he meant – and saw about my hair:
I mind of him, beld-heidit, wi a kyte.

Ane sneerit quarterly – I cuidna square
my savings bank – and sniftert in his spite.
Weill, gin they arena deid, it's time they were.

---

aa mowdert and agley – all mouldering and awry; *wycelike, bienlie*
– sensible, pleasant; *taiglie* – entangling; *weill-harnit, blate and fey*
– well-educated, shy and fated; *new-cleckit dominie* – just-hatched
schoolmaster; *ane tellt me* – one told me; *I mind of him* – I
remember him well; *kyte* – paunch; *gin they arena deid* – if they
aren't dead.

Norman MacCaig, 1910–96

MacCaig was born in Edinburgh, and studied Classics at Edinburgh University. A long career as a primary school teacher was followed by work as a lecturer and then Reader in English at the new University of Stirling. MacCaig was a conscientious objector during the Second World War. He disowned his early work, which was much influenced by the hysterical and often incoherent prophetic manner of the 1940s New Apocalypse school. What he called 'the long haul back to lucidity' began with *Riding Lights* (1956), after which he published prolifically. MacCaig's central themes were perception, the nature of reality and identity, usually examined in his beloved Scots landscapes and handled in a briskly concrete manner with humour and a taste for paradox. His modesty of scale should not disguise the seriousness of his intent. The highly formal manner of his middle phase gave way to an equally accomplished free-verse mode. Latterly he became Scotland's most popular poet, much in demand as a reader of his work. See *Selected Poems*, edited by Douglas Dunn (1997).

Summer Farm

Straws like tame lightnings lie about the grass
And hang zigzag on hedges. Green as glass
The water in the horse-trough shines.
Nine ducks go wobbling by in two straight lines.

A hen stares at nothing with one eye,
Then picks it up. Out of an empty sky
A swallow falls and, flickering through
The barn, dives up again into the dizzy blue.

I lie, not thinking, in the cool, soft grass,
Afraid of where a thought might take me – as
This grasshopper with plated face
Unfolds his legs and finds himself in space.

Self under self, a pile of selves I stand
Threaded on time, and with metaphysic hand
Lift the farm like a lid and see
Farm within farm, and in the centre, me.

The Shore Road

The sea pursued
Its beastlike amours, rolling in its sweat
And beautiful under the moon; and a leaf was
A lively architecture in the light.

The space between
Was full, to splitting point, of presences
So oilily adjustable a walking man
Pushed through and trailed behind no turbulence.

The walking man
With octaves in his guts was a quartertone
In octaves of octaves that climbed up and down
Beyond his hearing, to back parts of the moon.

As though things were
Perpetual chronologies of themselves,
He sounded his small history, to make complete
The interval of leaf and rutting waves.

Or so he thought,
And heard his hard shoes scrunching in the grit,
Smelt salt and iodine in the wind and knew
The door was near, the supper, the small lamplight.

Notations of Ten Summer Minutes

A boy skips flat stones out to sea – each does fine
till a small wave meets it head on and swallows it.
The boy will do the same.

The schoolmaster stands looking out of the window
with one Latin eye and one Greek one.
A boat rounds the point in Gaelic.

Out of the shop comes a stream
of Omo, Weetabix, BiSoDol tablets and a man
with a pocket shaped like a whisky bottle.

Lord V. walks by with the village in his pocket.
Angus walks by
spending the village into the air.

A melodeon is wheezing a clear-throated jig
on the deck of the *Arcadia*. On the shore hills Pan
cocks a hairy ear; and falls asleep again.

The ten minutes are up, except they aren't.
I leave the village, except I don't.
The jig fades to silence, except it doesn't.

Sorley MacLean, 1911–96

Sorley MacLean (Somhairle Macgill-Eain) was born on the island of Raasay into a Gaelic-speaking crofter family, and studied English at Edinburgh University. He served in the Second World War and was wounded at the Battle of El Alamein in 1942. In civilian life, he became an English teacher and later headmaster of Plockton School. Though MacLean wrote some early poems in English, he soon turned to Gaelic. His awareness of both tradition and modernity, and his sense of the political and moral conflicts of the modern era, produced poems which have assured Gaelic a place in modern poetry, and his own major status. MacLean's *From Wood to Ridge: Collected Poems in Gaelic and English* was published in 1989.

Hallaig

'Time, the deer, is in the wood of Hallaig'

The window is nailed and boarded
through which I saw the West
and my love is at the Burn of Hallaig,
a birch tree, and she has always been

between Inver and Milk Hollow,
here and there about Baile-chuirn:
she is a birch, a hazel,
a straight, slender young rowan.

In Screapadal of my people
where Norman and Big Hector were,
their daughters and their sons are a wood
going up beside the stream.

Proud tonight the pine cocks
crowing on the top of Cnoc an Ra,
straight their backs in the moonlight –
they are not the wood I love.

I will wait for the birch wood
until it comes up by the cairn,
until the whole ridge from Beinn na Lice
will be under its shade.

If it does not, I will go down to Hallaig,
to the Sabbath of the dead,
where the people are frequenting,
every single generation gone.

They are still in Hallaig,
MacLeans and MacLeods,
all who were there in the time of Mac Gille Chaluim
the dead have been seen alive.

The men lying on the green
at the end of every house that was,
the girls a wood of birches,
straight their backs, bent their heads.

Between the Leac and Fearns
the road is under mild moss
and the girls in silent bands
go to Clachan as in the beginning,

and return from Clachan,
from Suisnish and the land of the living;
each one young and light-stepping,
without the heartbreak of the tale.

From the Burn of Fearns to the raised beach
that is clear in the mystery of the hills,
there is only the congregation of the girls
keeping up the endless walk,

coming back to Hallaig in the evening,
in the dumb living twilight,
filling the steep slopes,
their laughter a mist in my ears,

and their beauty a film on my heart
before the dimness comes on the kyles,
and when the sun goes down behind Dun Cana
a vehement bullet will come from the gun of Love;

and will strike the deer that goes dizzily,
sniffing at the grass-grown ruined homes;
his eye will freeze in the wood,
his blood will not be traced while I live.

Roy Fuller, 1912–91

Born in Failsworth, Lancashire, Fuller trained as a solicitor and served in Africa during the Second World War. He became a director of the Woolwich Building Society and was Oxford Professor of Poetry 1968–73. Though Fuller lived and worked through the 1930s, the War and the 1950s Movement, his work cannot be 'placed' in any of them. He addresses large themes such as the meaning of history (see 'The Historian') and the value of art while maintaining strong roots in domesticity. Urbane, realistic yet at times visionary ('poetry is something between the dream / and its interpretation'), he was formally ingenious, experimenting with free verse and the sixteen-line 'Meredithian' sonnet. Fuller was also a respected novelist. See *New and Collected Poems 1934–84* (1985).

Poem out of Character

Rapidly moving from the end
To the middle of anthologies,
The poet starts to comprehend
The styles that never can be his.

The dreams of tremendous statements fade,
Inchoate still the passionate rhymes
Of men, the novel verse form made
To satirize and warn the times.

And yet at moments, as in sleep,
Beyond his book float images –
Those four great planets swathed in deep
Ammoniac and methane seas.

He walks the ruined autumn scene –
The trees a landscape painter's brown,
And through the foreground rags, serene
The faded sky, palladian town.

Or thinks of man, his single young,
The failure of the specialized,
Successful type; the curious, long
Years before earth was dramatized:

The West Wind Drift, that monstrous belt
Of sea below the planet's waist:
The twenty-one world cultures felt
Like fathers, doomed to be defaced.

Yes, these vast intimations rise
And still I merely find the words
For symbols of a comic size –
Ambiguous cats and sweets and birds.

Viewed through such tiny apertures
The age presents a leaf, a hair,
An inch of skin; while what enures,
In truth, behind the barrier,

Weltering in blood, enormous joys
Lighting their faces, is a frieze
Of giantesses, gods and boys;
And lions and inhuman trees.

R. S. (Ronald Stuart) Thomas, 1913–

Born in Cardiff, Thomas read Classics at University College, Bangor, and trained for the Anglican ministry at St Michael's college, Llandaff. Like his hero the Metaphysical poet George Herbert, Thomas spent his working life as a parish priest. Learning Welsh as a young man, Thomas immersed himself in Welsh life and history, and his early work combines a vivid sense of landscape and constricted small-farm life with an often bitter historical perspective on the decay of Welsh nationhood ('We fought and were always in retreat / like snow thawing'). From the early 1970s the poems take on a more abstract, speculative cast, emphasizing a theology as bleak as the upland landscape itself. Thomas has controversially expressed sympathy with violent resistance to further English colonization and exploitation of Wales. His brooding, painfully honest work is the major achievement of post-war Anglo-Welsh poetry and he has been spoken of as a possible Nobel laureate. See Complete *Poems* (1993).

Welsh Landscape

To live in Wales is to be conscious
At dusk of the spilled blood
That went to the making of the wild sky,
Dyeing the immaculate rivers
In all their courses.
It is to be aware,
Above the noisy tractor
And hum of the machine
Of strife in the strung woods,
Vibrant with sped arrows.
You cannot live in the present,
At least not in Wales.
There is the language for instance,
The soft consonants
Strange to the ear.
There are cries in the dark at night
As owls answer the moon,
And thick ambush of shadows,
Hushed at the fields' corners.
There is no present in Wales,
And no future;
There is only the past,
Brittle with relics,
Wind-bitten towers and castles
With sham ghosts;
Mouldering quarries and mines;
And an impotent people,
Sick with inbreeding,
Worrying the carcase of an old song.

Evans

Evans? Yes, many a time
I came down this bare flight
Of stairs into the gaunt kitchen
With its wood fire, where crickets sang
Accompaniment to the black kettle's
Whine, and so into the cold
Dark to smother in the thick tide
Of night that drifted about the walls
Of his stark farm on the hill ridge.

It was not the dark filling my eyes
And mouth appalled me; not even the drip
Of rain like blood from the one tree
Weather-tortured. It was the dark
Silting the veins of that sick man
I left stranded upon the vast
And lonely shore of his bleak bed.

On the Farm

There was Dai Puw. He was no good.
They put him in the fields to dock swedes,
And took the knife from him, when he came home
At late evening with a grin
Like the slash of a knife on his face.

There was Llew Puw, and he was no good.
Every evening after the ploughing
With the big tractor he would sit in his chair,
And stare into the tangled fire garden,
Opening his slow lips like a snail.

There was Huw Puw, too. What shall I say?
I have heard him whistling in the hedges
On and on, as though winter
Would never again leave those fields,
And all the trees were deformed.

And lastly there was the girl:
Beauty under some spell of the beast.
Her pale face was the lantern
By which they read in life's dark book
The shrill sentence: God is love.

Reservoirs

There are places in Wales I don't go:
Reservoirs that are the subconscious
Of a people, troubled far down
With gravestones, chapels, villages even;
The serenity of their expression
Revolts me, it is a pose
For strangers, a watercolour's appeal
To the mass, instead of the poem's
Harsher conditions. There are the hills,
Too; gardens gone under the scum
Of the forests; and the smashed faces
Of the farms with the stone trickle
Of their tears down the hills' side.

Where can I go, then, from the smell
Of decay, from the putrefying of a dead
Nation? I have walked the shore
For an hour and seen the English
Scavenging among the remains
Of our culture, covering the sand
Like the tide and, with the roughness
Of the tide, elbowing our language
Into the grave that we have dug for it.

Norman Nicholson, 1914–87

Nicholson was born and lived all his life in the Cumbrian steel town of Millom. His meticulous work is founded on religious faith and his fascination with the local setting. Nicholson is comparable to Charles Causley, in that the affection in which his poems are held grows out of a sense of his loyalties to his 'local habitation'. He is in the best sense a provincial poet. *Collected Poems*, edited by Neil Curry (1994), contains a useful introductory essay.

To the Memory of a Millom Musician

Harry Pelleymounter,
Day by half-pay day,
Served saucepans, fire-lighters, linseed oil
Over his father's counter;
But hard on shutting-up time
He snapped the yale and stayed
Alone with the rolled linoleum
And made the shop-dusk twang.

Harry played
Saxophone, piano,
Piano-accordion
At Christmas party and Saturday hop,
While we in the after-homework dark
Rang smut-bells, sang
'Yes, yes, YES, we have no',
And clicked ink-smitted fingers
At a down-at-heel decade.

The crumbling thirties
Were fumbled and riddled away;
Dirty ten bob coupons
Dropped from the pockets of war.
And Harry, dumped in the lateral
Moraine of middle age,
Strummed back the golden dole-days
When the boys with never a chance
Went without dinner
For a tanner for the dance.

Now Harry's daughter,
Fatherless at fifteen,
Is knitting a history thesis
Of Millom in between

Her youth and Harry's: –
Statistics of gas and water
Rates, percentage of unemployed,
Standard of health enjoyed
By the bare-foot children the police ran dances
To buy boots for – and Harry played.

Pulling at threads of the dead years,
The minutes taken as read –
Spectacled, earnest, unaware
That what the Chairman left unsaid,
The print in the dried-up throat, the true
Breath of the paper bones, once blew
Through Harry's soft-hummed, tumbled tunes
She never listened to.

C. H. (Charles Hubert) Sisson, 1914–

C. H. Sisson was born in Bristol and worked as a senior civil servant. His poems came to attention late. They are grave and sardonic, combining a music which accords with Ezra Pound's dictum 'Compose in sequence of the musical phrase' and an intense Englishness in the treatment of places. Classicist and conservative, Sisson is an acquired taste, and he seems inclined to warn off many who might acquire it. *Collected Poems* appeared in 1998.

Eastville Park

I sat on a bench in Eastville Park
It was Monday the 28th of October
I am your old intentions she said
And all your old intentions are over.

She stood beside me, I did not see her
Her shadow fell on Eastville Park
Not precise or shapely but spreading outwards
On the tatty grass of Eastville Park.

A swan might buckle its yellow beak
With the black of its eye and the black of its mouth
In a shepherd's crook, or the elms impend
Nothing of this could be said aloud.

I did not then sit on a bench
I was a shadow under a tree
I was a leaf the wind carried
Around the edge of the football game.

No need for any return for I find
Myself where I left myself – in the lurch
There are no trams but I remember them
Wherever I went I came here first.

Sidney Goodsir Smith, 1915–75

Sidney Goodsir Smith was born in New Zealand and studied at Oxford. His use of Scots differs from both McDiarmid's and Burns's, looking back to the fifteenth and sixteenth centuries. As a lyric poet, Goodsir Smith was pithy, economical and capable of great poignancy (see 'The Mither's Lament'). He was also an amply gifted comedian, as 'Slugabed' shows. *Collected Poems* was published in 1975. His verse play *The Wallace* appeared in 1960.

Slugabed

from *Under the Eildon Tree*

Here I ligg, Sydney Slugabed Godless Smith,
The Smith, the Faber, ποιητής and Makar,
And Oblomov has nocht to learn me,
Auld Oblomov has nocht on me
Liggan my lane in bed at nune
Gantan at gray December haar,
A cauld, scummie, hauf-drunk cup o' tea
      At my bed-side,
      Luntan Virginian fags
– The New World thus I haud in fief
And levie kyndlie tribute. Black men slave
Aneath a distant sun to mak for me
Cheroots at hauf-a-croun the box.
   Wi ase on the sheets, ase on the cod,
And crumbs of toast under my bum,
Scrievan the last great coronach
O' the westren flickeran bourgeois world.
   Eheu fugaces!
                  Lacrimæ rerum!
Nil nisi et cætera ex cathedra
          Requiescat up your jumper.

O, michtie Stalin in the Aist!
Could ye but see me nou,
The type, endpynt and final blume
O' decadent capitalistical thirldom
   – It took five hunder year to produce me –
Och, could ye but see me nou

here I ligg – here I lie; ποιητής – and poet; *my lane* – alone;
gantan – gaping; *haar* – mist; *luntan* – smoking; *ase* – ash; *cod* –
pillow; *coronach* – elegy; *thirldom* – servitude.

What a sermon could ye gie
    Further frae the Hailie Kremlin
Athort the mountains o' Europe humman
Till Swack! at my front door, the great *Schloss Schmidt*
That's *Numéro Cinquante* (ПЯТЬДЕСЯТ* ye ken)
In the umquhile pairk o' Craigmillar House
Whar Marie Stewart o the snawie blee
Aince plantit ane o' a thousand treen.

    Losh, what a sermon yon wad be!
For Knox has nocht on Uncle Joe
And Oblomov has nocht on Smith
    And sae we come by a route maist devious
    Til the far-famed Aist-West Synthesis!
    Beluved by Hugh that's beluved by me
And the baith o' us loe the barley-bree –
But wha can afford to drink the stuff?
    Certies no auld Oblomov!
    – And yet he does! Whiles!
But no as muckle as Uncle Joe – I've smaa dout!
НА ЗГОРОВЬЕ† then, auld Muscovite!

Thus are the michtie faaen,
Thus the end o' a michtie line,
Dunbar til Smith the Slugabed
Whas luve burns brichter nor them aa
And whas dounfaain is nae less,
    Deid for a ducat deid
By the crueltie o' his ain maistress.

---

bummlan – bustling; *humman* – humming; *umquhile* – former;
v*blee* – complexion; *loe* – love; *barley-bree* – whisky; *no as muckle*
– not as much; *whas luve burns brichter nor them aa* – whose love
burns no less bright than anyone's; *dounfain* – fall from
respectability.

* *piat' desiat* – fifty; † *Na zdorovye* – good health

Gavin Ewart, 1916–95

While still at school Ewart published poems in Geoffrey Grigson's *New Verse*, the leading magazine of the 1930s. *Poems and Songs* appeared in 1938, but he published no more collections until the mid-sixties, after which a torrent of work continued until his death, making Ewart the best-loved light-verse poet of the post-war period. A determined breaking of sexual taboos was his major theme, and Ewart relished an ingenious handling of matter-of-fact physical vulgarity. His preoccupation was matched by an immense versatility: few other poets can have tried as many stanzas and metres. See *The Collected Ewart 1933–1980* (1980) and *Collected Poems 1980–1990* (1991).

Fiction: A Message

'My dear fellow!' said the great poet, putting his arm
                          affably round Ponsonby's neck,
'I respect your feelings for Gertrude. I realize they have
                          something to do with sec
or secs or whatever they call it. Of course in my little
                   backwater I haven't moved with the times –
just listen to the bells of St Josef – how I love those chimes!'

Down below, the Austrian lake reflected his agonized
                        incomprehension sleepily in the sun.
'I'm at the end of my tether!' cried Ponsonby. 'But you –
                        your race is nearly run –
I look to you for a message. I know that behind her
                spectacles she has the most beautiful eyes,
I've heard her playing Chopin at midnight with rapt,
                        adoring cries!'

'These things are sent to try us' said Anzeiger. 'You'll
                  find something in Apollonius of Rhodes,
or one of the Desert Fathers, that proves fairly
                conclusively that women are toads.'
'I've told myself so, yet I often have the most
                incomprehensible puzzling dreams.
I dream of the Kaiserhof, of milk churns, of chocolate
                        creams.

Sometimes I run into a dark wood of feathery soft
                     perfumed aromatic trees
or I'm sinking in unimaginable sweetness like honey,
                   right up to my knees,
or I see Gertrude waving from a cottage with a very
                 attractive rose-circled door.
I'm wearing my Norfolk jacket and, I'm ashamed to say,
                        nothing more!'

'That sounds like the Flesh' pondered Anzeiger, fingering
                              gently Ponsonby's fair curls.
'We know well that St Anthony was tempted in dreams
                              by demons and dancing girls.
Though these apparitions, old fellow, seem so irrational,
                              so disturbing, So unaccountably odd,
I think we can safely assume, in your case, they don't
                              come from God.

Though, of course, He has been known to work in some
                              really very mysterious ways.'
'But what shall I do?' cried Ponsonby. 'Offer it up. Just
                              pray and give praise.
We'll take the pony and trap and go down on Sunday,
                              dear boy, to Linz.
The Lord will lend a kindly ear to your account of your
                              sins.'

They turned and walked towards the house, arm in arm.
                              The sun had nearly set.
As they approached the pretty garden, by the last dark
                              sentinel pine trees they met
Gertrude in a light summer dress, confidently smiling,
                              friendly and demure.
Ponsonby smiled back. He was above her. Of that he was
                              now sure.

Charles Causley, 1917–

Apart from war service in the Navy, Causley spent his working life in his birthplace, Launceston in Cornwall, where he was a teacher before taking up full-time writing in the 1950s. War, Cornish life and legend, and stories from the Bible are the important sources of his work. He has forged a ballad style which is at once clear and mysterious, 'traditional' and highly individual. His work is often accessible to and much enjoyed by children ('The Ballad of the Bread Man', 'Timothy Winters') and driven by an adult sense of loss and horror, as in 'Devonport' and, included here, 'Armistice Day'. He is one of a small number of post-war poets to achieve genuine popularity. See *Collected Poems* (1997).

Armistice Day

I stood with three comrades in Parliament Square
November her freights of grey fire unloading,
No sound from the city upon the pale air,
Above us the sea-bell eleven exploding.

Down by the bands and the burning memorial
Beats all the brass in a royal array,
But at our end we are not so sartorial:
Out of (as usual) the rig of the day.

Starry is wearing a split pusser's flannel
Rubbed, as he is, by the regular tide;
Oxo the ducks that he ditched in the Channel
In June, 1940 (when he was inside).

Kitty recalls his abandon-ship station,
Running below at the Old Man's salute
And (with a deck-watch) going down for duration
Wearing his oppo's pneumonia-suit.

Comrades, for you the black captain of carracks
Writes in Whitehall his appalling decisions,
But as was often the case in the Barracks
Several ratings are not at Divisions.

Into my eyes the stiff sea-horses stare,
Over my head sweeps the sun like a swan.
As I stand alone in Parliament Square
A cold bugle calls, and the city moves on.

pusser's flannel: naval-issue shirt
ducks: white duck-suit
oppo: from 'opposite number'; friend, comrade
pneumonia-suit: tropical rig; or canvas suit worn while painting
ship, etc.

My Young Man's a Cornishman

My young man's a Cornishman
   He lives in Camborne town,
I met him going up the hill
   As I was coming down.

His eye is bright as Dolcoath tin,
   His body as china clay,
His hair as dark as Werrington Wood
   Upon St Thomas's Day.

He plays the rugby football game
   On Saturday afternoon,
And we shall walk on Wilsey Down
   Under the bouncing moon.

My young man's a Cornishman,
   Won't leave me in the lurch,
And one day we shall married be
   Up to Trura church.

He's bought me a ring of Cornish gold,
   A belt of copper made,
At Bodmin Fair for my wedding-dress
   A purse of silver paid.

And I shall give him scalded cream
   And starry-gazy pie,
And make him a saffron cake for tea
   And a pasty for by and by.

My young man's a Cornishman,
   A proper young man is he,
And a Cornish man with a Cornish maid
   Is how it belongs to be.

Martin Bell, 1918–78

Born in Southampton, and educated at the city's University College, Bell was influenced by Auden, by French poets such as Nerval and Laforgue, and by surrealism. A Communist in youth, he remained a man of the Left. Not until 1962 did he receive proper publication (in *Penguin Modern Poets 3*). Bell's friend Peter Porter edited and introduced the posthumous *Complete Poems* (1988).

Winter Coming On

A caricature from Laforgue
(*for Peter Porter*)

Fine feelings under blockade! Cargoes just in from
                                        Kamchatka!
Rain falling and falling and night falling
And how the wind howls . . .
Hallowe'en, Christmas, New Year's Day
Sodden in drizzle – all my tall chimneys –
Industrial smoke through the rain!

No sitting down, all the park-benches are wet.
It's finished, I tell you, till next season.
Park-benches wet and all the leaves rust-eaten,
Horns and their echoes – dying, dying . . .

Rally of rain-clouds! Procession from the Channel –
You certainly spoiled our last free Sunday.

Drizzles:
And in wet woods the spiders' webs
Weigh down with rain-drops: and that's their lot.
O golden delegates from harvest festivals,
Broad suns from cattle-shows,
Where have they buried you?
This evening a sun lies, shagged, on top of the hill,
On a tramp's mattress, rags in the gorse –
A sun as white as a blob of spittle
On tap-room saw-dust, on a litter of yellow gorse,
Of yellow October gorse.
And the horns echo and call to him –
Come back! Won't you come back?

View halloo, Tally-ho . . . Gone away.
O oratorio chorus, when will you be done?

Carrying on like mad things . . .
And there he lies, like a torn-out gland on a neck,
Shivering, with no one by.
Tally-ho, then, and get on with it.
It's good old Winter coming, we know that.

By-passes empty, turnings on main roads
With no Red Riding Hood to be picked up.
Ruts from the wheels of last month's traffic –
Quixotic tram-lines to the rescue of
Cloud-patrols scurrying
Bullied by winds to transatlantic sheep-folds.
Get a move on, it's the well-known season coming, now.
And the wind last night, on top of its form,
Smashing suburban front-gardens – what a mess!
Disturbing my night's sleep with dreams of axes.

These branches, yesterday, had all their dead leaves –
Nothing but compost now, just lying about.
Dear leaves of various shapes and sizes
May a good breeze whirlpool you away
To lie on ponds, decorative,
To glow in the park-keeper's fire,
To stuff ambulance mattresses, comforts
For our soldiers overseas.

Time of year, time of year: the rust is eating,
The rust is gnawing long miles of ennui,
Telegraph-wires along main roads, deserted.

Horns, again horns . . . the echoes dying,
Dying . . .
Now changing key, going north
With the North Wind, Wagnerian,
Up to all those bloody skalds and Vikings . . .

Myself, I can't change key; too many echoes!
What beastly weather! Goodbye autumn, goodbye
                                        ripeness . . .
And here comes the rain with the diligence of an angel.
Goodbye harvest, good-bye baskets for nutting,
And Watteau picnics under the chestnut trees.
It's barrack-room coughing again,
The landlady's horrible herbal tea –
It's TB in the garden suburb,
All the sheer misery of satellite towns.

Wellingtons, long underwear, cash chemists, dreams,
Undrawn curtains over verandas, shores
Of the red-brick sea of roofs and chimney-pots,
Lamp-shades, tea and biscuits, all the picture papers –
You'll have to be my only loves!
(And known them, have you? ritual more portentous
Than the sad pianos tinkling through the dusk,
The registrar's returns of births and deaths,
In small type weekly in the press.)

No! It's the time of year, and this clown of a planet!
O please let the wind, let the high wind
Unknit the bed-socks Time is knitting herself!
Time of year, things tearing, time of year!
O let me every year, every year, just at this time
Join in the chorus, sound the right sour note.

W. S. Graham, 1918–86

W. S. Graham was born in Greenock, Scotland, and later lived in London and Cornwall. His early work shares some of the intense, decorative manner of Dylan Thomas, but Graham gradually purged his writing to its essentials. The book that initially made his name was *The Nightfishing* (1955), a visionary account of a trawler voyage. Recent readers have been more intrigued by *Malcolm Mooney's Land* (1970) and *Implements in their Places* (1977), with their enquiries into the workings of language and the mind – a dry description of a passionate, strangely exposed and finally inimitable style. Graham was also a fine poet of love and friendship. The importance of Graham's work is gradually being recognized. *Selected Poems* (1996) is a good introduction.

Loch Thom

1

Just for the sake of recovering
I walked backward from fifty-six
Quick years of age wanting to see,
And managed not to trip or stumble
To find Loch Thom and turned round
To see the stretch of my childhood
Before me. Here is the loch. The same
Long-beaked cry curls across
The heather-edges of the water held
Between the hills a boyhood's walk
Up from Greenock. It is the morning.

And I am here with my mammy's
Bramble jam scones in my pocket.
The Firth is miles and I have come
Back to find Loch Thom maybe
In this light does not recognize me.

This is a lonely freshwater loch.
No farms on the edge. Only
Heather grouse-moor stretching
Down to Greenock and One Hope
Street or stretching away across
Into the blue moors of Ayrshire.

2

And almost I am back again
Wading the heather down to the edge
To sit. The minnows go by in shoals
Like iron-filings in the shallows.

My mother is dead. My father is dead
And all the trout I used to know
Leaping from their sad rings are dead.

3

I drop my crumbs into the shallow
Weed for the minnows and pinheads.
You see that I will have to rise
And turn round and get back where
My running age will slow for a moment
To let me on. It is a colder
Stretch of water than I remember.

The curlew's cry travelling still
Kills me fairly. In front of me
The grouse flurry and settle. GOBACK
GOBACK GOBACK FAREWELL LOCH THOM.

Lines on Roger Hilton's Watch

Which I was given because
I loved him and we had
Terrible times together.

O tarnished ticking time
Piece with your bent hand,
You must be used to being
Looked at suddenly
In the middle of the night
When he switched the light on
Beside his bed. I hope
You told him the best time
When he lifted you up
To meet the Hilton gaze.

I lift you up from the mantel
Piece here in my house
Wearing your verdigris.
At least I keep you wound
And put my ear to you
To hear Botallack tick.

You realize your master
Has relinquished you
And gone to lie under
The ground at St Just.

Tell me the time. The time
Is Botallack o'clock.
This is the dead of night.

He switches the light on
To find a cigarette
And pours himself a Teachers.
He picks me up and holds me

Near his lonely face
To see my hands. He thinks
He is not being watched.

The images of his dream
Are still about his face
As he spits and tries not
To remember where he was.

I am only a watch
And pray time hastes away.
I think I am running down.

Watch, it is time I wound
You up again. I am
Very much not your dear
Last master but we had
Terrible times together.

Johann Joachim Quantz's Five Lessons

The First Lesson

So that each person may quickly find that
Which particularly concerns him, certain metaphors
Convenient to us within the compass of this
Lesson are to be allowed. It is best I sit
Here where I am to speak on the other side
Of language. You, of course, in your own time
And incident (I speak in the small hours.)
Will listen from your side. I am very pleased
We have sought us out. No doubt you have read
My Flute Book. Come. The Guild clock's iron men
Are striking out their few deserted hours
And here from my high window Brueghel's winter
Locks the canal below. I blow my fingers.

The Second Lesson

Good morning, Karl. Sit down. I have been thinking
About your progress and my progress as one
Who teaches you, a young man with talent
And the rarer gift of application. I think
You must now be becoming a musician
Of a certain calibre. It is right maybe
That in our lessons now I should expect
Slight and very polite impatiences
To show in you. Karl, I think it is true,
You are now nearly able to play the flute.

Now we must try higher, aware of the terrible
Shapes of silence sitting outside your ear
Anxious to define you and really love you.

Remember silence is curious about its opposite
Element which you shall learn to represent.

Enough of that. Now stand in the correct position
So that the wood of the floor will come up through you.
Stand, but not too stiff. Keep your elbows down.
Now take a simple breath and make me a shape
Of clear unchained started and finished tones.
Karl, as well as you are able, stop
Your fingers into the breathing apertures
And speak and make the cylinder delight us.

The Third Lesson

Karl, you are late. The traverse flute is not
A study to take lightly. I am cold waiting.
Put one piece of coal in the stove. This lesson
Shall not be prolonged. Right. Stand in your place.

Ready? Blow me a little ladder of sound
From a good stance so that you feel the heavy
Press of the floor coming up through you and
Keeping your pitch and tone in character.

Now that is something, Karl. You are getting on.
Unswell your head. One more piece of coal.
Go on now but remember it must be always
Easy and flowing. Light and shadow must
Be varied but be varied in your mind
Before you hear the eventual return sound.

Play me the dance you made for the barge-master.
Stop stop Karl. Play it as you first thought
Of it in the hot boat-kitchen. That is a pleasure
For me. I can see I am making you good.
Keep the stove red. Hand me the matches. Now
We can see better. Give me a shot at the pipe.

Karl, I can still put on a good flute-mouth
And show you in this high cold room something
You will be famous to have said you heard.

The Fourth Lesson

You are early this morning. What we have to do
Today is think of you as a little creator
After the big creator. And it can be argued
You are as necessary, even a composer
Composing in the flesh an attitude
To slay the ears of the gentry, Karl,
I know you find great joy in the great
Composers. But now you can put your lips to
The messages and blow them into sound
And enter and be there as well. You must
Be faithful to who you are speaking from
And yet it is all right. You will be there.

Take your coat off. Sit down. A glass of Bols
Will help us both. I think you are good enough
To not need me anymore. I think you know
You are not only an interpreter.

What you will do is always something else
And they will hear you simultaneously with
The Art you have been given to read. Karl,
I think the Spring is really coming at last.
I see the canal boys working. I realize
I have not asked you to play the flute today.
Come and look. Are the barges not moving?
You must forgive me. I am not myself today.
Be here on Thursday. When you come, bring
Me five herrings. Watch your fingers. Spring
Is apparent but it is still chilblain weather.

The Last Lesson

Dear Karl, this morning is our last lesson.
I have been given the opportunity to
Live in a certain person's house and tutor
Him and his daughters on the traverse flute.
Karl, you will be all right. In those recent
Lessons my heart lifted to your playing.

I know. I see you doing well, invited
In a great chamber in front of the gentry. I
Can see them with their dresses settling in
And bored mouths beneath moustaches sizing
You up as you are, a lout from the canal
With big ears but an angel's tread on the flute.

But you will be all right. Stand in your place
Before them. Remember Johann. Begin with good
Nerve and decision. Do not intrude too much
Into the message you carry and put out.

One last thing, Karl, remember when you enter
The joy of those quick high archipelagoes,
To make to keep your finger-stops as light
As feathers but definite. What can I say more?
Do not be sentimental or in your Art.
I will miss you. Do not expect applause.

Elma Mitchell, 1919–

Born in Airdrie, Scotland, Elma Mitchell worked in libraries and publishing. Like U. A. Fanthorpe's, Mitchell's work found publication in mid-life, and her carefully observed, occasionally tart poems have won a similarly devoted audience. *People Et Cetera: Poems New and Selected* appeared from Peterloo Poets in 1987 and there is a selection in *Penguin Modern Poets 6* (1996).

Thoughts After Ruskin

Women reminded him of lilies and roses.
Me they remind rather of blood and soap,
Armed with a warm rag, assaulting noses,
Ears, neck, mouth and all the secret places:

Armed with a sharp knife, cutting up liver,
Holding hearts to bleed under a running tap,
Gutting and stuffing, pickling and preserving,
Scalding, blanching, broiling, pulverizing,
– All the terrible chemistry of their kitchens.

Their distant husbands lean across mahogany
And delicately manipulate the market,
While safe at home, the tender and the gentle
Are killing tiny mice, dead snap by the neck,
Asphyxiating flies, evicting spiders,
Scrubbing, scouring aloud, disturbing cupboards,
Committing things to dustbins, twisting, wringing,
Wrists red and knuckles white and fingers puckered,
Pulpy, tepid. Steering screaming cleaners
Around the snags of furniture, they straighten
And haul out sheets from under the incontinent
And heavy old, stoop to importunate young,
Tugging, folding, tucking, zipping, buttoning,
Spooning in food, encouraging excretion,
Mopping up vomit, stabbing cloth with needles,
Contorting wool around their knitting needles,
Creating snug and comfy on their needles.

Their huge hands! their everywhere eyes! their voices
Raised to convey across the hullabaloo,
Their massive thighs and breasts dispensing comfort,
Their bloody passages and hairy crannies,
Their wombs that pocket a man upside down!

And when all's over, off with overalls,
Quickly consulting clocks, they go upstairs,
Sit and sigh a little, brushing hair,
And somehow find, in mirrors, colours, odours,
Their essences of lilies and of roses.

Keith Douglas, 1920–44

Douglas was born in Kent and educated at Christ's Hospital and Merton College, Oxford. He served in the Sherwood Rangers as a tank commander in North Africa and Normandy, and was killed shortly after D-Day. On the severest assessment, Douglas is the only English poet of the Second World War to rival his major predecessors in the Great War, Wilfred Owen and Isaac Rosenberg. While aware of their achievement (remarking 'Rosenberg I only repeat what you were saying'), in a brief, cruelly accelerated writing life he discovered a manner apt to his own experience – grimly realistic but with a metaphysical intensity of perception. What began as an adolescent courting of death became the focus for his best work – the poems printed here, as well as 'Sportsmen' and 'On a Return from Egypt'. It is painful to consider what he might have achieved, had he lived. While Douglas did publish in his lifetime, it was many years before accurate texts of his work became known. His importance to his successors is indicated by essays on Douglas written by Ted Hughes and Geoffrey Hill. See *Complete Poems* (1987); *A Prose Miscellany* (1985) and Desmond Graham's biography, *Keith Douglas* (1974).

Vergissmeinicht

Three weeks gone and the combatants gone,
returning over the nightmare ground
we found the place again, and found
the soldier sprawling in the sun.

The frowning barrel of his gun
overshadowing. As we came on
that day, he hit my tank with one
like the entry of a demon.

Look. Here in the gunpit spoil
the dishonoured picture of his girl
who has put: *Steffi. Vergissmeinicht*
in a copybook gothic script.

We see him almost with content
abased, and seeming to have paid
and mocked at by his own equipment
that's hard and good when he's decayed.

But she would weep to see today
how on his skin the swart flies move;
the dust upon the paper eye
and the burst stomach like a cave.

For here the lover and killer are mingled
who had one body and one heart.
And death who had the soldier singled
has done the lover mortal hurt.

How to Kill

Under the parabola of a ball,
a child turning into a man,
I looked into the air too long.
The ball fell in my hand, it sang
in the closed fist: *Open Open*
Behold a gift designed to kill.

Now in my dial of glass appears
the soldier who is going to die.
He smiles, and moves about in ways
his mother knows, habits of his.
The wires touch his face: I cry
NOW. Death, like a familiar, hears

and look, has made a man of dust
of a man of flesh. This sorcery
I do. Being damned, I am amused
to see the centre of love diffused
and the waves of love travel into vacancy.
How easy it is to make a ghost.

The weightless mosquito touches
her tiny shadow on the stone,
and with how like, how infinite
a lightness, man and shadow meet.
They fuse. A shadow is a man
when the mosquito death approaches.

Edwin Morgan, 1920–

Born in Glasgow, Morgan served in the Medical Corps during the Second World War and for many years taught at Glasgow University. Now the leading older Scots poet, his work has a breathtaking scope and variety and its influence can be felt in the work of younger writers such as Robert Crawford and W. N. Herbert. He has published translations from Anglo-Saxon (*Beowulf*, 'The Seafarer'), the famous Glasgow reportage-poems, concrete poetry, science-fiction poetry and a good deal that defies categorization. The vast 1997 *Collected Poems* confirms what Morgan's light touch and playful approach may at times have disguised – that he is a poet for the European and world stage. He is an experimentalist of the best sort, firmly in possession of tradition and able to combine an immense local and structural ingenuity with a deep charge of feeling. *About Edwin Morgan* (1990), edited by Robert Crawford and Hamish Whyte, surveys his work.

Stanzas of the Jeopardy

It may be at midday, limousines in cities, the groaning
Derrick and hissing hawser alive at dockyards,
Liners crawling with heat-baked decks, their élite
Drinking languid above the hounded turbines,
Doorways and crossroads thronged with a hundred
                                        rendezvous,
Planes low over spire and cupola with screaming
Jet-streams or soaring inaudible in disembodied calm,
Plough-teams on headlands in the sweat of noon, the warm
Earth up-ruffled swarming for crow and gull,
Boys whistling and calling at play in the sea-caves,
Cables humming, telephonists sighing, sirens
Wailing twelve from workshop and factory, tar
Bubbling in the skin of the street, shopfronts shimmering,
In Times Square, Leicester Square, Red Square – that the
                                        roar, the labour,
The onset and the heat, the engine and the flurry and the
                                        errand,
The plane and the phone and the plough and the farm,
                                        the farmer
And the stoker and the airman and the docker and the
                                        shopper and the boy
Shall all be called to a halt:
In the middle of the day, and in the twinkling of an eye.

It could be at midnight, braziers smouldering on wharves,
Watchmen dozing by the tar-boiler's hulk, warehouses
Planted gloomily in bloodless night-idleness,
Desolate siding and shed and circuit littered
With the truck and trash marooned by ebbing daytime,
Astronomers at their mirrors in zodiacal quiet, dancers
Swept through the rosy fantasy of muted waltzes,
Children speaking to the wind and stars in dream,

Great lakes of darkness mountain-locked and moonless
Breaking to the meagre splash of angler's oar,
Badger and hedgehog rooting among the beech-mast, gardens
Swirling with scents disessenced by the dawn,
Lovers lying in the dunes of summer, swimmers
Flashing like sudden fire in the bay – that the play,
The sleep and the pleasure, the tryst, the glow, the
                                        tranquillity,
The water and the silence, the fragrance, the vigil and the
                                        kiss,
The fishermen and the slumberers and the whisperers and
                                the creatures of the wood
Shall craze to an intolerable blast
And hear at midnight the very end of the world.

'Shall the trumpet sound before the suns have cooled?
Shall there not be portents of blood, sea-beds laid bare,
Concrete and girder like matchwood in earthquake and
                                        whirlwind?
Shall we not see the angels, or the creeping icecap, or the
                                        moon
Falling, or the wandering star, feel veins boiling
Or fingers freezing or the wind thickening with wings?'
The earth may spin beyond apocalypse;
Long before entropy the worlds may stop.
The heart praises its own intentions, while the moment,
The neighbour, the need, the face of love and the tears
Have passed unseized, at some day they will pass
Beyond all action, beyond despair and redemption,
When matter has uttered its last sound, when the eye
That roved around the universe goes blind, when lips
To lips are numb, when space is rolled away
And time is torn from its rings, and the door of life
Flies open on unimaginable things –
At noon, at midnight, or at no time,
As you receive these verses, O Corinthians.

from **The Video Box**

25

If you ask what my favourite programme is
it has to be that strange world jigsaw final.
After the winner had defeated all his rivals
with harder and harder jigsaws, he had to prove his mettle
by completing one last absolute mindcrusher
on his own, under the cameras, in less than a week.
We saw, but he did not, what the picture would be:
the mid-Atlantic, photographed from a plane,
as featureless a stretch as could be found,
no weeds, no flotsam, no birds, no oil, no ships,
the surface neither stormy nor calm, but ordinary,
a light wind on a slowly rolling swell.
Hand-cut by a fiendish jigger to simulate,
but not to have, identical beaks and bays,
it seemed impossible; but the candidate –
he said he was a stateless person, called himself Smith –
was impressive: small, dark, nimble, self-contained.
The thousands of little grey tortoises were scattered
on the floor of the studio; we saw the clock; he started.
His food was brought to him, but he hardly ate.
He had a bed, with the light only dimmed to a weird blue
never out. By the first day he had established
the edges, saw the picture was three metres long
and appeared to represent (dear God!) the sea.
Well, it was a man's life, and the silence
(broken only by sighs, click of wood, plop of coffee
in paper cups) that kept me fascinated.
Even when one hand was picking the edge-pieces
I noticed his other hand was massing sets
of distinguishing ripples or darker cross-hatching or
incipient wave-crests; his mind,

if not his face, worked like a sea.
It was when he suddenly rose from his bed
at two, on the third night, went straight over
to one piece and slotted it into a growing central patch,
then back to bed, that I knew he would make it.
On the sixth day he looked haggard and slow,
with perhaps a hundred pieces left,
of the most dreary unmarked lifeless grey.
The camera showed the clock more frequently.
He roused himself, and in a quickening burst
of activity, with many false starts, began
to press that inhuman insolent remnant together.
He did it, on the evening of the sixth day.
People streamed onto the set. Bands played.
That was fine. But what I liked best
was the last shot of the completed sea,
filling the screen; then the saw-lines disappeared,
till almost imperceptibly the surface moved
and it was again the real Atlantic, glad
to distraction to be released, raised
above itself in growing gusts, allowed
to roar as rain drove down and darkened,
allowed to blot, for a moment, the orderer's hand.

from Stobhill

The Porter

Ah know ah tellt them lies at the enquiry.
Ah sayed ah thought the wean wis dead
when ah took it tae the incinerator.
Ah didny think the wean wis dead,
but ah didny ken fur shair, did ah?
It's no fur me tae question the doctors.
Ah get a bag fae the sister, right?
She says take that an burn it. She's only
passin on the doctor's instructions,
but she seen the wean, she thought it wis dead,
so ye canny blame her. And the doctor says
ye canny blame him. Everybody wants
tae come doon on me like a tonna bricks.
Ah canny go aboot openin disposal bags –
if ah did ah'd be a nervous wreck.
Ah passed two electricians in the corridor
and ah tellt them the wean wis alive
but they thought ah wis jokin. Efter that
ah jist shut up, an left it tae the boilerman
tae fin oot fur hissel – he couldny miss it
could he? The puir wee thing wis squeelin
through the bag wis it no? Ah canny see
ah had tae tell him whit wis evident.
– Ah know ah'm goin on aboot this.
But suppose the kiddy could've been saved –
or suppose the boilerman hadny noticed it –
mah wee lassie's gote a hamster, ye ken? –
and ah fixed up a treadmill fur it
and it goes roon an roon an roon –
it's jist like that. Well ah'm no in court noo.
Don't answer nothing incriminatin, says the sheriff.

And that's good enough fur yours truly.
And neither ah did, neither ah did,
neither ah did, neither ah did.

On John MacLean

'I am not prepared to let Moscow dictate to Glasgow.'
Failures may be interesting, but it is the firmness
of what he wanted and did not want
that raises eyebrows: when does the quixotic
begin to gel, begin to impress, at what point
of naked surprise?
                              'I for one will not follow
a policy dictated by Lenin until he knows
the situation more clearly.'
                                        Which Lenin hadn't time to
and parties never did – the rock of nations
like the rock of ages, saw-toothed, half-submerged,
a cranky sputtering lighthouse somewhere, as often
out as lit, a wreck of ships all round,
there's the old barnacled 'Workingclass Solidarity',
and 'International Brotherhood' ripped open and awash,
while you can see the sleekit 'Great-Power Chauvinism'
steaming cannily past on the horizon
as if she had never heard of *cuius regio*.
MacLean wanted neither the maimed ships
nor the paradox of not wanting them
while he painfully trimmed the lighthouse lamp
to let them know that Scotland was not Britain
and writs of captains on the Thames
would never run in grey Clyde waters.

Well, nothing's permanent. It's true he lost –
a voice silenced in November fog. Party
is where he failed, for he believed in people,
not in *partiinost'* that as everyone knows
delivers the goods. Does it? Of course.
And if they're damaged in transit you make do?
You do – and don't be so naive about this world!

MacLean was not naive, but
                              'We are out
for life and all that life can give us'

was what he said, that's what he said.

The Sheaf

My life, as a slant of rain
on the grey earth fields
is gathered in thirsty silence, disappears.
I cannot even guess
the roots, but feel them sighing
in the stir of the soil I die to. Let this rain
be on the children of my heart,
I have no other ones.
                              On the generations,
on the packed cells and dreaming shoots,
the untried hopes, the waiting good
I send this drop to melt.

George Mackay Brown, 1921–96

George Mackay Brown was born in the Orkney Islands and educated at Edinburgh University. A scholar as well as singer, his poetry serves and re-imagines the world of Orcadian experience and is fed by Norse sagas, Catholicism and ballads. The result is a poetry strangely immune to time, where ancient and modern fuse in a rhetoric much given to names and lists. Here the elemental facts of love, death and ocean weather allow the reader sight and sound of a life at once ampler and simpler than that of familiar late modernity. See *Selected Poems 1954–83* (1991). Mackay Brown's novels include *Greenvoe* (1972) and *Time in a Red Coat* (1984).

Hamnavoe Market

They drove to the Market with ringing pockets.

Folster found a girl
Who put wounds on his face and throat,
Small and diagonal, like red doves.

Johnston stood beside the barrel.
All day he stood there.
He woke in a ditch, his mouth full of ashes.

Grieve bought a balloon and a goldfish.
He swung through the air.
He fired shotguns, rolled pennies, ate sweet fog from a
                                                    stick.

Heddle was at the Market also.
I know nothing of his activities.
He is and always was a quiet man.

Garson fought three rounds with a negro boxer,
And received thirty shillings,
Much applause, and an eye loaded with thunder.

Where did they find Flett?
They found him in a brazen circle,
All flame and blood, a new Salvationist.

A gypsy saw in the hand of Halcro
Great strolling herds, harvests, a proud woman.
He wintered in the poorhouse.

They drove home from the Market under the stars
Except for Johnston
Who lay in a ditch, his mouth full of dying fires.

Seven Translations of a Lost Poem

1

At the door marked with the sign Bordel
I was expensively entertained.
For that rich hour I hobble on a stick.

At the door marked Poet
I never sat with such a dull spiteful creature.
Yet harp can cancel crippledom.

When I come to the door marked Death
It will be sorrow to me
I had not been carried through it, a small
                         white wordless statue.

2

She was a very luxurious lady.
She rotted my leg.

This man made street-stones jade and diamond.
I did not like him.

An old ploughman, that's what I'd like to be,
                    near my death,
Ignorant of ode and perfume.

3

I still get angry at the loss of five gold pieces
And my boyhood
And my ability to dance, to that madam.

'I am poor. Nobody understands genius.
What are you wanting here?'
After the stings and blunderings, honey.

Death is a stroke of fire
Or a slow withering.
Some say, a circling magnificence like the ocean.

4

'I charge more than most
Because my love
Will make you a lord or a beggar.'
That's what the witch said
And I naked among the webs of silk.

'One poem, price one silver denarius.
Then off with you.
My shirt is torn. Look. I must see to it.'
That's what the enchanter said
One morning, among privy noises.

Death, lord, my inheritance is squandered
Among courtesans and artists.
Never a thought I gave to you
Until now, when I stand at your door
Without greeting or a proper gift.

5

The address given was Peacock House.
I came to Full Moon House.
Each girl had an ivory box, for gifts.
In one room a silver mirror.
Toothlessness, scant hairs, peered back at me.

Also by mistake I called on the wrong poet
For instruction in verse-craft.
The man could explain nothing.
He took the fee. He sent me home early.
He is said to be the best poet in all that long street.

I hope, when I am summoned by death
That – sick and one-legged as I am –
Once more I will be directed to the wrong door.

6

If Sandra would open her blue robe,
Nothing more. There is nothing
I would ask or desire from the gods.

If Sator would recite The Hill Song
I would seek, a ghost,
That same day, the marble.

She showed the silk under the silk.
He uttered 'plough-to-oven', a spell.
Why have I lived another half-century?

7

With a golden key I opened a door
On a bowl of dead rose-leaves.

In a house of withered webbed stone
The harp is hidden.

Be patient now, near the end –
Fold hands.
Bid the stone enter.

                    Love and Beauty,
One old April, cut epitaphs.

Donald Davie, 1922–95

Davie was born in Barnsley and educated at St Catherine's College, Cambridge. He did war service in the Navy. He held professorships at Essex, Stanford and Vanderbilt. His progress from the provinces to the academy made him almost the model poet of the Movement. His critical book *Purity of Diction in English Verse* (1953) was in some ways a manifesto for its rational, plain-language aspirations. Davie described himself as 'a pasticheur of late Augustan styles' and depicted himself as a poet of the made rather than the given poem; but he was capable of great emotional delicacy and intensity. Accomplished in traditional forms, he also wrote sinewy free verse. A prolific critic and controversialist, Davie represented the conservative strain in English poetic thought and in culture as a whole and was a presiding presence in the magazine *PN Review*. Passionately engaged with the modernism of Ezra Pound, he lamented the supposed shortcomings of the Hardy–Larkin line in English poetry (see *Thomas Hardy and British Poetry*, 1973) – a sentiment which carried him beyond the reach of the Movement he had worked hard to define. Dissenting Christianity is another important feature of his outlook. His energetic convictions latterly made him somewhat neglected outside the circle of the like-minded, and his work is due for reassessment. See *Collected Poems 1950–1970* (1972), *Collected Poems 1970–83* (1983) and the selection in *Penguin Modern Poets 7* (1996).

Remembering the Thirties

I

Hearing one saga, we enact the next.
We please our elders when we sit enthralled;
But then they're puzzled; and at last they're vexed
To have their youth so avidly recalled.

It dawns upon the veterans after all
That what for them were agonies, for us
Are high-brow thrillers, though historical;
And all their feats quite strictly fabulous.

This novel written fifteen years ago,
Set in my boyhood and my boyhood home,
These poems about 'abandoned workings', show
Worlds more remote than Ithaca or Rome.

The Anschluss, Guernica – all the names
At which those poets thrilled or were afraid
For me mean schools and schoolmasters and games;
And in the process some-one is betrayed.

Ourselves perhaps. The Devil for a joke
Might carve his own initials on our desk,
And yet we'd miss the point because he spoke
An idiom too dated, Audenesque.

Ralegh's Guiana also killed his son.
A pretty pickle if we came to see
The tallest story really packed a gun,
The Telemachiad an Odyssey.

II

Even to them the tales were not so true
As not to be ridiculous as well;
The ironmaster met his Waterloo,
But Rider Haggard rode along the fell.

'Leave for Cape Wrath tonight!' They lounged away
On Fleming's trek or Isherwood's ascent.
England expected every man that day
To show his motives were ambivalent.

They played the fool, not to appear as fools
In time's long glass. A deprecating air
Disarmed, they thought, the jeers of later schools;
Yet irony itself is doctrinaire,

And curiously, nothing now betrays
Their type to time's derision like this coy
Insistence on the quizzical, their craze
For showing Hector was a mother's boy.

A neutral tone is nowadays preferred.
And yet it may be better, if we must,
To praise a stance impressive and absurd
Than not to see the hero for the dust.

For courage is the vegetable king,
The sprig of all ontologies, the weed
That beards the slag-heap with his hectoring,
Whose green adventure is to run to seed.

Time Passing, Beloved

Time passing, and the memories of love
Coming back to me, carissima, no more mockingly
Than ever before; time passing, unslackening,
Unhastening, steadily; and no more
Bitterly, beloved, the memories of love
Coming into the shore.

How will it end? Time passing, and our passages of love
As ever, beloved, blind
As ever before; time binding, unbinding
About us; and yet to remember
Never less chastening, nor the flame of love
Less like an ember.

What will become of us? Time
Passing, beloved, and we in a sealed
Assurance unassailed
By memory. How can it end,
This siege of a shore that no misgivings have steeled,
No doubts defend?

Philip Larkin, 1922–85

Larkin grew up in Coventry and read English at St John's College, Oxford. Unfit for military service, he began his career in librarianship in Wellington, Shropshire. After work in Leicester and Belfast he became Librarian of Hull University and is indelibly associated with his adopted city. Although his first, heavily Yeatsian, collection *The North Ship* appeared in 1945, Larkin seemed most powerfully drawn to fiction, publishing two novels, *Jill* (1946) and *A Girl in Winter* (1947). His second book of poems, *The Less Deceived* (1955), established him as the leading poet of the Movement, and *The Whitsun Weddings* (1964) made him 'the unofficial laureate of England' (he declined the actual Laureateship).

Larkin's poems can seem to subvert the definitions they have helped to create, but it is fair to say that the poem of the Movement in his hands is often concerned with an enquiry into right or possible behaviour; with the conflict between dreams and obligations ('Toads'); with the bottomlessly problematic character of relationships ('No Road', 'Wild Oats'); with the decline of faith ('An Arundel Tomb', 'Church Going'); and with death ('Ambulances', 'The Building', 'Aubade'). For a man convicted by his detractors of misogyny, he shows remarkable sympathy with women's lives ('Love Songs in Age', 'Maiden Name', 'Broadcast'). And for a poet of supposedly narrow range, he could achieve remarkable combinations of scale and detail ('Here', 'The Whitsun Weddings', 'Show Saturday'), transmitting the image of English life back into the world that provided it. Larkin could also be variously comic – in the light-verse 'Vers de Societe' and the gleeful peasant uproar of 'The Card Players'. In his last book, *High Windows* (1974), the comedy coarsens and darkens, but equally the transcendent potential of the imagination becomes apparent – as does a love of fiction. At every stage Larkin's fascinated skill in verse technique is apparent – something largely lost among his many later imitators.

Like his friend Kingsley Amis, Larkin in later life revealed a gradually intensifying conservatism (although his actual political engagement was minimal) and a philistinism quite at odds with his subtle and well-stocked literary mind. This, together with revelations about his personal life, has in recent years produced a clouding of his reputation and an attempt to marginalize him. Had he not written poems whose skill and compassion are undeniable, these efforts would succeed; as it is, he seems to form part of the permanent literary consciousness. *Collected Poems*, edited by Anthony Thwaite, appeared in 1988, *Selected Letters 1940–1985*, edited by Anthony Thwaite, in 1992, and Andrew Motion's *Philip Larkin: A Writer's Life* in 1993.

Ambulances

Closed like confessionals, they thread
Loud noons of cities, giving back
None of the glances they absorb.
Light glossy grey, arms on a plaque,
They come to rest at any kerb:
All streets in time are visited.

Then children strewn on steps or road,
Or women coming from the shops
Past smells of different dinners, see
A wild white face that overtops
Red stretcher-blankets momently
As it is carried in and stowed,

And sense the solving emptiness
That lies just under all we do,
And for a second get it whole,
So permanent and blank and true.
The fastened doors recede. *Poor soul,*
They whisper at their own distress;

For borne away in deadened air
May go the sudden shut of loss
Round something nearly at an end,
And what cohered in it across
The years, the unique random blend
Of families and fashions, there

At last begin to loosen. Far
From the exchange of love to lie
Unreachable inside a room
The traffic parts to let go by
Brings closer what is left to come,
And dulls to distance all we are.

The Whitsun Weddings

That Whitsun, I was late getting away:
   Not till about
One-twenty on the sunlit Saturday
Did my three-quarters-empty train pull out,
All windows down, all cushions hot, all sense
Of being in a hurry gone. We ran
Behind the backs of houses, crossed a street
Of blinding windscreens, smelt the fish-dock; thence
The river's level drifting breadth began,
Where sky and Lincolnshire and water meet.

All afternoon, through the tall heat that slept
   For miles inland,
A slow and stopping curve southwards we kept.
Wide farms went by, short-shadowed cattle, and
Canals with floatings of industrial froth;
A hothouse flashed uniquely: hedges dipped
And rose: and now and then a smell of grass
Displaced the reek of buttoned carriage-cloth
Until the next town, new and nondescript,
Approached with acres of dismantled cars.

At first, I didn't notice what a noise
   The weddings made
Each station that we stopped at: sun destroys
The interest of what's happening in the shade,
And down the long cool platforms whoops and skirls
I took for porters larking with the mails,
And went on reading. Once we started, though,
We passed them, grinning and pomaded, girls
In parodies of fashion, heels and veils,
All posed irresolutely, watching us go,

As if out on the end of an event
	Waving goodbye
To something that survived it. Struck, I leant
More promptly out next time, more curiously,
And saw it all again in different terms:
The fathers with broad belts under their suits
And seamy foreheads; mothers loud and fat;
An uncle shouting smut; and then the perms,
The nylon gloves and jewellery-substitutes,
The lemons, mauves, and olive-ochres that

Marked off the girls unreally from the rest.
	Yes, from cafés
And banquet-halls up yards, and bunting-dressed
Coach-party annexes, the wedding-days
Were coming to an end. All down the line
Fresh couples climbed aboard: the rest stood round;
The last confetti and advice were thrown,
And, as we moved, each face seemed to define
Just what it saw departing: children frowned
At something dull; fathers had never known

Success so huge and wholly farcical;
	The women shared
The secret like a happy funeral;
While girls, gripping their handbags tighter, stared
At a religious wounding. Free at last,
And loaded with the sum of all they saw,
We hurried towards London, shuffling gouts of steam.
Now fields were building-plots, and poplars cast
Long shadows over major roads, and for
Some fifty minutes, that in time would seem

Just long enough to settle hats and say
	I nearly died,
A dozen marriages got under way.
They watched the landscape, sitting side by side

– An Odeon went past, a cooling tower,
And someone running up to bowl – and none
Thought of the others they would never meet
Or how their lives would all contain this hour.
I thought of London spread out in the sun,
Its postal districts packed like squares of wheat:

There we were aimed. And as we raced across
    Bright knots of rail
Past standing Pullmans, walls of blackened moss
Came close, and it was nearly done, this frail
Travelling coincidence; and what it held
Stood ready to be loosed with all the power
That being changed can give. We slowed again,
And as the tightened brakes took hold, there swelled
A sense of falling, like an arrow-shower
Sent out of sight, somewhere becoming rain.

Livings

I

I deal with farmers, things like dips and feed.
Every third month I book myself in at
The —— Hotel in —ton for three days.
The boots carries my lean old leather case
Up to a single, where I hang my hat.
One beer, and then 'the dinner', at which I read
The —shire Times from soup to stewed pears.
Births, deaths. For sale. Police court. Motor spares.

Afterwards, whisky in the Smoke Room: Clough,
Margetts, the Captain, Dr Watterson;
Who makes ends meet, who's taking the knock,
Government tariffs, wages, price of stock.
Smoke hangs under the light. The pictures on
The walls are comic – hunting, the trenches, stuff
Nobody minds or notices. A sound
Of dominoes from the Bar. I stand a round.

Later, the square is empty: a big sky
Drains down the estuary like the bed
Of a gold river, and the Customs House
Still has its office lit. I drowse
between ex-Army sheets, wondering why
I think it's worth while coming. Father's dead:
He used to, but the business now is mine.
It's time for change, in nineteen twenty-nine.

II

Seventy feet down
The sea explodes upwards,
Relapsing, to slaver
Off landing-stage steps –
Running suds, rejoice!

Rocks writhe back to sight.
Mussels, limpets,
Husband their tenacity
In the freezing slither –
Creatures, I cherish you!

By day, sky builds
Grape-dark over the salt
Unsown stirring fields.
Radio rubs its legs,
Telling me of elsewhere:

Barometers falling,
Ports wind-shuttered,
Fleets pent like hounds,
Fires in humped inns
Kippering sea-pictures –

Keep it all off!
By night, snow serves
(O loose moth world)
Through the stare travelling
Leather-black waters.

Guarded by brilliance
I set plate and spoon,
And after, divining-cards.
Lit shelved liners
Grope like mad worlds westward.

III

Tonight we dine without the Master
(Nocturnal vapours do not please);
The port goes round so much the faster,
Topics are raised with no less ease –
Which advowson looks the fairest,
What the wood from Snape will fetch,
Names for *pudendum mulieris*,
Why is Judas like Jack Ketch?

The candleflames grow thin, then broaden:
Our butler Starveling piles the logs
And sets behind the screen a jordan
(Quicker than going to the bogs).
The wine heats temper and complexion:
Oath-enforced assertions fly
On rheumy fevers, resurrection,
Regicide and rabbit pie.

The fields around are cold and muddy,
The cobbled streets close by are still,
A sizar shivers at his study,
The kitchen cat has made a kill;
The bells discuss the hour's gradations,
Dusty shelves hold prayers and proofs:
Above, Chaldean constellations
Sparkle over crowded roofs.

Money

Quarterly, is it, money reproaches me:
   'Why do you let me lie here wastefully?
I am all you never had of goods and sex.
   You could get them still by writing a few cheques.'

So I look at others, what they do with theirs:
   They certainly don't keep it upstairs.
By now they've a second house and car and wife:
   Clearly money has something to do with life

– In fact, they've a lot in common, if you enquire:
   You can't put off being young until you retire,
And however you bank your screw, the money you save
   Won't in the end buy you more than a shave.

I listen to money singing. It's like looking down
   From long french windows at a provincial town,
The slums, the canal, the churches ornate and mad
   In the evening sun. It is intensely sad.

Dannie Abse, 1923–

Born in Wales of a Jewish background, Abse has spent his working life as a doctor. The widely popular poems of his maturity combine meticulous observation of everyday life with an interest in art, myth and parable. At his best, as in 'Case History' or 'The Evening Road', he achieves a kind of mysterious clarity. *Selected Poems* (1994) is the best introduction to his work. Abse has written several volumes of autobiography and edited the important anthology, *Twentieth Century Anglo-Welsh Poetry* (1997).

Epithalamion

Singing, today I married my white girl
beautiful in a barley field.
Green on thy finger a grass blade curled,
so with this ring I thee wed, I thee wed,
and send our love to the loveless world
of all the living and all the dead.

Now, no more than vulnerable human,
we, more than one, less than two,
are nearly ourselves in a barley field –
and only love is the rent that's due
though the bailiffs of time return anew
to all the living but not the dead.

Shipwrecked, the sun sinks down harbours
of a sky, unloads its liquid cargoes
of marigolds, and I and my white girl
lie still in the barley – who else wishes
to speak, what more can be said
by all the living against all the dead?

Come then all you wedding guests:
green ghost of trees, gold of barley,
you blackbird priests in the field,
you wind that shakes the pansy head
fluttering on a stalk like a butterfly;
come the living and come the dead.

Listen flowers, birds, winds, worlds,
tell all today that I married
more than a white girl in the barley –
for today I took to my human bed
flower and bird and wind and world,
and all the living and all the dead.

Case History

'Most Welshmen are worthless,
an inferior breed, doctor.'
He did not know I was Welsh.
Then he praised the architects
of the German death-camps –
did not know I was a Jew.
He called liberals, 'White blacks',
and continued to invent curses.

When I palpated his liver
I felt the soft liver of Goering;
when I lifted my stethoscope
I heard the heartbeats of Himmler;
when I read his encephalograph
I thought, *'Sieg heil, mein Führer.'*

In the clinic's dispensary
red berry of black bryony,
cowbane, deadly nightshade, deathcap.
Yet I prescribed for him
as if he were my brother.

Later that night I must have slept
on my arm: momentarily
my right hand lost its cunning.

James Berry, 1924–

Born in Jamaica, James Berry came to Britain in 1948 and for many years worked as an international telephone operator. Also a short-story writer, teacher of writing in schools and all-round advocate, Berry has done much to raise awareness of black writing in Britain. His anthology *News for Babylon* (1984) was a ground-breaking work. The best introduction to his poetry is *Hot Earth Cold Earth* (1995). Berry combines standard and black English in dealing with themes of freedom and prejudice, with strong comic touches and pungent sensuous evocation. He is also a popular writer for children (see *A Thief in the Village*, 1987 and *Anancy-Spiderman*, 1989).

On an Afternoon Train from
Purley to Victoria, 1955

Hello, she said and startled me.
Nice day. Nice day I agreed.
I am a Quaker she said and Sunday
I was moved in silence
to speak a poem loudly
for racial brotherhood.

I was thoughtful, then said
what poem came on like that?
One the moment inspired she said.
I was again thoughtful.

Inexplicably I saw
empty city streets lit dimly
in a day's first hours.
Alongside in darkness
was my father's big banana field.

Where are you from? she said.
Jamaica I said.
What part of Africa is Jamaica? she said.
Where Ireland is near Lapland I said.
Hard to see why you leave
such sunny country she said.
Snow falls elsewhere I said.
So sincere she was beautiful
as people sat down around us.

Elizabeth Jennings, 1926–

Born in Lincolnshire and educated at Oxford, Elizabeth Jennings was the only woman poet represented in the famous Movement anthology *New Lines* (1956). Her early work is marked by a limpid anxiety to discern order in experience – anxiety not wholly assuaged by religious faith. Her best work – such as 'My Grand-mother', 'Song at the Beginning of Autumn' and 'One Flesh' – marries this feeling with a graceful discretion. *Collected Poems* appeared in 1987.

One Flesh

Lying apart now, each in a separate bed,
He with a book, keeping the light on late,
She like a girl dreaming of childhood,
All men elsewhere – it is as if they wait
Some new event: the book he holds unread,
Her eyes fixed on the shadows overhead.

Tossed up like flotsam from a former passion,
How cool they lie. They hardly ever touch,
Or if they do it is like a confession
Of having little feeling – or too much.
Chastity faces them, a destination
For which their whole lives were a preparation.

Strangely apart, yet strangely close together,
Silence between them like a thread to hold
And not wind in. And time itself's a feather
Touching them gently. Do they know they're old,
These two who are my father and my mother
Whose fire from which I came, has now grown cold?

Christopher Middleton, 1926–

Christopher Middleton was born in Cornwall and educated at Oxford. He has lived for many years in the United States, where he was Professor of German at the University of Texas at Austin. Although Alvarez included Middleton in *The New Poetry*, Middleton has never quite had his due on this side of the Atlantic – partly as a result of the restless experimentalism which has led him from the romantic realism of 'At Porthcothan' towards expressionism, surrealism and various uncategorizable approaches. He is perhaps more famous as a translator from German, often in collaboration with Michael Hamburger. 'Briefcase History' can suggest the vein of grim humour which sometimes surfaces from the many layers of his work. See *Selected Writings* (1989).

Briefcase History

This briefcase was made on the Baltic coast
in 1946
some prize pig was flayed for the leather
metal stripped from a seaplane
silk for the stitching picked from parachute cord

People say where did you get that singular briefcase
and then I notice it
people ask how much did it cost
and when I say fifty cigarettes not many understand
once the leather was flying wrapped
around seaplane fuel tanks the space between
wadded with two inches of rubber
this briefcase might stop a bullet I wonder

For twenty-five years I have carried in it
books of poems battered or new
cosmic mountain notebooks plays with broken spines
bread and cheese a visiting card from Bratislava
and a pliable cranny for anything to be pocketed
at the last moment

The handle ribbed with stitches of parachute silk
anchored by clasps of seaplane metal
is worn shiny and dark with sweat
the whole thing has an unspeakable gray colour
running a fingertip over a surface
leprous one might say
various tones of gray flickering mould green
the scored leather looks to me like the footsole
of an old aborigine bowman earth in a space photo
nerve webs of a bat's wing

The two side pockets have their seams intact
two straps happily slip through buckles and hold there

Furthermore this briefcase has contained
a dynasty of shirts mostly now extinct nothing to declare
my Venus relics old stones believed
animal figures carved back of beyond in France

Everywhere
this briefcase has been with me somehow
I find reason to celebrate it today

Briefcase helping friend
ploughshare beaten from the sword
briefcase bag of tricks peaceful seaplane spirit
ocean wanderer
you have never contained an explosive device
never have you contained an explosive device
yet

Frank Redpath, 1927–90

Frank Redpath grew up in Hull and spent his working life first as a writer of picture stories for girls' comics and then as a college lecturer. He published little during his lifetime. *How it Turned Out*, edited by John Wakeman (1996), is a substantial selection which shows Redpath to be a fellow traveller of the Movement – sceptical, formalist – but one driven by his own speculative and often celebratory imagination. The sombre and powerful 'Transit Camp' recasts themes of threat and uncertainty in the context of army life.

Transit Camp

. . . came to a place – funny – I felt I half remembered,
With some sort of shed or factory, on the farther side
Of a cinder track by the railway siding, with dismembered
Bits of machinery, being rained on, dumped outside.
Blank walls, sliding doors, windows blacked out with
                                            metal sheeting,
Unpainted and greasy, welded to angle-iron frames.

Well, they got us off, lined us up, got the names
Of our units, then gave the usual order: stand over there
                                            and wait.
No idea where we were, of course; been some sort of fun
                                            and games
Back down the line; they'd taken the officers off. It was late
When we got there, pitch black, pissing down. The only
                                            lighting
Was three lamps on poles. It looked like the arsehole of
                                            hell.

After a bit, they sent up rations and somebody to tell
Us to carry on waiting. Rations! A mess-tin half full of tea
That tasted like yesterday's warm-up, and a wad that was
                                            well
Soaked in the pissing-down rain; we ate it lined up in the
                                            lee
Of the wall. Then somebody opened a door and I got a
                                            fleeting
Glimpse inside: a dozen blokes, big bastards, Staff, I
                                            suppose,
Clearing up after a shift it looked like. One was coiling a
                                            hose
And the rest were sweeping up some sort of muck from
                                            the floor,

Stripped to the waist, wearing oilskin aprons. There were
                                                        rows
Of flat-bed trolleys on trackways that went across to a
                                                        door
In the far wall. The bloke said *Fuck! Still fucking raining*,
Then slammed the door shut again. We waited there half
                                                        the night

And, after a bit, the noises started: a sort of tight
Screeching sound from the trolleys, then something
                                                clanging.
Once somebody inside yelled *Keep it moving on the right!*
And we could hear this shuffling sound and something
                                                        banging.
There were pipes, jutting out overhead, that kept on
                                                spurting
Jets of steam, and a smell that was sort of shitty and flat.

Then some sort of officer came up in a car and told us that
We shouldn't be where we were and marched us five
                                                bloody miles,
Down the track, through a wood, with the officer sat on
                                                        his fat
Arse in the car in front, to some huts. They gave us piles
Of straw and sacks to sleep on but we weren't
                                        complaining;
We'd have slept on the floor, by then, to be out of the rain.

Three bloody days they kept us there. We kept hearing
                                                the train
Whistling in the distance but nobody could tell us where
We were supposed to be. Nothing but rumours, no plain
Answers: *It's nothing to do with us; we're not going there;
We're moving on tomorrow; somebody said it's a home
                                                        posting.*
Still, you can get used to just about anything. Anyway . . .

Charles Tomlinson, 1927–

Tomlinson was born in Stoke-on-Trent and educated at Cambridge. He became Professor of English at Bristol University. Tomlinson stands out against the supposed conformities of the Movement by engaging with international modernism, including Ungaretti, Wallace Stevens and William Carlos Williams, and condemning the 'suburban mental ratio' of much English poetry. A visual artist as well as a poet, Tomlinson is most exercised by the visible world. Whether his vast descriptive powers compensate for the lack of a human presence in this work is open to debate, but *Collected Poems* (1985) is a substantial achievement.

The Weathercocks

Bitten and burned into mirrors of thin gold,
the weathercocks, blind from the weather,
have their days of seeing as they
grind round on their swivels.

A consciousness of pure metal
begins to melt when (say)
that light 'which never was'
begins to be

And catches the snow's accents
in each dip and lap, and the wide
stains on the thawed ploughland are like continents
across a rumpled map.

Their gold eyes hurt
at the corduroy lines come clear whose grain
feels its way over the shapes of the rises
joining one brown accord of stain and stain.

And the patterning stretches, flown
out on a wing of afternoon cloud that the sun
is changing to sea-wet sandflats,
hummocked in tiny dunes like the snow half-gone –

As if the sole wish of the light
were to harrow with mind matter, to shock
wide the glance of the tree-knots and the stone-eyes
the sun is bathing, to waken the weathercocks.

Thomas Kinsella, 1928–

Thomas Kinsella was born in Dublin and worked for many years in the Irish Ministry of Finance, after which he taught in American universities. He runs the Peppercanister Press. Kinsella's work is at times heavily allusive, even cryptic, a sign that, beginning to write in the generation before Heaney and Mahon, he felt that Irish poetry should accept the cultural obligations of modernism. Perhaps as a result, his poems are often studied and strenuous, with lyricism and drama in thrall to a larger seriousness which is also shadowed by W. B. Yeats. With *Poems 1956–1994* (1996), his collections have included *From Centre City* (1994) and *Blood and Family* (1988). Editor of *The New Oxford Book of Irish Verse* (1986), he has also translated widely from Irish poetry, including *The Tain* (1970) and *An Duanaire, 1600–1900: Poems of the Dispossessed* (1981).

In the Ringwood

As I roved out impatiently
Good Friday with my bride
To drink in the rivered Ringwood
The draughty season's pride
A fell dismay held suddenly
Our feet on the green hill-side.

The yellow Spring on Vinegar Hill,
The smile of Slaney water,
The wind that swept the Ringwood,
Grew dark with ancient slaughter.
My love cried out and I beheld her
Change to Sorrow's daughter.

'Ravenhair, what rending
Set those red lips a-shriek,
And dealt those locks in black lament
Like blows on your white cheek,
That in your looks outlandishly
Both woe and fury speak?

As sharp a lance as the fatal heron
There on the sunken tree
Will strike in the stones of the river
Was the gaze she bent on me.
O her robe into her right hand
She gathered grievously.

'Many times the civil lover
Climbed that pleasant place,
Many times despairing
Died in his love's face,
His spittle turned to vinegar,
Blood in his embrace.

Love that is every miracle
Is torn apart and rent.
The human turns awry
The poles of the firmament.
The fish's bright side is pierced
And good again is spent.

Though every stem on Vinegar Hill
And stone on the Slaney's bed
And every leaf in the living Ringwood
Builds till it is dead
Yet heart and hand, accomplished,
Destroy until they dread.

Dread, a grey devourer,
Stalks in the shade of love.
The dark that dogs our feet
Eats what is sickened of.
The End that stalks Beginning
Hurries home its drove.'

I kissed three times her shivering lips.
I drank their naked chill.
I watched the river shining
Where the heron wiped his bill.
I took my love in my icy arms
In the Spring on Ringwood Hill.

Ian Crichton Smith, 1928–98

Ian Crichton Smith (Iain Mac a'Ghobhainn) was born in Glasgow and grew up on the island of Lewis. He studied at Aberdeen University and was a schoolteacher before taking up full-time writing. Prolific (he was also a novelist) in both English and Gaelic, Crichton Smith was a lyric and satirical poet, with a range from the local to the international, a humanist crying out against narrow, ignorant and materialistic modernity as against the constrictions of his Free Presbyterian upbringing; a member of the Gaelic world aware of the threats to its survival. *Collected Poems* was published in 1992, *Selected Essays* in 1986.

from The White Air of March

1

This is the land God gave to Andy Stewart –
        we have our inheritance.
There shall be no ardour, there shall be indifference.
There shall not be excellence, there shall be the average.
We shall be the intrepid hunters of golf balls.
Have you not known, have you not heard, has it not been
                                                reported
that Mrs Macdonald has given an hour-long lecture on
                                                Islay
and at the conclusion was presented with a bouquet of
                                                flowers
by Marjory, aged five?
                        Have you not noted
the photograph of the whist drive, skeleton hands,
rings on skeleton fingers?
                        Have you not seen
the glossy weddings in the glossy pages,
champagne and a 'shared joke'.
                                Do you not see
the Music Hall's still alive here in the North? and on the
                                                stage
the yellow gorse is growing.
            'Tragedy,' said Walpole, 'for those who feel.
For those who think, it's comic.'
                                Pity then those who feel
and, as for the Scottish Soldier, off to the wars!
The Cuillins stand and will forever stand.
Their streams scream in the moonlight.

How Often I Feel Like You

Ah, you Russians, how often I feel like you
full of ennui, hearing the cry of wolves
on frontiers of green glass.
In the evening
one dreams of white birches and of bears.
There are picnics in bright glades and someone talking
endlessly of verse as if mowing grass,
endlessly of philosophy round and round
like a red fair with figures of red soldiers
spinning forever at their 'Present Arms'.
How long it takes for a letter to arrive.
Postmen slog heavily over the steppes
and drop their dynamite through the letter-box.
For something is happening everywhere but here.
Here there are Hamlets and old generals.
Everyone sighs and says 'Ekh' and in the stream
a girl is swimming naked among gnats.
This space is far too much for us like time.
Even the clocks have asthma. There is honey,
herring and jam and an old samovar.
Help us, let something happen, even death.
God has forgotten us. We are like fishers
with leather leggings dreaming in a stream.

U. A. Fanthorpe, 1929–

Born in Kent and educated at Oxford, U. A. Fanthorpe taught at Cheltenham Ladies College before becoming 'a middle-aged drop-out' and doing clerical work in the National Health Service. With the publication of *Side Effects* (1978), Fanthorpe achieved the wide popularity she has enjoyed ever since. Her poems offer poignant or comic observations of ordinary life faced with mess, unhappiness and mortality, sometimes with a mythic undertow. Her most recent collection is *Standing To* (1995). There is a good introductory selection in *Penguin Modern Poets 6* (1996).

Rising Damp

(*for C. A. K. and R. K. M.*)

'A river can sometimes be diverted, but it is a very hard
thing to lose it altogether.'
– J. G. Head, paper read to the Auctioneers' Institute in 1907

At our feet they lie low,
The little fervent underground
Rivers of London

Effra, Graveney, Falcon, Quaggy,
Wandle, Walbrook, Tyburn, Fleet

Whose names are disfigured,
Frayed, effaced.

These are the Magogs that chewed the clay
To the basin that London nestles in.
These are the currents that chiselled the city,
That washed the clothes and turned the mills,
Where children drank and salmon swam
And wells were holy.

They have gone under.
Boxed, like the magician's assistant.
Buried alive in earth.
Forgotten, like the dead.

They return spectrally after heavy rain,
Confounding suburban gardens. They infiltrate
Chronic bronchitis statistics. A silken
Slur haunts dwellings by shrouded
Watercourses, and is taken
For the footing of the dead.

Being of our world, they will return
(Westbourne, caged at Sloane Square,
Will jack from his box),
Will deluge cellars, detonate manholes,
Plant effluent on our faces,
Sink the city.

Effra, Graveney, Falcon, Quaggy,
Wandle, Walbrook, Tyburn, Fleet

It is the other rivers that lie
Lower, that touch us only in dreams
That never surface. We feel their tug
As a dowser's rod bends to the source below

Phlegethon, Acheron, Lethe, Styx.

Thom Gunn, 1929–

Raised in London and educated at Cambridge, Gunn has lived for many years in the United States, dividing his time between writing and university teaching. He was included in the *New Lines* anthology without quite seeming part of that company. In *Fighting Terms* (1954) and *The Sense of Movement* (1957) he displayed an interest in existentialism matched with a manner heavily influenced by Elizabethan and metaphysical poetry. Aggression, eroticism, display and self-conscious heroism – metaphors of Gunn's gay concerns – all figured in these impressive early books, culminating in *My Sad Captains* (1961), a collection divided between traditional English and American/syllabic prosody. Later volumes, including *Touch* (1967) and *Moly* (1971), maintained this dual approach, but Gunn's work in the 1960s and 70s often seemed to lack the intellectual drive and stylishness of his early poems. The 1993 *Collected Poems* revealed a poet with a willingness to change and take risks. *Shelf-Life* (1993) is an illuminating selection of Gunn's critical writing.

On the Move

The blue jay scuffling in the bushes follows
Some hidden purpose, and the gust of birds
That spurts across the field, the wheeling swallows,
Has nested in the trees and undergrowth.
Seeking their instinct, or their poise, or both,
One moves with an uncertain violence
Under the dust thrown by a baffled sense
Or the thunder of approximate words.

On motorcycles, up the road, they come:
Small, black, as flies hanging in heat, the Boys,
Until the distance throws them forth, their hum
Bulges to thunder held by calf and thigh.
In goggles, donned impersonality,
In gleaming jackets trophied with the dust,
They strap in doubt – by hiding it, robust –
And almost hear a meaning in their noise.

Exact conclusion of their hardiness
Has no shape yet, but from known whereabouts
They ride, direction where the tyres press.
They scare a flight of birds across the field:
Much that is natural, to the will must yield.
Men manufacture both machine and soul,
And use what they imperfectly control
To dare a future from the taken routes.

It is a part solution, after all.
One is not necessarily discord
On earth; or damned because, half animal,
One lacks direct instinct, because one wakes
Afloat on movement that divides and breaks.
One joins the movement in a valueless world,

Choosing it, till, both hurler and the hurled,
One moves as well, always toward, toward.

A minute holds them, who have come to go:
The self-defined, astride the created will
They burst away; the towns they travel through
Are home for neither bird nor holiness,
For birds and saints complete their purposes.
At worst, one is in motion; and at best,
Reaching no absolute, in which to rest,
One is always nearer by not keeping still.

My Sad Captains

One by one they appear in
the darkness: a few friends, and
a few with historical
names. How late they start to shine!
but before they fade they stand
perfectly embodied, all

the past lapping them like a
cloak of chaos. They were men
who, I thought, lived only to
renew the wasteful force they
spent with each hot convulsion.
They remind me, distant now.

True, they are not at rest yet,
but now that they are indeed
apart, winnowed from failures,
they withdraw to an orbit
and turn with disinterested
hard energy, like the stars.

John Montague, 1929–

John Montague was born in New York and grew up in Co. Tyrone. His importance for his Northern Irish successors lies in his poems of place names and local history – the means of tracing conflict and dispossession. Montague's best work has an incantatory element, singing the dead 'into the dark permanence of ancient forms'. See *New Selected Poems* (1990). He has also translated a good deal of poetry from the Irish: see *The Faber Book of Irish Verse* (1974).

A Lost Tradition

All around, shards of a lost tradition:
From the Rough Field I went to school
In the Glen of the Hazels. Close by
Was the bishopric of the Golden Stone;
The cairn of Carleton's homesick poem.

Scattered over the hills, tribal –
And placenames, uncultivated pearls.
No rock or ruin, dun or dolmen
But showed memory defying cruelty
Through an image-encrusted name.

The heathery gap where the Rapparee,
Shane Barnagh, saw his brother die –
On a summer's day the dying sun
Stained its colours to crimson:
So breaks the heart, Brish-mo-Cree.

The whole landscape a manuscript
We had lost the skill to read,
A part of our past disinherited;
But fumbled, like a blind man,
Along the fingertips of instinct.

The last Gaelic speaker in the parish
When I stammered my school Irish
One Sunday after mass, crinkled
A rusty litany of praise:
*Tá an Ghaeilge againn arís . . .**

* We have the Irish again

Tír Eoghain: Land of Owen,
Province of the O'Niall;
The ghostly tread of O'Hagan's
Barefoot gallowglasses marching
To merge forces in Dun Geanainn

Push southward to Kinsale!
Loudly the war-cry is swallowed
In swirls of black rain and fog
As Ulster's pride, Elizabeth's foemen,
Founder in a Munster bog.

Peter Porter, 1929–

Porter was born in Brisbane, coming to Britain in 1951, where he worked in advertising for some years before writing full-time. He participated in the meetings of the Group organized by Philip Hobsbaum and Edward Lucie-Smith, which held regular sessions of close reading and analysis of members' work; but like his fellow attenders (who included Alan Brownjohn, Peter Redgrove, George MacBeth and, latterly, Fleur Adcock) he was a highly individual poet, not confined to any school or style. His first books (*Once Bitten, Twice Bitten*, 1961 and *Poems Ancient and Modern*, 1964) revealed a poet of omnivorous cultural interests who could display high seriousness alongside a capacity to be, in Auden's phrase, 'among the filthy filthy too'. At times Jacobean in the vehemence of his manner, Porter is also influenced by Browning, and the dramatic monologue has remained the operating basis of his work – whether in satire, elegy or fantasy. Consciously or not, Porter has achieved a range of reference and a readiness for life more generally associated with the nineteenth-century novel than with poetry. He reads London as if it were Rome and treats works of art and music as actualities. A poet of the European city, he also writes passionately of the landscapes of his native Australia. In recent years the influence of Wallace Stevens has become stronger. Forbiddingly allusive at times, and probably uncategorizable, Porter combines the talkative drive of Auden with a Modernist sense of catastrophe. *A Porter Selected* (1989) is a good introduction. A new two-volume *Collected Poems* is imminent. Bruce Bennett's *Spirit in Exile: Peter Porter and His Poetry* (1991) is a detailed critical and biographical study.

Soliloquy at Potsdam

There are always the poor –
Getting themselves born in crowded houses,
Feeding on the parish, losing their teeth early
And learning to dodge blows, getting
Strong bodies – cases for the warped nut of the mind.
The masterful cat-o'-nine-tails, the merciful
Discipline of the hours of drill – better
Than being poor in crowded Europe, the swan-swept
Waters where the faces dredge for bread
And the soggy dead are robbed on their way to the grave.
I can hear it from this window, the musket-drill
On the barrack square. Later today I'll visit
The punishment block. Who else in Europe
Could take these verminous, clutching creatures
And break them into men? What of the shredded back
And the broken pelvis, when the side-drum sounds,
When the uniformed wave tilts and overwhelms
The cheese-trading burghers' world, the aldermanic
Principalities. The reformers sit at my table,
They talk well but they've never seen a battle
Or watched the formed brain in the flogged body
Marching to death on a bellyful of soup and orders.
There has to be misery so there can be discipline.
People will have to die because I cannot bear
Their clinging to life. Why are the best trumpeters
Always French? Watch the west, the watershed
Of revolution. Now back to Quantz. I like to think
That in an afternoon of three sonatas
A hundred regiments have marched more miles
Than lie between here and Vienna and not once
Has a man broken step. Who would be loved
If he could be feared and hated, yet still
Enjoy his lust, eat well and play the flute?

The Last of England

It's quiet here among the haunted tenses:
Dread Swiss germs pass the rabbit's throat,
Chemical rain in its brave green hat
Drinks at a South Coast Bar, the hedgehog
Preens on nylon, we dance in Tyrolean
Drag whose mothers were McGregors,
Exiled seas fill every cubit of the bay.

Sailing away from ourselves, we feel
The gentle tug of water at the quay –
Language of the liberal dead speaks
From the soil of Highgate, tears
Show a great water table is intact.
You cannot leave England, it turns
A planet majestically in the mind.

The Future

It is always morning in the big room
but the inhabitants are very old.
Crooking her finger on a watering-can,
a precise figure of regret, no wisp
of her silver hair disturbed, drips succour
on a cat-predated plant. Words here
are shredded like its silver leaves,
they are epitomes of chanciness,
none will get you through the day.
When the sun fills the windows with its
misleading call to truth, the old woman
changes to a young girl, then to a man
from a novel looking up to ask
why things have gone so very wrong.
I am allowed, as if this were a dream,
to join them on their tableau.
We do not die, they say, but harden
into frescoes. This is what the future means,
her seeking me on her knees, poignant
as a phrase from a Victorian novel
or farewell spoken beyond a watercourse,
lyrical erotica I have no talent for –
Just the one room brightening, to which
hasten all the relatives of insecurity,
talking of my brief Bohemian days:
To be poised as the long-necked swan
or collared badger while the work
of worldliness is done, to stay the same
after the sun has gone, waiting merely
for light to show us up; the future
is to stand still with one gesture held,
a white glove entering a confluence.

And No Help Came

Where would you look for blessing who are caught
In published acres of millennia
By ravishments of salt and raucous saints
Or janissaries drilling a Big Bang?
The parish of the poor you'd seek, far from
The high grandstands of words and notes and paints.

And when you drove your flagged and honking jeep
Among the huts of starving, brutalized
Dependents, you might chance to hear them playing
Sentimental songs of flowers and moons
Chiefly to keep them safe from art, whose gods
Build palaces adorned with scenes of flaying.

Roy Fisher, 1930–

Roy Fisher was born in Handsworth, Birmingham, and educated at Birmingham University. For many years he taught American Studies at Keele University. He is also a jazz pianist. It is often said, with truth, that Fisher provides a bridge between the mainstream and the *avant-garde*; what is less often remarked is that he is a rare *avant-gardiste*: one who can write as well as theorize. Influences such as the Black Mountain poet Charles Olson, and Objectivists such as Louis Zukofsky and Lorine Niedecker can be sought in his work, but there is another – and a very English – aspect of modernity in his poems: the great industrial city of Birmingham, to whose massive brick landscapes, blind walls and roadways Fisher has devoted much of his curiosity from the 1950s on. Fisher calls himself 'a realist', but there is a romantic element in his mental mapping of Birmingham through *City* (1961), 'Handsworth Liberties', 'Wonders of Obligation', *A Furnace* (1986) and *Birmingham River* (1994). As well as place, Fisher wants to understand the role of perception and representation in writing, so that much of his work is an attempt to understand itself as well as its objects. Fisher's publishing history is complicated. The best place to start is *The Dow Low Drop: New and Selected Poems* (1996). *The Thing About Roy Fisher: Critical Studies*, edited by John Kerrigan and Peter Robinson, will appear in 1999.

By the Pond

from *City*

This is bitter enough: the pallid water
With yellow rushes crowding toward the shore,
That fishermen's shack.

The pit-mound's taut and staring wire fences,
The ashen sky. All these can serve as conscience.
For the rest, I'll live.

Brick-dust in sunlight. That is what I see now in the city, a dry epic flavour, whose air is human breath. A place of walls made straight with plumbline and trowel, to desiccate and crumble in the sun and smoke. Blistered paint on cisterns and girders, cracking to show the priming. Old men spit on the paving slabs, little boys urinate; and the sun dries it as it dries out patches of damp on plaster facings to leave misshapen stains. I look for things here that make old men and dead men seem young. Things which have escaped, the landscapes of many childhoods.

Wharves, the oldest parts of factories, tarred gable ends rearing to take the sun over lower roofs. Soot, sunlight, brick-dust; and the breath that tastes of them.

At the time when the great streets were thrust out along the old high-roads and trackways, the houses shouldering towards the country and the back streets filling in the widening spaces between them like webbed membranes, the power of will in the town was more open, less speciously democratic, than it is now. There were, of course, cottage railway stations, a jail that pretended to be a castle out of Grimm, public urinals surrounded by screens of cast-iron lacework painted green and scarlet; but there was also an arrogant ponderous architecture that dwarfed and terrified the people by its sheer size and functional brutality: the work-houses and the older hospitals, the thick-walled abattoir, the long vaulted market-halls, the striding canal bridges and railway viaducts. Brunel was welcome here. Compared with these structures the straight white blocks and concrete roadways of today are a fairground, a clear dream just before waking, the creation of salesmen rather than of engineers. The new city is bred out of a hard will, but as it appears, it shows itself a little ingratiating, a place of arcades, passages, easy ascents, good light. The eyes twinkle, beseech and veil themselves; the full, hard mouth, the broad jaw – these are no longer made visible to all.

A street half a mile long with no buildings, only a continuous embankment of sickly grass along one side, with railway signals on it, and strings of trucks through whose black-spoked wheels you can see the sky; and for the whole length of the other a curving wall of bluish brick, caked with soot and thirty feet high. In it, a few wicket gates painted ochre, and fingermarked, but never open. Cobbles in the roadway.

A hundred years ago this was almost the edge of town. The goods yards, the gasworks and the coal stores were established on tips and hillocks in the spare fields that lay among the houses. Between this place and the centre, a mile or two up the hill, lay a continuous huddle of low streets and courts, filling the marshy valley of the meagre river that now flows under brick and tarmac. And this was as far as the railway came, at first. A great station was built, towering and stony. The sky above it was southerly. The stately approach, the long curves of wall, still remain, but the place is a goods depot with most of its doors barred and pots of geraniums at those windows that are not shuttered. You come upon it suddenly in its open prospect out of tangled streets of small factories. It draws light to itself, especially at sunset, standing still and smooth faced, looking westwards at the hill. I am not able to imagine the activity that must once have been here. I can see no ghosts of men and women, only the gigantic ghost of stone. They are too frightened of it to pull it down.

For Realism

For 'realism':
the sight of Lucas's
lamp factory on a summer night;
a shift coming off about nine,
pale light, dispersing,
runnels of people chased,
by pavements drying off
quickly after them,
away among the wrinkled brown houses
where there are cracks for them to go;
sometimes, at the corner of Farm and Wheeler Streets,
standing in that stained, half-deserted place

– pale light for staring up
four floors high
through the blind window walls
of a hall of engines,
shady humps left alone,
no lights on in there
except the sky –

there presses in
– and not as conscience –
what concentrates down in the warm hollow:

plenty of life there still,
the foodshops open late, and people
going about constantly, but not far;

there's a man in a blue suit
facing into a corner,
straddling to keep his shoes dry;
women step, talking, over the stream,
and when the men going by call out, he answers.

Above, dignity. A new precinct
comes over the scraped hill,
flats on the ridge get the last light.

Down Wheeler Street, the lamps
already gone, the windows have
lake stretches of silver
gashed out of tea green shadows,
the after-images of brickwork.

A conscience
builds, late, on the ridge. A realism
tries to record, before they're gone,
what silver filth these drains have run.

It is Writing

Because it could do it well
the poem wants to glorify suffering.
I mistrust it.

I mistrust the poem in its hour of success,
a thing capable of being
tempted by ethics into the wonderful.

Ted Hughes, 1930–98

Ted Hughes was born in Mytholmroyd, Yorkshire, and grew up in Mexborough. After National Service he studied at Cambridge. Hughes's first book, *The Hawk in the Rain* (1957), made an immediate impact, combining intimate, exultant, Lawrentian observations of the natural world with a smoky, swaggering Shakespearean-Jacobean manner. *Lupercal* (1960) fixed him in the public mind as the author of 'An Otter' and 'Hawk Roosting' – at once a brilliant animator of the world and at some level troublingly complicit in its violence. The suicide of Hughes's wife, the American poet Sylvia Plath, in 1963, had an incalculable effect on Hughes's work. *Wodwo* (1967) is a sprawling book in several parts presented as a unity, including a play, short stories and visionary poems such as 'Gog'. It foreshadowed the through-composed mythopoeic works of the 1970s, *Crow* (revised edition, 1972) and *Gaudete* (1977). *Crow*, a horror-movie book about the indomitable brutality of creation, showed Hughes ready to discard his strengths of precision and image for a thrashing if admittedly potent rhetoric. *Gaudete* involved myths of fertility and sacrifice, while shamanistic overtones often accompanied Hughes's work. Prolific and apparently unedited, Hughes by the 1990s had accumulated a vast body of poetry, which can be sampled in *New Selected Poems* (1995). Appointed Poet Laureate in 1984 in succession to Sir John Betjeman, he approached his duties with typical seriousness and energy. The resulting book, *Rain-Charm for the Duchy* (1992) provided a clearer-than-usual illustration of his beliefs – atavistic, royalist, conservative. Hughes also wrote many books for children. His critical work *Shakespeare and the Goddess of Complete Being* appeared in 1992 and *Winter Pollen: Occasional Prose*, edited by William Scammell, in 1994. Recent publications include *Tales from Ovid* (1996) and *Birthday Letters* (1998), a book of poems about and addressed to Sylvia Plath, which attracted interest far beyond the normal poetry readership and became a bestseller. He died in October 1998.

Pike

Pike, three inches long, perfect
Pike in all parts, green tigering the gold.
Killers from the egg: the malevolent aged grin.
They dance on the surface among the flies.

Or move, stunned by their own grandeur
Over a bed of emerald, silhouette
Of submarine delicacy and horror.
A hundred feet long in their world.

In ponds, under the heat-struck lily pads –
Gloom of their stillness:
Logged on last year's black leaves, watching upwards.
Or hung in an amber cavern of weeds

The jaws' hooked clamp and fangs
Not to be changed at this date;
A life subdued to its instrument;
The gills kneading quietly, and the pectorals.

Three we kept behind glass,
Jungled in weed: three inches, four,
And four and a half: fed fry to them –
Suddenly there were two. Finally one.

With a sag belly and the grin it was born with.
And indeed they spare nobody.
Two, six pounds each, over two feet long,
High and dry and dead in the willow-herb –

One jammed past its gills down the other's gullet:
The outside eye stared: as a vice locks –
The same iron in this eye
Though its film shrank in death.

A pond I fished, fifty yards across,
Whose lilies and muscular tench
Had outlasted every visible stone
Of the monastery that planted them –

Stilled legendary depth:
It was as deep as England. It held
Pike too immense to stir, so immense and old
That past nightfall I dared not cast

But silently cast and fished
With the hair frozen on my head
For what might move, for what eye might move.
The still splashes on the dark pond,

Owls hushing the floating woods
Frail on my ear against the dream
Darkness beneath night's darkness had freed,
That rose slowly towards me, watching.

Thistles

Against the rubber tongues of cows and the hoeing hands
                                                    of men
Thistles spike the summer air
Or crackle open under a blue-black pressure.

Every one a revengeful burst
Of resurrection, a grasped fistful
Of splintered weapons and Icelandic frost thrust up

From the underground stain of a decayed Viking.
They are like pale hair and the gutturals of dialects.
Every one manages a plume of blood.

Then they grow grey, like men.
Mown down, it is a feud. Their sons appear,
Stiff with weapons, fighting back over the same ground.

Sunstruck

The freedom of Saturday afternoons
Starched to cricket dazzle, nagged at a theorem –
Shaggy valley parapets
Pending like thunder, narrowing the spin-bowler's angle.

The click, disconnected, might have escaped –
A six! And the ball slammed flat!
And the bat in flinders! The heart soaring!
And everybody jumping up and running –

Fleeing after the ball, stampeding
Through the sudden hole in Saturday – but
Already clapped into hands and the trap-shout
The ball jerked back to the stumper on its elastic.

Everything collapsed that bit deeper
Towards Monday.

Misery of the brassy sycamores!
Misery of the swans and the hard ripple!

Then again Yes Yes a wild YES –
The bat flashed round the neck in a tight coil,
The stretched shout snatching for the North Sea –
But it fell far short, even of Midgley.

And the legs running for dear life, twinkling white
In the cage of wickets
Were cornered again by the ball, pinned to the crease,
Blocked by the green and white pavilion.

Cross-eyed, mid-stump, sun-descending headache!
Brain sewn into the ball's hide
Hammering at four corners of abstraction
And caught and flung back, and caught, and again caught

To be bounced on baked earth, to be clubbed
Toward the wage-mirage sparkle of mills
Toward Lord Savile's heather
Toward the veto of the poisonous Calder

Till the eyes, glad of anything, dropped
From the bails
Into the bottom of a teacup,
To sandwich crusts for the canal cygnets.

The bowler had flogged himself to a dishclout.
And the burned batsmen returned, with changed faces,
'Like men returned from a far journey',
Under the long glare walls of evening

To the cool sheet and the black slot of home.

Tiger

At the junction of beauty and danger
The tiger's scroll becomes legible.
In relief, he moves through an impotent chaos.
The Creator is his nearest neighbour.
The mild, frosty, majestic mandala
Of his face, to spirit hospitable
As to flesh. With easy latitude
He composes his mass.
He exhales benediction,
Malediction. Privileged
At the paradoxical cross-junction
Of good and evil, and beyond both.
His own ego is unobtrusive
Among the jungle babblers,
His engineering faultlessly secure.
In a fate like an allegory
Of God-all-but-forgotten, he balances modestly
The bloodmarks of his canvas
And the long-grass dawn beauty
As the engraved moment of lightning
On the doomsday skin of the Universe.

Anthony Thwaite, 1930–

Anthony Thwaite spent his childhood in Yorkshire and was evacuated to the United States during the war. Following National Service, he studied at Christ Church, Oxford, thereafter combining university teaching overseas with work in broadcasting, publishing and as an editor of *The New Statesman* and *Encounter*. His first book, *Home Truths* (1957), suggested that he was a latecomer to the Movement, but while his language has often sought a modest, proverbial pitch, the range of his poetic interests and approaches has always been wide. Archaeology, Japanese history and literature, and the culture of the Victorian period, have prompted his most ambitious poems. *Selected Poems* (1997) is an unusually brutal pruning of forty years' work. Thwaite's role as editor of the *Collected Poems* and the *Letters* of Philip Larkin has led him into public controversy. He is also the author of the several times revised, opinionated but very useful *Poetry Today*, whose latest incarnation, *A Critical Guide to British Poetry 1960–95*, appeared in 1996.

Imagine a City

Imagine a city. It is not a city you know.
You approach it either by river or by one of four roads,
Never by air. The river runs through the city.
The roads enter at the four points of the compass.
There are city walls, old ones, now long decayed
But they are still there, bits of a past it once had.

Approach it now (shall we say) by the road from the east.
You can see the ruined gate from a mile away,
And, beyond the gate, towers that may be temples or
                                                    tombs.
It is evening, and smoke here and there is rising in drifts,
So meals are being prepared, you suppose, in thousands
                                                    of houses.
There is a smell of roast meat, a succulent odour.

Now enter the city, go through the eastern gate.
Great birds, like vultures, shift on its broken tiles.
The street in front of you is obscured by the setting sun,
A yellow-red ball in a dazzling haze of brilliance.
The paving under your feet is uneven. You stumble,
Clutching a door that leans to your hand as you take it.

And now for the first time you are uneasy.
No one is in the street, or in the side-turnings,
Or leaning out from the windows, or standing in
                                                    doorways.
The fading sunlight conspires with the drifting smoke,
Yet if there were people here surely you'd see them,
Or, at the least, hear them. But there is silence.

Yet you go on, if only because to go back now
Seems worse – worse (shall we say) than whatever
Might meet you ahead, as the street narrows, and alleys
Flow in hither and thither, a dead-end of tangles

Looping forwards and sideways, neither here nor there,
                                             but somehow
Changing direction like water wind-caught abruptly.

And there you are, now. You may find the western gate.
It must lie straight ahead, the north to your right,
The south to your left. But where is the river
You heard about (you say) at the beginning?
That is for you to find out, or not to find out.
It may not, in any case, serve as a way of escape.

You imagined a city. It is not a city you know.

Alan Brownjohn, 1931–

Alan Brownjohn was born in London and educated at Merton College, Oxford. After working as teacher and college lecturer, he became a freelance writer. Brownjohn's scrupulous, morally exact early work could be placed in the Movement, though he attended meetings of the Group, but a dimension of fiction, and a wide range of free verse forms, enter his poems in the 1970s. The Movement concern for order and truthfulness is offset by a sense of bottomless alarm, and the measured, reasonable voice that inhabits the poems becomes precisely attuned to the unease it can suggest, as well as its humorous potential. Brownjohn is a political poet as well as a moralist. His work might be read as a biography of English left-liberal belief in the post-war era. A substantial *Collected Poems* appeared in 1988, followed by *The Observation Car* (1990), containing the long, ambitious 'Sea Pictures', and *The Cruel Arcade* (1994). Among Brownjohn's other books is a novel, *The Long Shadows* (1997), inspired by his frequent visits to Romania.

An Elegy on Mademoiselle Claudette

Mourning the final death from disbelief of one
Who lies now farther out than her rival's sword;
The sea, having had her at last, being
A fit receptacle and outcome. She
Was thirty-two when she died, I having
Given her first credulity when I was eight,

And the ideal reader. Somewhere they met,
Her fatalism, my childhood, and made strange friends:
She held her world with fingertips of ice
On chalices of poison. She was in the eyes
Pulling mine at fifteen over café floors, she stared
Out from trains, she dared in time to come near and be

No different, even when she undressed. The spell didn't
Break, because she was always gone next morning,
A skyline figure on horseback, not leaving a note.
And this continued some while, her cloak
Flowed at numberless parties, and she nurtured
Linguistic codes beyond mine, and had flats

(Which I never went to) all mauve lights and white divans,
Acting indestructible enough to be
A life-force in her way, a fuel for one kind
Of imagination. But what could she keep when
Life coarsened, and truth walked in? Well,
She thrived for a while by updating her devices,

Like – playing the metropolis, all the sleights of
Communications, the trick of the very new:
She was good at sudden taxis, away, in the small hours,
Had a dreadful skill with things like the letter
Never sent because of the promise to phone,
Never kept. And she had this vague gallery of

'Friends' to refer to, in a sensual, significant abstract,
No names vouchsafed. She was trying hard, was
                                        desperately
Applying the cosmetics of decline. – But she's
Abstract herself now; finally dead; not
Struck down by some other in contest, not replaced
By odder enchantments, not vanquished by any

Conversion from Snow Queens to Earth Mothers, none
Of that: she just couldn't keep up the pose.
It was not so long back that her last departure
Took place. She put out one entreating hand in velvet,
But it looked like something ghost-written for her.
I tried to feed those plaintive metaphors, I searched

The depths of my compassionate soul for faith
To keep her alive; but all the same she died.
And sad the way daylight lastly saw her sink,
Poor Mademoiselle Claudette: leaving shadows of
                                        stances only,
Vague rags of garments, tawdry stage properties,
And terribly dry pink tissues on bedroom floors.

The Ship of Death

First, prolonged and weird estuarial waters,
    And so wide before you realize: full of rusted,
Sunken, purposeless objects; or creaking guide-lights
    Offering unclear channels, curving paths
Of a grey water greyer than the rest. And now the eager
    Sea-birds that followed have dropped back for the
                            shore.
The strip-lighting blinks on in the Dining Room, the
                            cutlery
    Scintillates. But you don't enjoy their small-talk at the
                            table, as
The white-coated band on the platform lilts into selections,
    Selections: it's a musical about your life they
Are playing them from, and it could not have run long
                            in town.
    Now the ship tilts, and the crockery slides downhill; and
There is a tannoy announcement from the captain:
    Welcoming you to the ship, hoping you will be
Comfortable, and reminding you there is no destination.
    You leave the table for the bar. Already it's dark, which
Might be more interesting; though you expected,
                      looking out,
    That a scattering of stars might show; and the sky's dull.
Far off, is it west, you can pick out an esplanade
    With lights like a frippery of beads; you
Never attained that one, wherever. Your drink hasn't
                          lasted,
    The print in your newspaper blurs and you can't see
                            faces
Very clearly. The map, of the route of the ship in
    The frame on the wall, is practically blank. Is there a
                        rest room?
The stewards don't attend to you, they are attending

To the bed-makers in the cabins. The duty-free shop
Is a shut grille. The handrail in the corridor misses
    Your hand, upstairs both sides of the deck cant you into
The bullets of the spray. The wake is dark, the prow is
                                    chained off.
    You go to the Engine Room for the monotone of the
                                    drone.
But that is no anaesthetic. There should be
    Amusements aboard, surely? What about the staterooms
Looking so sumptuous in the brochures? And the gilt
                            lounges?
    Something worth having this ticket for? God, this
                            ship feels
No different from being alive; because
    Your seaboard walk shakes like your walk on land, and
All your thinking ends at the same advice: it's time, no
    Other choice, to go down the metal steps to
Where it says Men, and lock the door; be alone, alone,
    You may find, there, what's wrong that you couldn't
Name, that nobody found out.
                        – So this you do, except
    That when you have closed the door, the door locks
On you. Rust runs in lifelong trickles from the welded
    Bolts of this cubicle; everything shudders, even more,
In you and the whole ship. No hammering for help,
    Or calling, it's H.M.S. Death, death: the eternal
Accumulated store of everything life became: just
    Yourself, as you are, and your face in that bowl.
                            Smile, you're free
To vomit your self-regard for the rest of the voyage.

Tony Conran, 1931–

Tony Conran was born in West Bengal and grew up in North Wales. He studied at the University College of North Wales, Bangor, where he later taught. Since the 1950s, Conran has been a prolific and highly regarded translator of poetry in Welsh (*The Penguin Book of Welsh Verse*, 1967). His immersion in Welsh idioms is reflected in his poetry in English, much of which retains a sustaining sense of community and combines modernist and traditional Welsh practice. His earlier poetry is collected in *Poems 1951–1967* (1974). Subsequent work included *Blodeuwedd* (1988) and *Castles* (1993), the translations of *Eighteen Poems of Dante Alighieri* (1975) and *The Cost of Strangeness* (1982), his critical study of Anglo-Welsh poetry.

Elegy for the Welsh Dead, in the Falkland Islands, 1982

Gwŷr a aeth Gatraeth oedd ffraeth eu llu.
Glasfedd eu hancwyn, a gwenwyn fu.
– *Y Gododdin* (6th century)

(Men went to Catraeth, keen was their company.
They were fed on fresh mead, and it proved poison.)

Men went to Catraeth. The luxury liner
For three weeks feasted them.
They remembered easy ovations,
Our boys, splendid in courage.
For three weeks the albatross roads,
Passwords of dolphin and petrel,
Practised their obedience
Where the killer whales gathered,
Where the monotonous seas yelped.
Though they went to church with their standards
Raw death has them garnished.

Men went to Catraeth. The Malvinas
Of their destiny greeted them strangely,
Instead of affection there was coldness,
Splintering iron and the icy sea,
Mud and the wind's malevolent satire.
They stood nonplussed in the bomb's indictment.

Malcolm Wigley of Connah's Quay. Did his helm
Ride high in the war-line?
Did he drink enough mead for that journey?
The desolated shores of Tegeingl,
Did they pig this steel that destroyed him?
The Dee runs silent beside empty foundries.
The way of the wind and the rain is adamant.

Clifford Elley of Pontypridd. Doubtless he feasted.
He went to Catraeth with a bold heart.
He was used to valleys. The shadow held him.
The staff and the fasces of tribunes betrayed him.
With the oil of our virtue we have anointed
His head, in the presence of foes.

Philip Sweet of Cwmbach. Was he shy before girls?
He exposes himself now to the hags, the glance
Of the loose-fleshed whores, the deaths
That congregate like gulls on garbage.
His sword flashed in the wastes of nightmare.

Russell Carlisle of Rhuthun. Men of the North
Mourn Rheged's son in the castellated vale.
His nodding charger neighed for the battle.
Uplifted hooves pawed at the lightning.
Now he lies down. Under the air he is dead.

Men went to Catraeth. Of the forty-three
Certainly Tony Jones of Carmarthen was brave.
What did it matter, steel in the heart?
Shrapnel is faithful now. His shroud is frost.

With the dawn men went. Those forty-three,
Gentlemen all, from the streets and byways of Wales,
Dragons of Aberdare, Denbigh and Neath –
Figment of empire, whore's honour, held them.
Forty-three at Catraeth died for our dregs.

Geoffrey Hill, 1932–

Geoffrey Hill was born in Bromsgrove, Worcestershire, and educated at Oxford. He has taught at the universities of Leeds, Cambridge and Boston. *For the Unfallen* (1959) introduced a poet quite incompatible with Movement domesticity, beginning with a telling of Creation and continuing through compact, resonant poems rooted in English history. *King Log* (1968) made Hill's interests clearer – belief, barbarism both ancient and modern, and the responsibilities of the artist. 'Funeral Music', a sequence set in the Wars of the Roses, is widely regarded as a contemporary classic. So too is 'The Songbook of Sebastian Arrurruz', the work of an imaginary modernist poet. *Mercian Hymns* (1971) is a set of chiselled, vivid prose poems on the life of the half-legendary Offa, King of Mercia: as is Hill's habit, contemporary parallels are pursued, sometimes to humorous effect. *Tenebrae* (1978) is a densely allusive book, with meditations on faith and Englishness, while *The Mystery of the Charity of Charles Peguy* (1983) contemplates the life, and the death in battle in the First World War, of the Catholic intellectual Peguy. *Collected Poems* appeared in 1985. *Canaan* (1996) seemed to some readers to mark a decline in concentration and authority.

Hill is a learned poet, and a conscientious one. What often shadows his work is a concern with the propriety of art. In maintaining a continuity with modernism he has endeared himself to many academics, while others feel that there is something factitious in the extreme self-consciousness of his poems. His gifts of image, phrase and orchestration can hardly be denied, however. Hill's essays, *The Lords of Limit*, appeared in 1984. Among the critical literature on his work are essays by Christopher Ricks in *The Force of Poetry* (1984), *Geoffrey Hill: Essays on His Work*, edited by Peter Robinson (1985) and the scornfully dissenting Tom Paulin's 'A Visionary Nationalist: Geoffrey Hill' in *Minotaur: Poetry and the Nation State* (1992).

from Funeral Music

3

They bespoke doomsday and they meant it by
God, their curved metal rimming the low ridge.
But few appearances are like this. Once
Every five hundred years a comet's
Over-riding stillness might reveal men
In such array, livid and featureless,
With England crouched beastwise beneath it all.
'Oh, that old northern business . . .' A field
After battle utters its own sound
Which is like nothing on earth, but is earth.
Blindly the questing snail, vulnerable
Mole emerge, blindly we lie down, blindly
Among carnage the most delicate souls
Tup in their marriage-blood, gasping 'Jesus'.

A Song from Armenia

from *The Songbook of Sebastian Arrurruz*

Roughly-silvered leaves that are the snow
On Ararat seen through those leaves.
The sun lays down a foliage of shade.

A drinking-fountain pulses its head
Two or three inches from the troughed stone.
An old woman sucks there, gripping the rim.

Why do I have to relive, even now,
Your mouth, and your hand running over me
Deft as a lizard, like a sinew of water?

The Naming of Offa

from *Mercian Hymns*

I

King of the perennial holly-groves, the riven sand-
    stone: overlord of the M5: architect of the his-
    toric rampart and ditch, the citadel at Tamworth,
    the summer hermitage in Holy Cross: guardian of
    the Welsh Bridge and the Iron Bridge: contractor
    to the desirable new estates: saltmaster: money-
    changer: commissioner for oaths: martyrologist:
    the friend of Charlemagne.

'I liked that,' said Offa, 'sing it again.'

The Death of Offa

from *Mercian Hymms*

XXVII

'Now when King Offa was alive and dead', they were
    all there, the funereal gleemen: papal legate and
    rural dean; Merovingian car-dealers, Welsh mercen-
    aries; a shuffle of house-carls.

He was defunct. They were perfunctory. The ceremony
    stood acclaimed. The mob received memorial vouch-
    ers and signs.

After that shadowy, thrashing midsummer hail-storm,
    Earth lay for a while, the ghost-bride of livid
    Thor, butcher of strawberries, and the shire-tree
    dripped red in the arena of its uprooting.

George MacBeth, 1932–92

George MacBeth was born in Shotts, Lanarkshire, grew up in Sheffield and studied at New College, Oxford. He was an influential member of the Group. For much of his career he was a radio talks producer for the BBC, where he offered much encouragement to emergent writers. Opinion divides over MacBeth. To some readers, MacBeth is a virtuoso stylist of formidable range and depth; to others a rhetorical poseur, indulging the horrors of modernity. There seems to be truth in both views. *Collected Poems 1958–82* (1990) was followed by *Trespassing: Poems from Ireland* (1991). *A Child of the War* (1987) is a fascinating prose memoir.

The God of Love

The musk-ox is accustomed to near-Arctic conditions.
When danger threatens, these beasts cluster together to
form a defensive wall or a 'porcupine' with the calves in
the middle.
– Dr Wofgang Engelhardt, *Survival of the Free*

I found them between far hills, by a frozen lake,
    On a patch of bare ground. They were grouped
In a solid ring, like an ark of horn. And around
    Them circled, slowly closing in,
Their tongues lolling, their ears flattened against the wind,

A whirlpool of wolves. As I breathed, one fragment
                                    of bone and
    Muscle detached itself from the mass and
Plunged. The pad of the pack slackened, as if
    A brooch had been loosened. But when the bull
Returned to the herd, the revolving collar was tighter.
                                    And only

The windward owl, uplifted on white wings
    In the glass of air, alert for her young,
Soared high enough to look into the cleared centre
    And grasp the cause. To the slow brain
Of each beast by the frozen lake what lay in the cradle of
                                    their crowned

Heads of horn was a sort of god-head. Its brows
    Nudged when the ark was formed. Its need
Was a delicate womb away from the iron collar
    Of death, a cave in the ring of horn
Their encircling flesh had backed with fur. That the collar
                                    of death

Was the bone of their own skulls: that a softer womb
 Would open between far hills in a plunge
Of bunched muscles: and that their immortal calf lay
 Dead on the snow with its horns dug into
The ice for grass: they neither saw nor felt. And yet if

 That hill of fur could split and run – like a river
  Of ice in thaw, like a broken grave –
 It would crack across the icy crust of withdrawn
  Sustenance and the rigid circle
Of death be shivered: the fed herd would entail its
                                              under-fur

 On the swell of a soft hill and the future be sown
  On grass, I thought. But the herd fell
 By the bank of the lake on the plain, and the pack
                                              closed,
  And the ice remained. And I saw that the god
In their ark of horn was a god of love, who made them die.

Sylvia Plath, 1932–63

Sylvia Plath was born in Boston, Massachusetts, and studied at Smith College. In January 1963 she committed suicide. A brilliant student and precocious writer, Plath was tormented by her father's early death and her relationship with her mother. There had been earlier suicide attempts. It is part of the great sadness of Plath's career that considerations of her work seem inextricably but not always constructively linked to analyses of her life and psyche. Enlisted by some as a patron saint of feminism, she was in some respects a strongly conventional figure, as concerned with home-making as with literature, driven by a need to excel in all areas of life. This may be thought sufficient strain in itself. Whatever the detailed truth of the matter, her studious poetic apprenticeship, in which she took on set forms and themes, absorbing the lessons of Wallace Stevens, Marianne Moore and Theodore Roethke (see *The Colossus*, 1960), put her in a very strong position when her own true and terrible subject matter – suffering, depression, the collapse of marriage – made itself known in a usuable form. The poems of *Ariel* (1963) and some others published posthumously are a great achievement, combining an Expressionist force with absolute precision. They are also unrepeatable, which is why Plath has been valuable as an inspiration but rarely as a direct influence. *Collected Poems*, edited by Ted Hughes, appeared in 1981. Plath's novel, *The Bell Jar*, appeared in 1963. There are numerous biographies but perhaps the most interesting work is itself a study of Plath's biographers, *The Silent Woman* by Janet Malcolm (1994).

Poppies in October

Even the sun-clouds this morning cannot manage such
skirts.
Nor the woman in the ambulance
Whose red heart blooms through her coat so
astoundingly –

A gift, a love gift
Utterly unasked for
By a sky

Palely and flamily
Igniting its carbon monoxides, by eyes
Dulled to a halt under bowlers.

O my God, what am I
That these late mouths should cry open
In a forest of frost, in a dawn of cornflowers.

Sheep in Fog

The hills step off into whiteness.
People or stars
Regard me sadly, I disappoint them.

The train leaves a line of breath.
O slow
Horse the color of rust,

Hooves, dolorous bells –
All morning the
Morning has been blackening,

A flower left out.
My bones hold a stillness, the far
Fields melt my heart.

They threaten
To let me through to a heaven
Starless and fatherless, a dark water.

The Moon and the Yew Tree

This is the light of the mind, cold and planetary.
The trees of the mind are black. The light is blue.
The grasses unload their griefs on my feet as if I were God,
Prickling my ankles and murmuring of their humility.
Fumy, spiritous mists inhabit this place
Separated from my house by a row of headstones.
I simply cannot see where there is to get to.

The moon is no door. It is a face in its own right,
White as a knuckle and terribly upset.
It drags the sea after it like a dark crime; it is quiet
With the O-gape of complete despair. I live here.
Twice on Sunday, the bells startle the sky –
Eight great tongues affirming the Resurrection.
At the end, they soberly bong out their names.

The yew tree points up. It has a Gothic shape.
The eyes lift after it and find the moon.
The moon is my mother. She is not sweet like Mary.
Her blue garments unloose small bats and owls.
How I would like to believe in tenderness –
The face of the effigy, gentled by candles,
Bending, on me in particular, its mild eyes.

I have fallen a long way. Clouds are flowering
Blue and mystical over the face of the stars.
Inside the church, the saints will be all blue,
Floating on their delicate feet over the cold pews,
Their hands and faces stiff with holiness.
The moon sees nothing of this. She is bald and wild.
And the message of the yew tree is blackness – blackness
                                        and silence.

Edge

The woman is perfected.
Her dead

Body wears the smile of accomplishment,
The illusion of a Greek necessity

Flows in the scrolls of her toga,
Her bare

Feet seem to be saying:
We have come so far, it is over.

Each dead child coiled, a white serpent,
One at each little

Pitcher of milk, now empty.
She has folded

Them back into her body as petals
Of a rose close when the garden

Stiffens and odors bleed
From the sweet, deep throats of the night flower.

The moon has nothing to be sad about,
Staring from her hood of bone.

She is used to this sort of thing.
Her blacks crackle and drag.

Peter Redgrove, 1932–

Peter Redgrove was educated at Taunton School and Queen's College, Cambridge, where he read Natural Sciences. He has held writing residencies in England and the United States. That Redgrove attended meetings of the Group and received encouragement from the Marxist-Symbolist Martin Bell is further indication of how broad a church the Group was. While Redgrove has sometimes been paired with Ted Hughes, a Cambridge contemporary, his bounding energy has a very different mood. Often erotic and comic, absurdly inventive and startlingly prolific, he embodies a kind of Muscular Pantheism which owes something to Christopher Smart. His scientific mysticism is celebrated in numerous collections, as well as plays and fiction. *Collected Poems* is soon to appear in an enlarged edition.

Under the Reservoir

The reservoir great as the weight
Of a black sun radiates through the cracks
In the concrete, expresses water supercharged

By pressure and darkness, the whole body
Of water leaning on the hairline cracks,
Water pumping itself through masonry

Like light through glass. Water charged
By the mystery of lying there in storeys
In transparent tons staring both upwards and downwards

(His coffee hand spills on his shirt the regalia
Of his worried mind in linked splashes like medals
Of a muddy war)

The reservoirs in their unending battle to flow
Turned into steely strain like hammered pewter
Endure their thousand tons of mud, as though

They held their surfaces open like Samson
To the dust that sifts on to their cold pewter,
And rejoice in their dark linings, as they might

Rejoice in plentiful seed,
Black seed of illimitable forest cracking
Open the stone rooms when the water has gone.

The Big Sleep

Sea, great sleepy
Syrup easing round the point, toiling
In two dials, like cogs

Of an immense sea-clock,
One roping in, the other out.
Salt honey, restless in its comb,

Ever-living, moving, salt sleep,
Sandy like the grains at eyes' corners
Of waking, or sleepiness, or ever-sleeping;

And when the sun shines, visited as by bees
Of the sun that glitter, and hum in every wave,
As though the honey collected the bees;

The honey that was before all flowers, sleepiness,
Deep gulfs of it, more of it than anything,
Except sleepy warm rock in the earth centre

Turning over slowly, creating magnetism,
Which is a kind of sleepiness, drowsy glue
Binding the fingers, weakly waking fingers,

Or fingers twitching lightly with the tides;
And the giant clock glides like portals, tics
Like eyelids of giants sleeping, and we lie

In Falmouth like many in a bed,
And when the big one turns
We all turn; some of us

Fall out of bed into the deep soil,
Our bones twitch to the tides,
Laid in their magnetic pattern, our waters

Rise like white spirits distilled by the moon,
Can get no further, and turn over
heavy as honey into the sea

To sleep and dream, and when the big one dreams
We all dream. And when she storms
We all weep and ache, and some fall

Into her gulfs as she tosses, and we weep
For the lifeboats toiling on the nightmares . . .
But in those beds waters touch each other

Coiling, in a certain way, and where they touch,
At the very point, a mineral spark,
A bone begins to grow, someone is

Putting bones together in the gulf,
In her accustomed patterns – and in their season
The women walk about the town, a big drop

Of the Dreamer in their bellies, and in the drop
A smaller dreamer, image of themselves,
Who are the image dreamed by the ocean's drop,

By the two clocks, one roping in, one out.

Rosemary Tonks, 1932–

Rosemary Tonks was born in London. Her two collections of poetry are *Notes on Cafés and Bedrooms* (1963) and *Iliad of Broken Sentences* (1967). 'The Sofas, Fogs and Cinemas', included here, is clearly written in the light of the late nineteenth-century French poet Jules Laforgue, also greatly influential on T. S. Eliot. Tonks, who has ceased to publish, is believed to have adopted evangelical Christianity in the early 1970s.

The Sofas, Fogs and Cinemas

I have lived it, and lived it,
My nervous, luxury civilization,
My sugar-loving nerves have battered me to pieces.

. . . Their idea of literature is hopeless.
Make them drink their own poetry!
Let them eat their gross novel, full of mud.

It's quiet; just the fresh, chilly weather . . . and he
Gets up from his dead bedroom, and comes in here
And digs himself into the sofa.
He stays there up to two hours in the hole – and talks
– Straight into the large subjects, he faces up to *everything*
It's . . . . . . damnably depressing.
(That great lavatory coat . . . the cigarillo burning
In the little dish . . . And when he calls out: 'Ha!'
Madness! – you no longer possess your own furniture.)

On my bad days (and I'm being broken
At this very moment) I speak of my ambitions . . . and he
Becomes intensely gloomy, with the look of something
                                                    jugged,
Morose, sour, mouldering away, with lockjaw . . .

I grow coarse; and more modern (*I*, who am driven mad
By my ideas; who go nowhere;
Who dare not leave my frontdoor, lest an idea . . .)
All right. I admit everything, everything!

Oh yes, the opera (Ah, but the cinema)
He particularly enjoys it, enjoys it *horribly*, when
                                            someone's ill
At the last minute; and they specially fly in
A new, gigantic, Dutch soprano. He wants to help her

With her arias. Old goat! Blasphemer!
He wants to help her with her arias!

No, I . . . go to the cinema,
I particularly like it when the fog is thick, the street
Is like a hole in an old coat, and the light is brown as
                                          laudanum,
. . . the fogs! the fogs! The cinemas
Where the criminal shadow-literature flickers over our
                                          faces,
The screen is spread out like a thundercloud – that bangs
And splashes you with acid . . . or lies derelict, with
                                          lighted waters in it,
And in the silence, drips and crackles – taciturn, luxurious.
. . . The drugged and battered Philistines
Are all around you in the auditorium . . .

And he . . . is somewhere else, in his dead bedroom clothes,
He wants to make me think his thoughts
And they will be *enormous*, dull – (just the sort
To keep away from).
. . . when I see that cigarillo, when I see it . . . smoking
And he wants to face the international situation . . .
Lunatic rages! Blackness! Suffocation!

– All this sitting about in cafés to calm down
Simply wears me out. And their idea of literature!
The idiotic cut of the stanzas; the novels, full up, gross.

I have lived it, and I know too much.
My café-nerves are breaking me
With black, exhausting information.

James Simmons, 1933–

James Simmons was born in Londonderry and studied at Leeds University. He taught at Leeds, in Africa and at the New University of Ulster in Coleraine. In 1968 he founded the long-lived magazine *The Honest Ulsterman*. Simmons is stylistically plainer than most of his Northern Irish colleagues, an assured and, in his phrase, 'dirty-minded' comic poet. His unpretentious clarity lends authenticity and, at times, poignancy to his poems of love and marriage, and in cultural matters he can be found siding with life against the massed forces of T. S. Eliot. *Poems 1956–86* appeared in 1986. Simmons has also made recordings of his songs.

Censorship

A crappy bookshop in a country town.
The manager sets five soiled copies down.
He doesn't care what honesty is worth.
Indifference is a virtue in the North.

'This is pure dirt,' he says. I shake my head:
'It's true, it's funny, and it should be read.'
He says, 'We get schoolchildren in the shop,
and people have complained. We'll have to stop
taking your magazine if you print dirt.'

I remonstrate, 'Look, can't you see how hurt
young Harrison would be to hear you talking
like that about his work . . . ?' but the man is walking
back to his lair. 'That poem will outlast
a wilderness of sermons from Belfast!'
I shout, and chase him, catch him as he darts
into his office, and grab his private parts.
He shrieks out, 'Jesus. Help!' I squeeze some more,
and two teenagers knock the office door.
We hear them whisper, 'Someone is in pain.'
Damn right. I squeeze his private parts again.
'What's wrong?' a girl's voice trembles. 'Christ! My balls!
He's trying to tear them off,' the critic calls.
'Shame on you, sir,' I whisper in his ear.
'Such language, when a young person can hear.'
'It's true. It's urgent. What else could I say?'

'That's how the poet feels,' I smile. 'Good day.'

Anne Stevenson, 1933–

The child of American parents, Stevenson was born in Cambridge and educated at the University of Michigan. *Correspondences* (1974) is an ambitious epistolary work about the history of an American family – and thus of American values – from 1829 until the 1960s. Her work elsewhere, as in *Enough of Green* (1977), shows the fruitful influence of Elizabeth Bishop – a connection taken up in recent years by numerous younger female poets. The distinguished *Collected Poems 1955–1995* appeared in 1996. Stevenson is also the author of a controversial biography of Sylvia Plath, *Bitter Fame* (1989).

North Sea off Carnoustie

You know it by the northern look of the shore,
by salt-worried faces,
an absence of trees, an abundance of lighthouses.
It's a serious ocean.

Along marram-scarred, sandbitten margins
wired roofs straggle out to where
a cold little holiday fair
has floated in and pitched itself
safely near the prairie of a golf course.
Coloured lights have sunk deep into the solid wind,
but all they've caught is a pair of lovers
and three silly boys.
Everyone else has a dog.
Or a room to get to.

The smells are of fish and of sewage and cut grass.
Oystercatchers, doubtful of habitation,
clamour *weep, weep, weep*, as they fuss over
scummy black rocks the tide leaves for them.

The sea is as near as we come to another world.

But there in your stony and windswept garden
a blackbird is confirming the grip of the land.
You, you, he murmurs, dark purple in his voice.

And now in far quarters of the horizon
lighthouses are awake, sending messages –
invitations to the landlocked,
warnings to the experienced,
but to anyone returning from the planet ocean,
candles in the windows of a safe earth.

Fleur Adcock, 1934–

Born in Auckland, New Zealand, Fleur Adcock spent the war in England. She studied Classics at Wellington University and worked as a librarian. In 1963 she moved to London. The progress of Adcock's work has consisted of a gradual simplification of style. Her best earlier poems have an exotic, bejewelled quality, dream-driven but precise (see 'The Ex-Queen among the Astronomers'), while the poems of family history from *Looking Back* (1997) attempt a conversational plainness. Adcock is a fine love poet – painfully honest, vengeful and funny by turns. *Selected Poems* (1991) represents six earlier volumes. Adcock has edited an important anthology, *The Faber Book of Twentieth-Century Women's Poetry* (1987) and, with Jacqueline Simms, *The Oxford Book of Creatures* (1995), as well as translating Romanian and medieval Latin poetry.

The Ex-Queen among the Astronomers

They serve revolving saucer eyes,
dishes of stars; they wait upon
huge lenses hung aloft to frame
the slow procession of the skies.

They calculate, adjust, record,
watch transits, measure distances.
They carry pocket telescopes
to spy through when they walk abroad.

Spectra possess their eyes; they face
upwards, alert for meteorites,
cherishing little glassy worlds:
receptacles for outer space.

But she, exile, expelled, ex-queen,
swishes among the men of science
waiting for cloudy skies, for nights
when constellations can't be seen.

She wears the rings he let her keep;
she walks as she was taught to walk
for his approval, years ago.
His bitter features taunt her sleep.

And so when these have laid aside
their telescopes, when lids are closed
between machine and sky, she seeks
terrestrial bodies to bestride.

She plucks this one or that among
the astronomers, and is become
his canopy, his occultation;
she sucks at earlobe, penis, tongue

mouthing the tubes of flesh; her hair
crackles, her eyes are comet-sparks.
She brings the distant briefly close
above his dreamy abstract stare.

Street Song

Pink Lane, Strawberry Lane, Pudding Chare:
someone is waiting, I don't know where;
hiding among the nursery names,
he wants to play peculiar games.

In Leazes Terrace or Leazes Park
someone is loitering in the dark,
feeling the giggles rise in his throat
and fingering something under his coat.

He could be sidling along Forth Lane
to stop some girl from catching her train,
or stalking the grounds of the RVI
to see if a student nurse goes by.

In Belle Grove Terrace or Fountain Row
or Hunter's Road he's raring to go –
unless he's the quiet shape you'll meet
on the cobbles in Back Stowell Street.

Monk Street, Friars Street, Gallowgate
are better avoided when it's late.
Even in Sandhill and the Side
there are shadows where a man could hide.

So don't go lightly along Darn Crook
because the Ripper's been brought to book.
Wear flat shoes, and be ready to run:
remember, sisters, there's more than one.

Brendan Kennelly, 1936–

Kennelly was born in Co. Kerry and educated at Trinity College, Dublin, where he became Professor of Modern English Literature. *My Dark Fathers* (1964) established his early reputation as an assured and attractive lyric poet. In mid-career he published the bestselling *Cromwell* (1983), a vast re-examination of Ireland's relations with its historical oppressor and with itself. Further ambitious works followed: *The Book of Judas* (1991), a violent, rawly comic set of commentaries on the theme of betrayal and self-interest; and *Poetry My Arse* (1995). Kennelly has also made translations from Lorca and Euripides. His selected prose, *Journey into Joy*, appeared in 1994. *Dark Fathers into Light*, edited by Richard Pine (1994), is a selection of essays on his work.

Oliver to His Brother

Loving brother, I am glad to hear of your welfare
And that our children have so much leisure
They can travel far to eat cherries.
This is most excusable in my daughter
Who loves that fruit and whom I bless.
Tell her I expect she writes often to me
And that she be kept in some exercise.
Cherries and exercise go well together.
I have delivered my son up to you.
I hope you counsel him; he will need it;
I choose to believe he believes what you say.
I send my affection to all your family.
Let sons and daughters be serious; the age requires it.
I have things to do, all in my own way.
For example, I take not kindly to rebels.
Today, in Burford Churchyard, Cornet Thompson
Was led to the place of execution.
He asked for prayers, got them, died well.
After him, a Corporal, brought to the same place
Set his back against the wall and died.
A third chose to look death in the face,
Stood straight, showed no fear, chilled into his pride.
Men die their different ways
And girls eat cherries
In the Christblessed fields of England.
Some weep. Some have cause. Let weep who will.
Whole floods of brine are at their beck and call.
I have work to do in Ireland.

Gillian Clarke, 1937–

Gillian Clarke was born in Cardiff, where she read English. After working in broadcasting and as an art historian, she took up writing full-time. She was for several years the editor of the *Anglo-Welsh Review* and is a leading figure in Anglo-Welsh literature. Her work is exquisitely detailed and strongly lyrical, often concentrating on Welsh landscapes, history and the lives of women. There is also a strand of humane political protest and environmental concern. *Collected Poems* appeared in 1997.

Llŷr

Ten years old, at my first Stratford play:
The river[1] and the king[2] with their Welsh names
Bore in the darkness of a summer night
Through interval and act and interval.
Swans moves double through glossy water
Gleaming with imponderable meanings.
Was it Gielgud on that occasion?
Or ample Laughton, crazily white-gowned,
Pillowed in wheatsheaves on a wooden cart,
Who taught the significance of little words?
All. Nothing. Fond. Ingratitude. Words
To keep me scared, awake at night. That old
Man's vanity and a daughter's 'Nothing',
Ran like a nursery rhyme in my head.

Thirty years later on the cliffs of Llŷn[3]
I watch how Edgar's crows and choughs still measure
How high cliffs are, how thrown stones fall
Into history, how deeply the bruise
Spreads in the sea where the wave has broken.
The turf is stitched with tormentil and thrift,
Blue squill and bird bones, tiny shells, heartsease.
Yellowhammers sing like sparks in the gorse.
The landscape's marked with figures of old men:
The bearded sea; thin-boned, wind-bent trees;
Shepherd and labourer and night-fisherman.
Here and there among the crumbling farms
Are lit kitchen windows on distant hills,
And guilty daughters longing to be gone.

1. Avon/Afon: river (Welsh)
2. Llŷr: Lear
3. Llŷn: N. W. peninsula of Wales

Night falls on Llŷn, on forefathers,
Old Celtic kings and the more recent dead,
Those we are still guilty about, flowers
Fade in jam jars on their graves; renewed
Refusals are heavy on our minds.
My head is full of sound, remembered speech,
Syllables, ideas just out of reach;
The close, looped sound of curlew and the far
Subsidiary roar, cadences shaped
By the long coast of the peninsula,
The continuous pentameter of the sea.
When I was ten a fool and a king sang
Rhymes about sorrow, and there I heard
That nothing is until it has a word.

John Fuller, 1937–

The son of Roy Fuller, John Fuller was born in Kent and educated at Oxford. He has been a Fellow of Magdalen College for many years. *Fairground Music* (1961) introduced a learned and accomplished poet with an interest in fable and fiction, indebted to Auden in the spirit rather than the letter. His ingenuity is typified by 'The Most Difficult Position' (*Lies and Secrets*, 1979), a long work about the nineteenth-century chess rivalry of Staunton and Morphy. There is a case for reading Fuller as the progenitor of postmodernist poetry in the English mainstream: his fictive, parodic, donnish manner, and his encouragement as a teacher, has influenced various younger poets, including James Fenton, Alan Jenkins and Mick Imlah. *Collected Poems* (1996) is vast, diverse and at times very distinguished. Fuller's novels include the brilliant *Flying to Nowhere* (1983) and *The Burning Boys* (1989). His long-awaited study of Auden appeared in 1998.

England

Falling towards the map is a controlled illusion,
The text scrolled to the cursor. It is England down there,
Tilted like a display. It is a living space
    Screened for observation,
A gravity-haunted logo, a significant shape
    From which there is no escape.

The shires are whitened with snow, old ploughing
Turned to Aztec friezes and museum crochet.
Between the rafters of weather and the granite flags
    Is a simulated surface
Of plot and portion that we only ever know
    As landscape from below.

It implicates our wish to be welcomed, our resolve
To enter the dull story and to make it remarkable,
To order the memory like a WAAF croupier
    Pushing her heroes across
Inches that are clouds and tiny villages recalling
    Our fear of falling.

At the heart of England we are pursuer and pursued,
Where frozen footprints are the history of that hunt
And towns we think we never visited are like
    Both past and future,
Tremendously distinguished in the willed notation
    Of our imagination.

At the heart of England the drivers are silently crawling
Bumper to bumper, the exits sealed off, the route
A duty to some present but long-forgotten intention
    And the lights are flashing
As if to warn us to keep to the dogged pace
    Of a wry acquisitive race.

At the heart of England we listen to old stories
With an amusement that guarantees their lack of any
                                              power
To direct our attention to what they may be saying
    And off we stolidly stump
Past the gingerbread cathedral and the factory blur
    To the scenery we prefer.

There the eye is of course directed upwards
As paths respect the mossy boulders and outcrop
Of the heights that induce their steady winding and
                                        climbing
    Until some point is reached
Where we see that heartland sprawled as in a lap,
    Half-asleep, half-map.

For the most part they are nibbled humps or great
                                        ledges
Swathed in rolling mist like experimental theatre:
It suits us to shade the eyes, to stare for coasts.
    From that isolation
On either side adventurous streams agree
    To part and find the sea.

We never join them. They are unjoinable.
And there is nothing much in the end to be done
Except to return either the way we came
    Or to find some other route,
Which with a monument or some woody confusion
    Maintains the illusion.

And time itself is like this, an elder dimension
Whose fondness for a particular country may turn
At a stroke to a sly or bullying disregard,
    Who knows that place is never
The involving predicate that something meant,
    Simply an accident.

And is after all where we truly belong,
Its present moments less comfortable than sofas
And the presences scattered on tables before them
    That say: 'We are England.
This memory. This book. This headline. And all the things
    That such belonging brings.'

As the very first move is the very first mistake,
Even the king's pawn, the dry kiss, the sinister
Lunge of the baby's toes like Johnson leaving
    The room when all has been said,
As what we are today depends on what we have been
    And all that we have seen,

As the bell while it rings has not ceased to summon us
Though we lose count of the strokes, as one match
Added to the whole becomes the Tower of London
    And we come to the end of the chapter,
As what we are today depends on what we are up to
    And all that we try to do,

As fingers reach where fruit must be before they know
The fruit is there, as the deafening tapes babble of love
And mothers not long out of childhood stitch shrouds
    At the cradle, as our star
Will give us short grace when it finally disappears
    And we know the prediction of tears,

As we find ourselves again in places that made us happy
And like bar-haunting actors on tour forget our cues,
As we rise in drowning with Greek cries of discovery,
    As we scribble our lucky numbers
And believe the oracle so that the hair lifts from our head
    As we shiver down in bed,

As time itself is unable to build its little Durham
Against anointed oblivion, and we are acknowledged
Its fool servitors, bearing enormous covered dishes

Into the hungry hall
Where we overhear the talk, seditious, immensely grand,
   That we hardly understand,

So we are left at last with only the hopeless instant,
The newborn innocent or wandering dressing-gowned
                                                victim
For whom the past must be a fable or abandoned
   Like an exhausted quarry,
For whom the future is that breath beyond the breath
   Taken at the moment of death,

So we are left in the thick of all our extended pleasures,
Hearing in the distance the popping guns moving over
England, and saying quietly, one to another:
   'Something is running for cover,
Something has nowhere to hide out there and likely as not
   Something is being shot,

'Such as the refined but shabby fox, left to die
As a gangster dies, arguing with balletic rhetoric
That when in the paleness of dawn the certainty of pain
   Is fully recognized
There will be no reasoning with it, no arguing at all,
   And we shall lie where we fall.'

Tony Harrison, 1937–

Tony Harrison was born in Leeds and educated at Leeds Grammar School and Leeds University, where he read Classics. He taught at universities in Nigeria and Czechoslovakia but has for many years made his living as a poet – on the page, in public recital, in the theatre and on film. 'Poetry is all I write,' he has remarked and his career has shown a dual concern – to bring serious poetry to a large audience and to analyse, satirize, master and throw off the historical conditions which, as he has also said, mean that 'poetry is not something I can take for granted'.

His first book, *The Loiners* (1970), was an accomplished collection, ranging from Spanish atrocities during the Dutch Revolt (see 'The Nuptial Torches') to sex on a Leeds gravestone, and the nature of literature ('Thomas Campey and the Copernican System'). The full exploration of class, language and power for which Harrison's poetry is most acclaimed is to be found in the continuing sequence *The School of Eloquence*. The use of the RP accent as a means of control and exclusion, the fate of the 'tongueless' man in history, the machine-breakers of the Industrial Revolution and the poet's vexed relationship with the inarticulate father from whom education separated him still further – these are a few of the themes which Harrison builds into a complex sequence where the satirist and elegist combine. The poems, in the sixteen-line 'Meredithian' sonnet, are a form of revenge on the excluders (including a cruelly immortalized English teacher) and an ambiguous celebration of access to the power of articulacy. Class and power also figure in the long and controversial poem-film *V* (1987). Set in a Leeds graveyard during the 1984–5 miners' strike, and taking the form of Gray's famous 'Elegy', the humanist Harrison confronts his anti-self, an unemployed skinhead whose only weapons are 'bad language' and vandalism. Harrison has in effect invented the film poem: other works include *The Blasphemers' Banquet*, set in an Indian restaurant after the Rushdie fatwa (1989) and the forthcoming cinema release *Prometheus*. He has also written with great success for the National Theatre. *Selected Poems* (1987) is a generous sample, including 'A Kumquat for John Keats'. See also *The Gaze of the Gorgon* (1992) and *Dramatic Works 1973–85. Tony Harrison*, edited by Neil Astley (1991), is an invaluable collection of critical writing about Harrison's earlier work.

The Nuptial Torches

'These human victims, chained and burning at the stake,
were the blazing torches which lighted the monarch to his
nuptial couch.'
– J. L. Motley, *The Rise of the Dutch Republic*

Fish gnaw the Flushing capons, hauled from fleeced
Lutheran Holland, for tomorrow's feast.
The Netherlandish lengths, the Dutch heirlooms,
That might have graced my movements and my groom's
Fade on the fat sea's bellies where they hung
Like cover-sluts. Flesh, wet linen wrung
Bone dry in a washerwoman's raw, red,
Twisting hands, bed-clothes off a lovers' bed,
Falls off the chains. At Valladolid
It fell, flesh crumpled like a coverlid.

Young Carlos de Sessa stripped was good
For a girl to look at and he spat like wood
Green from the orchards for the cooking pots.
Flames ravelled up his flesh into dry knots
And he cried at the King: *How can you stare
On such agonies and not turn a hair?*
The King was cool: *My friend, I'd drag the logs
Out to the stake for my own son, let dogs
Get at his testes for his sins; auto-da-fés
Owe no paternity to evil ways.*
Cabrera leans against the throne, guffaws
And jots down to the Court's applause
Yet another of the King's *bon mots*.

O yellow piddle in fresh fallen snow –
Dogs on the Guadarramas . . . dogs. Their souls
Splut through their pores like porridge holes.

They wear their skins like cast-offs. Their skin grows
Puckered round the knees like rumpled hose.

Doctor Ponce de la Fuente, you,
Whose gaudy, straw-stuffed effigy in lieu
Of members hacked up in the prison, burns
Here now, one sacking arm drops off, one turns
A stubble finger and your skull still croons
Lascivious catches and indecent tunes;
And croaks: *Ashes to ashes, dust to dust.*
Pray God be with you in your lust.
And God immediately is, but such a one
Whose skin stinks like a herring in the sun,
Huge from confinement in a filthy gaol,
Crushing the hooping on my farthingale.

O Holy Mother, Holy Mother, Ho-
ly Mother Church, whose melodious, low
Labour-moans go through me as you bear
These pitch-stained children to the upper air,
Let them lie still tonight, no crowding smoke
Condensing back to men float in and poke
their charcoaled fingers at our bed, and let
Me be his pleasure, though Philip sweat
At his rhythms and use those hateful tricks
They say he feels like after heretics.

O let the King be gentle and not loom
Like Torquemada in the torture room,
Those wiry Spanish hairs, these nuptial nights,
Crackling like lit tapers in his tights,
His seed like water spluttered off hot stone.
Maria, whose dark eyes very like my own
Shine on such consummations, Maria bless
My Philip just this once with gentleness.

The King's cool knuckles on my smoky hair!

Mare Mediterraneum, la mer, la mer
That almost got him in your gorge with sides
Of feastmeats, you must flush this scared bride's
Uterus with scouring salt. O cure and cool
The scorching birthmarks of his branding-tool.

Sweat chills my small breasts and limp hands.

They curled like foetuses, *maman*, and cried.

His crusted tunics crumple as he stands:

Come, Isabella. God *is satisfied.*

Them & [uz]

(for Professors Richard Hoggart & Leon Cortez)

I

αἰαῖ, ay, ay! . . . stutterer Demosthenes
gob full of pebbles outshouting seas –

4 words only of *mi 'art aches* and . . . 'Mine's broken,
you barbarian, T. W.!' *He* was nicely spoken.
'Can't have our glorious heritage done to death!'

I played the Drunken Porter in *Macbeth*.

'Poetry's the speech of kings. You're one of those
Shakespeare gives the comic bits to: prose!
All poetry (even Cockney Keats?) you see
's been dubbed by [ʌs] into RP,
Received Pronunciation, please believe [ʌs]
your speech is in the hands of the Receivers.'

'We say [ʌs] not [uz], T.W.!' That shut my trap.
I doffed my flat a's (as in 'flat cap')
my mouth all stuffed with glottals, great
lumps to hawk up and spit out . . . *E-nun-ci-ate*!

II

So right, yer buggers, then! We'll occupy
your lousy leasehold Poetry.

I chewed up Littererchewer and spat the bones
into the lap of dozing Daniel Jones,
dropped the initials I'd been harried as
and used my *name* and my voice: [uz] [uz] [uz],
ended sentences with by with, from,
and spoke the language that I spoke at home.
RIP RP, RIP T.W.
I'm *Tony* Harrison no longer you!

You can tell the Receivers where to go
(and not aspirate it) once you know
Wordsworth's *matter/water* are full rhymes,
[uz] can be loving as well as funny.

My first mention in the *Times*
automatically made Tony Anthony!

Continuous

James Cagney was the one up both our streets.
His was the only art we ever shared.
A gangster film and choc ice were the treats
that showed about as much love as he dared.

He'd be my own age now in '49!
The hand that glinted with the ring he wore,
his father's, tipped the cold bar into mine
just as the organist dropped through the floor.

He's on the platform lowered out of sight
to organ music, this time on looped tape,
into a furnace with a blinding light
where only his father's ring will keep its shape.

I wear it now to Cagneys on my own
and sense my father's hand cupped round my treat –

they feel as though they've been chilled to the bone
from holding my ice cream all through *White Heat*.

The Rhubarbarians

I

Those glottals glugged like poured pop, each
rebarbative syllable, remembrancer, raise
'mob' *rhubarb-rhubarb* to a tribune's speech
crossing the crackle as the hayricks blaze.

The gaffers' blackleg Boswells at their side.
Horsfall of Ottiwells, if the bugger could,
'd've liked to (exact words recorded) *ride
up to my saddle-girths in Luddite blood.*

What t'mob said to the cannons on the mills,
shouted to soldier, scab and sentinel
's silence, parries and hush on whistling hills,
shadows in moonlight playing knurr and spell.

It wasn't poetry though. Nay, wiseowl Leeds
pro rege et lege schools, nobody needs
your drills and chanting to parrot right
the *tusky-tusky* of the pikes that night.

II

(On translating Smetana's *Prodaná Nevěsta* for the
Metropolitan Opera, New York.)

One afternoon the Band Conductor up on his stand
Somehow lost his baton it flew out of his hand
So I jumped in his place and conducted the band
With mi little stick of Blackpool Rock!
George Formby

Finale of ACT II. Though I resist
blurring the clarity of *hanba* (shame)
not wanting the least nuance to be missed
syllables run to rhubarb just the same . . .

Sorry, dad, you won't get that quatrain
(I'd like to be the poet my father reads!)
It's all from you once saying on the train
how most of England's rhubarb came from Leeds.

Crotchets and quavers, rhubarb silhouettes,
dark-shy sea-horse heads through waves of dung!
Rhubarb arias, duets, quartets
soar to precision from our common tongue.

The uke in the attic manhole once was yours!

Watch me on the rostrum wave my arms –

mi little stick of Leeds grown *tusky* draws
galas of rhubarb from the MET-set palms.

Note. Tusky: the Leeds word for rhubarb.

200 – Tony Harrison

A Kumquat for John Keats

Today I found the right fruit for my prime,
not orange, not tangelo, and not lime,
nor moon-like globes of grapefruit that now hang
outside our bedroom, nor tart lemon's tang
(though last year full of bile and self-defeat
I wanted to believe no life was sweet)
nor the tangible sunshine of the tangerine,
and no incongruous citrus ever seen
at greengrocer's in Newcastle or Leeds
mis-spelt by the spuds and mud-caked swedes,
a fruit an older poet might substitute
for the grape John Keats thought fit to be Joy's fruit,
when, two years before he died, he tried to write
how Melancholy dwelled inside Delight,
and if he'd known the citrus that I mean
that's not orange, lemon, lime or tangerine,
I'm pretty sure that Keats, though he had heard
'of candied apple, quince and plum and gourd'
instead of 'grape against the palate fine'
would have, if he'd known it, plumped for mine,
this Eastern citrus scarcely cherry size
he'd bite just once and then apostrophize
and pen one stanza how the fruit had all
the qualities of fruit before the Fall,
but in the next few lines be forced to write
how Eve's apple tasted at the second bite,
and if John Keats had only lived to be,
because of extra years, in need like me,
at 42 he'd help me celebrate
that Micanopy kumquat that I ate
whole, straight off the tree, sweet pulp and sour skin –
or was it sweet outside, and sour within?
For however many kumquats that I eat

I'm not sure if it's flesh or rind that's sweet,
and being a man of doubt at life's mid-way
I'd offer Keats some kumquats and I'd say:
You'll find that one part's sweet and one part's tart:
say where the sweetness or the sourness start.
I find I can't, as if one couldn't say
exactly where the night became the day,
which makes for me the kumquat taken whole
best fruit, and metaphor, to fit the soul
of one in Florida at 42 with Keats
crunching kumquats, thinking, as he eats
the flesh, the juice, the pith, the pips, the peel,
that this is how a full life ought to feel,
its perishable relish prick the tongue,
when the man who savours life's no longer young,
the fruits that were his futures far behind.
Then it's the kumquat fruit expresses best
how days have darkness round them like a rind,
life has a skin of death that keeps its zest.

History, a life, the heart, the brain
flow to the taste buds and flow back again.
That decade or more past Keats's span
makes me an older not a wiser man,
who knows that it's too late for dying young,
but since youth leaves some sweetnesses unsung,
he's granted days and kumquats to express
Man's Being ripened by his Nothingness.
And it isn't just the gap of sixteen years,
a bigger crop of terrors, hopes and fears,
but a century of history on this earth
between John Keats's death and my own birth –
years like an open crater, gory, grim,
with bloody bubbles leering at the rim;
a thing no bigger than an urn explodes
and ravishes all silence, and all odes,

Flora asphyxiated by foul air
unknown to either Keats or Lemprière,
dehydrated Naiads, Dryad amputees
dragging themselves through slagscapes with no trees,
a shirt of Nessus fire that gnaws and eats
children half the age of dying Keats . . .

Now were you twenty five or six years old
when that fevered brow at last grew cold?
I've got no books to hand to check the dates.
My grudging but glad spirit celebrates
that all I've got to hand's the kumquats, John,
the fruit I'd love to have your verdict on,
but dead men don't eat kumquats, or drink wine,
they shiver in the arms of Proserpine,
not warm in bed beside their Fanny Brawne,
nor watch her pick ripe grapefruit in the dawn
as I did, waking, when I saw her twist,
with one deft movement of a sunburnt wrist,
the moon, that feebly lit our last night's walk
past alligator swampland, off its stalk.
I thought of moon-juice juleps when I saw,
as if I'd never seen the moon before,
the planet glow among the fruit, and its pale light
make each citrus on the tree its satellite.

Each evening when I reach to draw the blind
stars seem the light zest squeezed through night's black
rind;
the night's peeled fruit the sun, juiced of its rays,
first stains, then streaks, then floods the world with days,
days, when the very sunlight made me weep,
days, spent like the nights in deep, drugged sleep,
days in Newcastle by my daughter's bed,
wondering if she, or I, weren't better dead,
days in Leeds, grey days, my first dark suit,

my mother's wreaths stacked next to Christmas fruit,
and days, like this in Micanopy. Days!

As strong sun burns away the dawn's grey haze
I pick a kumquat and the branches spray
cold dew in my face to start the day.
The dawn's molasses make the citrus gleam
still in the orchards of the groves of dream.
The limes, like Galway after weeks of rain,
glow with a greenness that is close to pain,
the dew-cooled surfaces of fruit that spent
all last night flaming in the firmament.
The new day dawns. O days! My spirit greets
the kumquat with the spirit of John Keats.
O kumquat, comfort for not dying young,
both sweet and bitter, bless the poet's tongue!
I burst the whole fruit chilled by morning dew
against my palate. Fine, for 42!

I search for buzzards as the air grows clear
and see them ride fresh thermals overhead.
Their bleak cries were the first sound I could hear
when I stepped at the start of sunrise out of doors,
and a noise like last night's bedsprings on our bed
from Mr Fowler sharpening farmers' saws.

Roger McGough, 1937–

Born in Liverpool, Roger McGough read Modern Languages at Hull University. With Adrian Henri and Brian Patten McGough was a leading figure in the 1960s Liverpool pop poetry scene (see *Penguin Modern Poets: The Mersey Sound*, 1967). With its emphasis on live performance and accessible, funny, emotionally direct work, the trio reached audiences far beyond the normal poetic constituency. As if by a logical development, McGough was part of The Scaffold, a chart-topping pop group of the late 1960s. His work has gone on gaining popularity, partly through its widespread use in schools, and in recent years, while his poems have become more conscientious and conventional, McGough has become part of the establishment and a much-loved advocate for poetry. See *Penguin Modern Poets 4* (1995).

Ex Patria

After supper, we move out on to the veranda.
Moths flit between lamps. We drink, think about sex
and consider how best to wreck each other's lives.

At the river's edge, the kitchen maids are washing up.
In the age-old tradition, they slap the plates
against the side of a rock, singing tonelessly.

Like tiny chauffeurs, the mosquitoes will soon arrive
and drive us home. O England, how I miss you.
Ascot, Henley, Wimbledon. It's the little things.

Ken Smith, 1938–

Ken Smith was born in East Yorkshire and educated in Hull and at Leeds University. His first collection, *The Pity* (1967), established him as a compassionate, economical writer standing at an oblique angle to the fashionable nature poetry of the time. It was many years before his work was properly collected again, the mass of small-press publication resulting in *The Poet Reclining* (1982). Smith has discarded much of the image-based practice of English poetry in favour of a poetry of voice and fragmentary narration. A long narrative, 'Fox Running', a tale of near-destitution in London, showed him capable of sustained power. The subsequent *Terra* is a compelling reading of the 1980s, a set of themes with variations – power, paranoia, storytelling – again set mostly in London. Smith's work has always concerned itself with outcasts and drifters, and his time as writer in residence at HM Prison, Wormwood Scrubs, led to the harrowing *Wormwood* (1986). *The heart, the border* (1990) and *Tender to the Queen of Spain* (1993) followed. In 1998 a major new collection, *Wild Root*, appeared, containing the masterly 'The shadow of god', a poem of the Balkans.

Colden Valley

North I'm convinced of it: childhood's over,
in the narrow valley in the mist the frost
is silver in the veins and edge of leaves,
and last year's briar's coppered into stone.

Then more stone dragged to quarter fields
in which the miserable lives of beasts in winter
whiten into breath. The valley pulls –
poor pasture, poorer footage, water falling.

And all its children gone through millyards
into stone they chiselled *Billy, Emma, Jack*,
and gave their dates and shut the ground
in work and prayer. Or they are almost here,

their short days closing in an owl's hoot,
crows labouring over woods, along the road
a footstep always just about to fall
and all their voices just about to start.

Writing in Prison

Years ago I was a gardener.
I grew the flowers of my childhood,
lavender and wayside lilies
and my first love the cornflower.

The wind on the summer wheat.
The blue glaze in the vanished woods.
In the space of my yard I glimpsed again
all the lost places of my life.

I was remaking them. Here in a space
smaller still I make them again.

The Man Who Ran Away from the Circus

That one with the haircut round his ears,
the one that grins with the teeth and the glasses,
the little man holding a long umbrella –
or whichever one he is he's the shorter of the two.

It's been a hard road he says. As a kid
he remembers they were always on the move.
He'd sneak away to do his homework in the Fat Lady's
    tent.
He remembers roses, sawdust, llama spit, camel stink.

And he remembers how it was with his dad
on a bad night of muddy rain and a hatful of unsold
    tickets,
the takings slithering off into expenses, the books
unbalanced on the table and the whisky bottle out,
the dogs howling in the yard. Lenny the lion's sick
and the liontamer out on the razzle with the man/woman.
The ringmaster's run off with the cashflow
and the clowns are demanding a payrise and a pension
and Christmas is coming, it's all they can do
to find hay for the horses.

He's at the end of his endless tether again.

About then the old man would straighten up, pour a drink,
fix his bow-tie and collar, clear his throat,
look you right in the eye and say *There are signs
things are getting better. We're beginning to see
an upturn in our fortunes at last. The confidence rate
is well up this month. There are indications the worst
of this long bitter recession is over.*

That's how it was then. It was either that
or close down the zoo, sell the elephant,

auction off the tigers and the freak sheep,
the sideshows and the performing monkeys,
turn the zebras into handbags, the horses into glue,
lease the big top and develop the site, retire to Brighton
to sell takeaways, become a deck chair attendant,
watch the cricket and the bowls and the grey swilltub sea
from a window in his favourite seafront pub
and reminisce: *ah the good old days of the classless society,*
the world of every opportunity where everyone
could get to crack the whip. That again.

And he's away. Again the horses prance into the ring,
the pompons and the big drum and the trombone's
                                        oompah oompah
and the girls glittering in fishnet and sequins.
Here come the stiltmen and the clowns, the jugglers
and the human cannon ball, the rubber man, the singing
                                                    dog,
the giant and the dwarf and the thinnest man in England,
JoJo with her instruments and Suzy's little tricks,
the man who throws axes, the man who swallows knives
and the one who breathes fire, Manolito's highwire act
from Andalusia, the Russian pyramid, the invisible
                                        American,
the drunks, the grand finale of the troupe of South
                                American pickpockets
that did him in at last. Them and all those women.

Seamus Heaney, 1939–

Seamus Heaney was born into a farming family in Mossbawn, County Derry, and read English at Queen's University, Belfast, where he later lectured. Since moving to the Republic of Ireland in 1972, Heaney has held a professorship at Harvard, been appointed Oxford Professor of Poetry (1989), and in 1995 received the Nobel Prize for Literature.

It is apt that Heaney, a poet well read in the English 1950s (and the whole tradition), should have offered to his English contemporaries an expanded sense of poetic possibility in his large body of work. He exemplifies the vigour at the imperial margins which has distinguished our period. *Death of a Naturalist* (1966) and *Door into the Dark* (1969) were immediately popular for the vivid, sensuous renderings of farming life, and remain a staple of much English teaching. With *Wintering Out* (1973) and *North* (1975) Heaney undertook archaeologies of language and place, giving placenames a physical relish and producing the Bog poems ('Tollund Man', 'Punishment') which made him famous. It is in this phase that Heaney demonstrates the mastery of sound which lends his work its now-habitual authority.

Heaney's task is complex. He seeks to understand the past, to acknowledge tribalism and its violence; to balance Irish against the imperial tongue, English; to consider the post-1968 Troubles responsibly; and to ensure that art survives the tension between the claims of self-delighting creativity and those of history (see also *Field-Work*, 1979). Heaney's negotiation between artistic responsibility, ancestral republicanism and liberal accommodation parallels and dignify the labours of the Hulme–Mallon generation of constitutional nationalist politicians.

Station Island (1984) is an ambitious poem-of-passage in which a site of pilgrimage invokes the above questions; while in tandem, *Sweeney Astray* (1984), translated from the Irish, follows the mad king Sweeney in his Irish odyssey. What strikes the reader is the seeming naturalness with which Heaney moves between and unifies the roles of public and private poet, lyric and discursive writer, symbolist and allegorist. *The Haw Lantern* (1987) has a fine sequence on the death of his mother, as well as strange speculative 'Eastern European' poems such as 'From the Canton of Expectation'. *Seeing Things* (1991) includes elegies for the poet's father, while *The Spirit Level* (1996) strikes a note of celebration. *Opened Ground: Poems 1966–96* appeared in 1998.

Heaney, as much as T. S. Eliot or Wordsworth, has used his critical writing to promulgate and authorize a view of poetry and the poet's role. *Preoccupations: Selected Prose 1968–1978* (1980), *The Government of the Tongue* (1988) and *The Redress of Poetry* (1995) are absorbing in themselves, but also gradually present the poet as the wielder of a necessary freedom. From the large literature about Heaney, Neil Corcoran's *Seamus Heaney* (revised edition, 1998), Michael Parker's *Seamus Heaney: the Making of the Poet* (1993) and Bernard O'Donoghue's *Seamus Heaney and the Language of Poetry* (1994) are helpful starting points.

Punishment

I can feel the tug
of the halter at the nape
of her neck, the wind
on her naked front.

It blows her nipples
to amber beads,
it shakes the frail rigging
of her ribs.

I can see her drowned
body in the bog,
the weighing stone,
the floating rods and boughs.

Under which at first
she was a barked sapling
that is dug up
oak-bone, brain-firkin:

her shaved head
like a stubble of black corn,
her blindfold a soiled bandage,
her noose a ring

to store
the memories of love.
Little adulteress,
before they punished you

you were flaxen-haired,
undernourished, and your
tar-black face was beautiful.
My poor scapegoat,

I almost love you
but would have cast, I know,
the stones of silence.
I am the artful voyeur

of your brain's exposed
and darkened combs,
your muscles' webbing
and all your numbered bones:

I who have stood dumb
when your betraying sisters,
cauled in tar,
wept by the railings,

who would connive
in civilized outrage
yet understand the exact
and tribal, intimate revenge.

Exposure

It is December in Wicklow:
Alders dripping, birches
Inheriting the last light,
The ash tree cold to look at.

A comet that was lost
Should be visible at sunset,
Those million tons of light
Like a glimmer of haws and rose-hips,

And I sometimes see a falling star.
If I could come on meteorite!
Instead I walk through damp leaves,
Husks, the spent flukes of autumn,

Imagining a hero
On some muddy compound,
His gift like a slingstone
Whirled for the desperate.

How did I end up like this?
I often think of my friends'
Beautiful prismatic counselling
And the anvil brains of some who hate me

As I sit weighing and weighing
My responsible *tristia*.
For what? For the ear? For the people?
For what is said behind-backs?

Rain comes down through the alders,
Its low conducive voices
Mutter about let-downs and erosions
And yet each drop recalls

The diamond absolutes.
I am neither internee nor informer;
An inner émigré, grown long-haired
And thoughtful; a wood-kerne

Escaped from the massacre,
Taking protective colouring
From bole and bark, feeling
Every wind that blows;

Who, blowing up these sparks
For their meagre heat, have missed
The once-in-a-lifetime portent,
The comet's pulsing rose.

The Underground

There we were in the vaulted tunnel running,
You in your going-away coat speeding ahead
And me, me then like a fleet god gaining
Upon you before you turned to a reed

Or some new white flower japped with crimson
As the coat flapped wild and button after button
Sprang off and fell in a trail
Between the Underground and the Albert Hall.

Honeymooning, mooning around, late for the Proms,
Our echoes die in that corridor and now
I come as Hansel came on the moonlit stones
Retracing the path back, lifting the buttons

To end up in a draughty lamplit station
After the trains have gone, the wet track
Bared and tensed as I am, all attention
For your step following and damned if I look back.

Alphabets

I

A shadow his father makes with joined hands
And thumbs and fingers nibbles on the wall
Like a rabbit's head. He understands
He will understand more when he goes to school.

There he draws smoke with chalk the whole first week,
Then draws the forked stick that they call a Y.
This is writing. A swan's neck and swan's back
Make the 2 he can see now as well as say.

Two rafters and a cross-tie on the slate
Are the letter some call *ah*, some call *ay*.
There are charts, there are headlines, there is a right
Way to hold the pen and a wrong way.

First it is 'copying out' , and then 'English'
Marked correct with a little leaning hoe.
Smells of inkwells rise in the classroom hush.
A globe in the window tilts like a coloured O.

II

Declensions sang on air like a *hosanna*
As, column after stratified column,
Book One of *Elementa Latina*,
Marbled and minatory, rose up in him.

For he was fostered next in a stricter school
Named for the patron saint of the oak wood
Where classes switched to the pealing of a bell
And he left the Latin forum for the shade

Of new calligraphy that felt like home.
The letters of this alphabet were trees.
The capitals were orchards in full bloom,
The lines of script like briars coiled in ditches.

Here in her snooded garment and bare feet,
All ringleted in assonance and woodnotes,
The poet's dream stole over him like sunlight
And passed into the tenebrous thickets.

He learns this other writing. He is the scribe
Who drove a team of quills on his white field.
Round his cell door the blackbirds dart and dab.
Then self-denial, fasting, the pure cold.

By rules that hardened the farther they reached north
He bends to his desk and begins again.
Christ's sickle has been in the undergrowth.
The script grows bare and Merovingian.

III

The globe has spun. He stands in a wooden O.
He alludes to Shakespeare. He alludes to Graves.
Time has bulldozed the school and school window.
Balers drop bales like printouts where stooked sheaves

Made lambdas on the stubble once at harvest
And the delta face of each potato pit
Was patted straight and moulded against frost.
All gone, with the omega that kept

Watch above each door, the good luck horse-shoe.
Yet shape-note language, absolute on air
As Constantine's sky-lettered IN HOC SIGNO
Can still command him; or the necromancer

Who would hang from the domed ceiling of his house
A figure of the world with colours in it
So that the figure of the universe
And 'not just single things' would meet his sight

When he walked abroad. As from his small window
The astronaut sees all he has sprung from,
The risen, aqueous, singlar, lucent O
Like a magnified and buoyant ovum –

Or like my own wide pre-reflective stare
All agog at the plasterer on his ladder
Skimming our gable and writing our name there
With his trowel point, letter by strange letter.

from **Clearances**

3

When all the others were away at Mass
I was all hers as we peeled potatoes.
They broke the silence, let fall one by one
Like solder weeping off the soldering iron:
Cold comforts set between us, things to share
Gleaming in a bucket of clean water.
And again let fall. Little pleasant splashes
From each other's work would bring us to our senses.

So while the parish priest at her bedside
Went hammer and tongs at the prayers for the dying
And some were responding and some crying
I remembered her head bent towards my head,
Her breath in mine, our fluent dipping knives –
Never closer the whole rest of our lives.

from Lightenings

The annals say: when the monks of Clonmacnoise
Were all at prayers inside the oratory
A ship appeared above them in the air.

The anchor dragged along behind so deep
It hooked itself into the altar rails
And then, as the big hull rocked to a standstill,

A crewman shinned and grappled down the rope
And struggled to release it. But in vain.
'This man can't bear our life here and will drown,'

The abbot said, 'unless we help him.' So
They did, the freed ship sailed, and the man climbed back
Out of the marvellous as he had known it,

Michael Longley, 1939–

Michael Longley was born in Belfast and read Classics at Trinity College, Dublin. He worked as a schoolteacher and became Literature Officer of the Arts Council of Northern Ireland. He is married to the critic Edna Longley. Longley's work is that of a lyric and pastoral poet caught in a political crisis: pity and terror inform his poems of the Troubles – 'Wounds', 'The Linen Workers' – and 'Ghetto', about the fate of Polish Jews under the Nazis. He also writes celebratory poems of love, natural history and the landscapes of County Mayo, to which he brings a feathery, incantatory exactness. After the classicism of *No Continuing City* (1967), Longley has worked his way from high formalism towards an intimate address, in which the real and the dreamed appear to combine. Recent collections are *Gorse Fires* (1991) and *The Ghost Orchid* (1995). *Selected Poems* appeared in 1998. He edited the *Selected Poems* (1988) of Louis MacNeice.

Wounds

Here are two pictures from my father's head –
I have kept them like secrets until now:
First, the Ulster Division at the Somme
Going over the top with 'Fuck the Pope!'
'No Surrender!': a boy about to die,
Screaming 'Give 'em one for the Shankill!'
'Wilder than Gurkhas' were my father's words
Of admiration and bewilderment.
Next comes the London-Scottish padre
Resettling kilts with his swagger-stick,
With a stylish backhand and a prayer.
Over a landscape of dead buttocks
My father followed him for fifty years.
At last, a belated casualty,
He said – lead traces flaring till they hurt –
'I am dying for King and Country, slowly.'
I touched his hand, his thin head I touched.

Now, with military honours of a kind,
With his badges, his medals like rainbows,
His spinning compass, I bury beside him
Three teenage soldiers, bellies full of
Bullets and Irish beer, their flies undone.
A packet of Woodbines I throw in,
A lucifer, the Sacred Heart of Jesus
Paralysed as heavy guns put out
The night-light in a nursery for ever;
Also a bus-conductor's uniform –
He collapsed beside his carpet-slippers
Without a murmur, shot through the head
By a shivering boy who wandered in
Before they could turn the television down

Or tidy away the supper dishes.
To the children, to a bewildered wife,
I think 'Sorry Missus' was what he said.

Arrest

from *Mayo Monologues*

The sergeant called me by my christian name
And waited an hour while I tidied up.
Not once did he mention why he had come
Or when and where he would take me away.
He just moved quietly from wall to wall
As I swept the floor towards the flagstones
And leaned brush and shovel, the broken tongs
Next to the spade and hoe I'd brought inside.
I emptied the half-used packet of tea
Into the caddy and dusted the lid.
In the leaky basin with its brown ring
I washed knife, fork, spoon, the two teacups
And the saucer that does for an ashtray.
I put back the stools where they usually stand,
Hung the towel to dry over one of them
And spread fresh newspapers on the table.
When I'd thrown the water from the basin
I turned it upside down on the turf stack,
Then I packed my shaving brush and razor
And smoored the fire as though I might return.
They have locked me up in the institute
Because I made love to the animals.
I'd sooner stand barefoot, without a cap
And take in my acres from a distance,
From the rocky hilltops or the seashore,
From the purgatory of the windy gaps.

Peace

after Tibullus

Who was responsible for the very first arms deal –
The man of iron who thought of marketing the sword?
Or did he intend us to use it against wild animals
Rather than ourselves? Even if he's not guilty
Murder got into the bloodstream as gene or virus
So that now we give birth to wars, short cuts to death.
Blame the affluent society: no killings when
The cup on the dinner table was made of beechwood,
And no barricades or ghettos when the shepherd
Snoozed among sheep that weren't even thoroughbreds.

I would like to have been alive in the good old days
Before the horrors of modern warfare and warcries
Stepping up my pulse rate. Alas, as things turn out
I've been press-ganged into service, and for all I know
Someone's polishing a spear with my number on it.
God of my Fathers, look after me like a child!
And don't be embarrassed by this handmade statue
Carved out of bog oak by my great-great-grandfather
Before the mass-production of religious art
When a wooden god stood simply in a narrow shrine.

A man could worship there with bunches of early grapes,
A wreath of whiskery wheat-ears, and then say Thank you
With a wholemeal loaf delivered by him in person,
His daughter carrying the unbroken honeycomb.
If the good Lord keeps me out of the firing line
I'll pick a porker from the steamy sty and dress
In my Sunday best, a country cousin's sacrifice.
Someone else can slaughter enemy commanders
And, over a drink, rehearse with me his memoirs,
Mapping the camp in wine upon the table top.

It's crazy to beg black death to join the ranks
Who dogs our footsteps anyhow with silent feet –
No cornfields in Hell, nor cultivated vineyards,
Only yapping Cerberus and the unattractive
Oarsman of the Styx: there an anaemic crew
Sleepwalks with smoky hair and empty eye-sockets.
How much nicer to have a family and let
Lazy old age catch up on you in your retirement,
You keeping track of the sheep, your son of the lambs,
While the woman of the house puts on the kettle.

I want to live until the white hairs shine above
A pensioner's memories of better days. Meanwhile
I would like peace to be my partner on the farm,
Peace personified: oxen under the curved yoke;
Compost for the vines, grape-juice turning into wine,
Vintage years handed down from father to son;
Hoe and ploughshare gleaming, while in some dark corner
Rust keeps the soldier's grisly weapons in their place;
The labourer steering his wife and children home
In a hay cart from the fields, a trifle sozzled.

Then, if there are skirmishes, guerilla tactics,
It's only lovers quarrelling, the bedroom door
Wrenched off its hinges, a woman in hysterics,
Hair torn out, cheeks swollen with bruises and tears –
Until the bully-boy starts snivelling as well
In a pang of conscience for his battered wife:
Then sexual neurosis works them up again
And the row escalates into a war of words.
He's hard as nails, made of sticks and stones, the chap
Who beats his girlfriend up. A crime against nature.

Enough, surely, to rip from her skin the flimsiest
Of negligees, ruffle that elaborate hair-do,
Enough to be the involuntary cause of tears –
Though upsetting a sensitive girl when you sulk

Is a peculiar satisfaction. But punch-ups,
Physical violence, are out: you might as well
Pack your kit-bag, goose-step a thousand miles away
From the female sex. As for me, I want a woman
To come and fondle my ears of wheat and let apples
Overflow between her breasts. I shall call her Peace.

William Scammell, 1939–

William Scammell was born in Hampshire and educated at Bristol University. He has lived in Cumbria for many years and worked in adult education. Scammell is a witty, sensuous poet, a fine observer of landscape. His numerous collections include *Jouissance* (1985), *Bleeding Heart Yard* (1992) and *All Set to Fall off the Edge of the World* (1998). He has written a critical study, *Keith Douglas* (1988), and edited *Winter Pollen*, the occasional prose of Ted Hughes (1994).

Bleeding Heart Yard

Is where you go to buy the finest paper
gathered under an English sky.
The wiring looped up in the corner
is the scribbled ghost of Hokusai,
the rafters Dürer's signature.

They are keeping one eye on the rag trade
and one on the clientèle,
nails pointilliste in blue and red,
clothes flaring round them like a sail
let out to catch the lightest mood.

Nothing is lost either on the old Ralph
Roister Doister who mans the shop,
monkeying up to the topmost shelf
or naming the name of a fellowship
that's shy of people. 'Help yourself'

he says to the punters. They do and must,
stroking the paper as if it were
all the first things and the last,
a favourite daughter's thatch of hair,
thin flake of the moon, a creamy dust.

Their right hand itches, and the juice works
in their mouths. What invitations
to spill the beans, take lines for walks,
or post a statement to the nation,
blind Homer's eyes for a watermark

rough as justice, age-old, sore:
tablets for all the shapes and sizes
of wishes and wants edging round the door,
the artist's hurt, the model's poses,
the face that never lifts from the floor.

All four winds sough in the paper. Welcome
to their rich laurels and distresses.
Welcome to Tracy and Mnemosyne,
Hokusai's numberless addresses
sown like grain from a careless palm.

That girl will forever be flying her kite
over the rooftop of youth
while some old duffer falls for art
and the standing committee on God's truth
stumbles into the failing light.

Derek Mahon, 1941–

Derek Mahon was born in Belfast and studied French at Trinity College, Dublin. He has worked as a reviewer, a scriptwriter and a university teacher. Mahon's first book, *Night Crossing* (1968), introduced a formidable stylist – terse, ironic but intensely musical. The nature of his preoccupations grew clearer with *Lives* (1971) and *The Snow Party* (1974), which sketched the bleak coastal landscapes with which he has become indelibly associated – settings giving access to remote history and an exhausted future. Mahon traverses time, and moves between the atomic and the global level, lamenting the extinction of a magical world-view at the hands of economics. With 'A Disused Shed in Co. Wexford' he wrote one of the most influential poems of the period. *The Hunt By Night* (1982) was a formal *tour de force*, depicting a world and the poet's despair of it with a lens-maker's exactitude. With the brief *Antarctica* (1985) Mahon seemed on the brink of silence, offering what might be a final, magisterial dejection Ode in 'Death and the Sun', which addresses one of Mahon's exemplary clear thinkers, Albert Camus. *The Hudson Letter* (1995) was only a partial success, but in *The Yellow Book* (1997), Mahon builds triumphantly on the epistolary mode, including readings from the late nineteenth-century decadence, as well as versions from Baudelaire, a fine elegy for the poet's mother and a sense of renewed artistic vocation. Mahon's influence has been widespread; his Francophile blend of the laconic and lyric, the unillusioned and the impassioned, has come to seem representative of our period. *Selected Poems* (1991) is an accessible introduction. Mahon has also translated the *Selected Poems* of Philippe Jaccottet (1988) as well as Molière and Euripides.

A Disused Shed in Co. Wexford

Let them not forget us, the weak souls among the asphodels.
– Seferis, *Mythistorema*, tr. Keeley and Sherrard

(for J. G. Farrell)

Even now there are places where a thought might grow –
Peruvian mines, worked out and abandoned
To a slow clock of condensation,
An echo trapped for ever, and a flutter
Of wild-flowers in the lift-shaft,
Indian compounds where the wind dances
And a door bangs with diminished confidence,
Lime crevices behind rippling rain-barrels,
Dog corners for bone burials:
And in a disused shed in Co. Wexford,

Deep in the grounds of a burnt-out hotel,
Among the bathtubs and the washbasins
A thousand mushrooms crowd to a keyhole.
This is the one star in their firmament
Or frames a star within a star.
What should they do there but desire?
So many days beyond the rhododendrons
With the world waltzing in its bowl of cloud,
They have learnt patience and silence
Listening to the rooks querulous in the high wood.

They have been waiting for us in a foetor
Of vegetable sweat since civil war days,
Since the gravel-crunching, interminable departure
Of the expropriated mycologist.
He never came back, and light since then
Is a keyhole rusting gently after rain.
Spiders have spun, flies dusted to mildew

And once a day, perhaps, they have heard something –
A trickle of masonry, a shout from the blue
Or a lorry changing gear at the end of the lane.

There have been deaths, the pale flesh flaking
Into the earth that nourished it;
And nightmares, born of these and the grim
Dominion of stale air and rank moisture.
Those nearest the door grow strong –
'Elbow room! Elbow room!'
The rest, dim in a twilight of crumbling
Utensils and broken pitchers, groaning
For their deliverance, have been so long
Expectant that there is left only the posture.

A half century, without visitors, in the dark –
Poor preparation for the cracking lock
And creak of hinges. Magi, moonmen,
Powdery prisoners of the old regime,
Web-throated, stalked like triffids, racked by drought
And insomnia, only the ghost of a scream
At the flash-bulb firing-squad we wake them with
Shows there is life yet in their feverish forms.
Grown beyond nature now, soft food for worms,
They lift frail heads in gravity and good faith.

They are begging us, you see, in their wordless way,
To do something, to speak on their behalf
Or at least not to close the door again.
Lost people of Treblinka and Pompeii!
'Save us, save us,' they seem to say,
'Let the god not abandon us
Who have come so far in darkness and in pain.
We too had our lives to live.
You with your light meter and relaxed itinerary,
Let not our naive labours have been in vain!'

The Last of the Fire Kings

I want to be
Like the man who descends
At two milk churns

With a bulging
String bag and vanishes
Where the lane turns,

Or the man
Who drops at night
From a moving train

And strikes out over the fields
Where fireflies glow,
Not knowing a word of the language.

Either way, I am
Through with history –
Who lives by the sword

Dies by the sword.
Last of the fire kings, I shall
Break with tradition and

Die by my own hand
Rather than perpetuate
The barbarous cycle.

Five years I have reigned
During which time
I have lain awake each night

And prowled by day
In the sacred grove
For fear of the usurper,

Perfecting my cold dream
Of a place out of time,
A palace of porcelain

Where the frugivorous
Inheritors recline
In their rich fabrics
Far from the sea.

But the fire-loving
People, rightly perhaps,
Will not countenance this,

Demanding that I inhabit,
Like them, a world of
Sirens, bin-lids
And bricked-up windows –

Not to release them
From the ancient curse
But to die their creature and be thankful.

Leaves

The prisoners of infinite choice
Have built their house
In a field below the wood
And are at peace.

It is autumn, and dead leaves
On their way to the river
Scratch like birds at the windows
Or tick on the road.

Somewhere there is an afterlife
Of dead leaves,
A stadium filled with an infinite
Rustling and sighing.

Somewhere in the heaven
Of lost futures
The lives we might have led
Have found their own fulfilment.

Courtyards in Delft

– Pieter de Hooch, 1659

(*for Gordon Woods*)

Oblique light on the trite, on brick and tile –
Immaculate masonry, and everywhere that
Water tap, that broom and wooden pail
To keep it so. House-proud, the wives
Of artisans pursue their thrifty lives
Among scrubbed yards, modest but adequate.
Foliage is sparse, and clings. No breeze
Ruffles the trim composure of those trees.

No spinet-playing emblematic of
The harmonies and disharmonies of love;
No lewd fish, no fruit, no wide-eyed bird
About to fly its cage while a virgin
Listens to her seducer, mars the chaste
Precision of the thing and the thing made.
Nothing is random, nothing goes to waste.
We miss the dirty dog, the fiery gin.

That girl with her back to us who waits
For her man to come home for his tea
Will wait till the paint disintegrates
And ruined dykes admit the esurient sea;
Yet this is life too, and the cracked
Out-house door a verifiable fact
As vividly mnemonic as the sunlit
Railings that front the houses opposite.

I lived there as a boy and know the coal
Glittering in its shed, late-afternoon
Lambency informing the deal table,

The ceiling cradled in a radiant spoon.
I must be lying low in a room there,
A strange child with a taste for verse,
While my hard-nosed companions dream of war
On parched veldt and fields of rain-swept gorse;

For the pale light of that provincial town
Will spread itself, like ink or oil,
Over the not yet accurate linen
Map of the world which occupies one wall
And punish nature in the name of God.
If only, now, the Maenads, as of right,
Came smashing crockery, with fire and sword,
We could sleep easier in our beds at night.

Death and the Sun

(Albert Camus, 1913–1960)

Le soleil ni la mort ne se peuvent regarder fixement.

When the car spun from the road and your neck broke
I was hearing rain on the school bicycle shed
Or tracing the squeaky enumerations of chalk;
And later, while you lay in the *mairie*,
I pedalled home from Bab-el-Oued
To my mother silently making tea,
Bent to my homework in the firelight
Or watched an old film on television –
Gunfights under a blinding desert sun,
Bogartian urgencies in the cold Ulster night.

How we read you then, admiring the frank composure
Of a stranger bayed by dogs who could not hear
The interior dialogue of flesh and stone,
His life and death a work of art
Conceived in the silence of the heart.
Not that he would ever have said so, no,
He would merely have taken a rush-hour tram
To a hot beach white as a scream,
Stripped to a figure of skin and bone
And struck out, a back-stroke, as far as he could go.

Deprived though we were of his climatic privileges
And raised in a northern land of rain and muck,
We too knew the familiar foe, the blaze
Of headlights on a coast road, the cicadas
Chattering like watches in our sodden hedges;
Yet never imagined the plague to come,
So long had it crouched there in the dark –
The *cordon sanitaire*, the stricken home,

Rats on the pavement, rats in the mind,
'St James Infirmary' playing to the plague wind.

'An edifying abundance of funeral parlours',
The dead on holiday, cloth caps and curlers,
The shoe-shine and the thrice-combed wave
On Sunday morning and Saturday night;
Wee shadows fighting in a smoky cave
Who would one day be brought to light –
The modes of pain and pleasure,
These were the things to treasure
When times changed and your kind broke camp.
Diogenes in the dog-house, you carried a paraffin lamp.

Meanwhile in the night of Europe, the winter of faces,
Sex and opinion, a deft hand removes
The Just Judges from their rightful places
And hangs them behind a bar in Amsterdam –
A desert of fog and water, a cloudy dream
Where an antique Indonesian god grimaces
And relativity dawns like a host of doves;
Where the artist who refused suicide
Trades solidarity for solitude,
A night watch, a self-portrait, supper at Emmaus.

The lights are going on in towns that no longer exist.
Night falls on Belfast, on the just and the unjust,
On its Augustinian austerities of sand and stone –
While Sisyphus' descendants, briefly content,
Stand in the dole queues and roll their own.
Malraux described these preterite to you
As no longer historically significant;
And certainly they are shrouded in white dust.
All souls leprous, blinded by truth, each ghost
Steams on the shore as if awaiting rescue.

One cannot look for long at death or the sun.
Imagine Plato's neolithic troglodyte

Released from his dark cinema, released even
From the fire proper, so that he stands at last,
Absurd and anxious, out in the open air
And gazes, shading his eyes, at the world there –
Tangible fact ablaze in a clear light
That casts no shadow, where the vast
Sun gongs its lenity from a brazen heaven
Listening in silence to his rich despair.

Eiléan Ní Chuilleanáin, 1942–

Eiléan Ní Chuilleanáin was born in Cork and lectures in literature at Trinity College, Dublin. She is an editor of the magazine *Cyphers*. Vivid, evocative, crossing between the legendary and the real, Ní Chuilleanáin's poems have an imaginative confidence which lends her work a haunting authority. *The Second Voyage: Selected Poems* appeared in 1986, and *The Magdalene Sermon* in 1989.

Letter to Pearse Hutchinson

I saw the islands in a ring all round me
And the twilight sea travelling past
Uneasy still. Lightning over Mount Gabriel:
At such a distance no sound of thunder.
The mackerel just taken
Battered the floor, and at my elbow
The waves disputed with the engine.
Equally grey, the headlands
Crept round the rim of the sea.

Going anywhere fast is a trap:
This water music ransacked my mind
And started it growing again in a new perspective
And like the sea that burrows and soaks

In the swamps and crevices beneath
Made a circle out of good and ill.
So I accepted all the sufferings of the poor,
The old maid and the old whore
And the bull trying to remember
What it was made him courageous
As life goes to ground in one of its caves,
And I accepted the way love
Poured down a cul-de-sac
Is never seen again.

There was plenty of time while the sea-water
Nosed across the ruinous ocean floor
Inquiring for the ruinous door of the womb
And found the soul of Vercingetorix
Cramped in a jamjar
Who was starved to death in a dry cistern
In Rome, in 46 B.C.

Do not expect to feel so free on land.

The Second Voyage

Odysseus rested on his oar and saw
The ruffled foreheads of the waves
Crocodiling and mincing past: he rammed
The oar between their jaws and looked down
In the simmering sea where scribbles of weed defined
Uncertain depth, and the slim fishes progressed
In fatal formation, and thought
                                        If there was a single
Streak of decency in these waves now, they'd be ridged
Pocked and dented with the battering they've had,
And we could name them as Adam named the beasts,
Saluting a new one with dismay, or a notorious one
With admiration; they'd notice us passing
And rejoice at our shipwreck, but these
Have less character than sheep and need more patience.

I know what I'll do he said;
I'll park my ship in the crook of a long pier
(And I'll take you with me he said to the oar)
I'll face the rising ground and walk away
From tidal waters, up riverbeds
Where herons parcel out the miles of stream,
Over gaps in the hills, through warm
Silent valleys, and when I meet a farmer
Bold enough to look me in the eye
With 'where are you off to with that long
Winnowing fan over your shoulder?'
There I will stand still
And I'll plant you for a gatepost or a hitching-post
And leave you as a tidemark. I can go back
And organize my house then.
                                        But the profound
Unfenced valleys of the ocean still held him;

He had only the oar to make them keep their distance;
The sea was still frying under the ship's side.
He considered the water-lilies, and thought about fountains
Spraying as wide as willows in empty squares,
The sugarstick of water clattering into the kettle,
The flat lakes bisecting the rushes. He remembered
                                            spiders and frogs
Housekeeping at the roadside in brown trickles floored
                                                    with mud,
Horsetroughs, the black canal, pale swans at dark.
His face grew damp with tears that tasted
Like his own sweat or the insults of the sea.

Douglas Dunn, 1942–

Born in Renfrewshire, Dunn worked as a librarian before reading English at Hull University. He is Professor of English and founding Head of the School of Scottish Studies at St Andrews University. His debut, *Terry Street* (1970), attracted wide attention for its sequence of meticulously observed poems about life in a back street in Hull. It has taken a long time for the extent of the book's ambition, and its cultural and political ambiguity, to emerge. *The Happier Life* (1972) and *Love or Nothing* (1974) showed Dunn to be thematically wide-ranging and formally restless, incorporating influences as diverse as Laforgue and James Wright, while *Barbarians* (1979), with its ambitious 'pastorals' of class and power, established him as a leading political poet, a role maintained in *St Kilda's Parliament* (1981). After the death of his first wife, Dunn wrote the much-admired *Elegies* (1985). Scottish themes have been to the fore in his most recent books, *Northlight* (1988) and *Dante's Drumkit* (1993). He has also written a number of plays, a translation of Racine's *Andromache* (1990) and short stories (most recently *Boyfriends and Girlfriends*, 1995), as well as editing *The Faber Book of Twentieth-Century Scottish Poetry* (1992). *Reading Douglas Dunn*, edited by Robert Crawford and David Kinloch (1992), is a wide-ranging collection of essays on his work.

From the Night-Window

The night rattles with nightmares.
Children cry in the close-packed houses,
A man rots in his snoring.
On quiet feet, policemen test doors.
Footsteps become people under streetlamps.
Drunks return from parties,
Sounding of empty bottles and old songs.
Young women come home
And disappear into white beds
At the edge of the night.
All windows open, this hot night,
And the sleepless, smoking in the dark,
Making small red lights at their mouths,
Count the years of their marriages.

The River Through the City

The river of coloured lights, black stuff
The tired city rests its jewels on.
Bad carnival, men and women
Drown themselves under the bridges.
Death-splash, and after, the river wears
The neon flowers of suicides.
Prints of silence ripple where they went in.
An old man rows a black boat and slides past
Unnoticed, a god in an oilskin coat.
He feeds the uncatchable black fish.
They know where Hitler is hiding.
They know the secrets behind sordid events
In Central Europe, in America and Asia,
And who is doing what for money.
They keep files on petty thieves, spies,
Adulterers and their favourite bureaucrats.
That's one old man who's nobody's uncle.
That's one fish you don't want with your chips.
Iron doors bang shut in the sewers.

Empires

All the dead Imperia . . . They have gone
Taking their atlases and grand pianos.
They could not leave geography alone.
They conquered with the thistle and the rose.
To our forefathers it was right to raise
Their pretty flag at every foreign dawn
Then lower it at sunset in a haze
Of bugle-brass. They interfered with place,
Time, people, lives, and so to bed. They died
When it died. It had died before. It died
Before they did. They did not know it. Race,
Power, Trade, Fleet, a hundred regiments,
Postponed that final reckoning with pride,
Which was expensive. Counting up the cost
We plunder morals from the power they lost.
They ruined us. They conquered continents.
We filled their uniforms. We cruised the seas.
We worked their mines and made their histories.
You work, we rule, they said. We worked; they ruled.
They fooled the tenements. All men were fooled.
It still persists. It will be so, always
Listen. An out-of-work apprentice plays
God Save the Queen on an Edwardian flute.
He is, but does not know it, destitute.

Loch Music

I listen as recorded Bach
Restates the rhythms of a loch.
Through blends of dusk and dragonflies
A music settles on my eyes
Until I hear the living moors,
Sunk stones and shadowed conifers,
And what I hear is what I see,
A summer night's divinity.
And I am not administered
Tonight, but feel my life transferred
Beyond the realm of where I am
Into a personal extreme,
As on my wrist, my eager pulse
Counts out the blood of someone else.
Mist-moving trees proclaim a sense
Of sight without intelligence;
The intellects of water teach
A truth that's physical and rich.
I nourish nothing with the stars,
With minerals, as I disperse,
A scattering of quavered wash
As light against the wind as ash.

from **Europa's Lover**

VI

Shaped into this intimate suffering of death with life,
Past with present, living beneath a succession of coats
Until skin thickens into cloth, thread and blood, coarse
                                        immortality,
And blood thickens, and words melt on your tongue
As gourmet as a peppermint on a plate at Maxim's;
Shaped on a field behind the plough you were born to,
Shaped to these footprints, this size, in a drawing-room
Where you must sing before a brother of the bishop
Because aunt tells you to through her mouthful of cake;
Shaped as you sweep the gutter of its rejected trash –
How lonely is litter! – shaped as you sign a treaty
With the usurping nephew of a Maharajah or a Czar's
Bomb-crazy ambassador or a Kaiser's confidant;
Shaped before furnaces or dragging coal-carts with your
                                        back
In the mines of Yorkshire or Silesia, or shaped,
Shaped and indentured in the gardens of rhododendrons,
                                        peacocks
And exotic flora brought home by an eccentric uncle
Who commanded the firing-squads at Brazzaville or
                                        Hyderabad;
Shaped by decks and masts, spits and spars, that twiggery
Sprouting from warehouses before the continental wharves;
Shaped by regiment; shaped by evictions, shaped by
Rhetorical prelates and their torturing sectaries;
Shaped in the moulds of foundries in Glasgow and
                                        Düsseldorf,
From cleared crofts in Sutherland to Fontamara, shaped,
Shaped, shaped and ruled, in kingdoms and palatinates,
                                        by archon,

By tyrant, by imperial whim gathering spiderwebs
To please Heliogabalus, by parliament, by Bourbon, by
                                                    Tudor,
By Stewart, by Habsburg and Romanov, by democrat, by
                                              revolutionary
At his escritoire of apple-packings, by scythe and sabre,
By Capitalismus, by oligarch and plutocrat, by Socialismus,
By Trade, by Banks and the algebra of money,
Shaped in battle or by a kiss, shaped in the bed of your
                                                    parents,
Shaped to inherit or to labour in disciplined factories,
Shaped to administer in La Paz or Rangoon or the
                                              Islands . . .
All ways of being born, Europa, the chemistry of seed
                                              and cell,
And our millions plundered in their lands and cities,
Bullets searching them out like inquisitive half-wits from
The mitrailleuses of Europe, shreddings of men and
                                              women.
Now as two sit in a café in a French provincial town
Served by a descendant of métissage in Guadeloupe –
She is as beautiful as the wind on the Luberon –
There is no longer in our coffee that sensation of
                                        chains rattled
In offshore hulks, no longer in the sifts of our sugar
A slashing of docile machetes or orations by
Abolitionists in Chambers of Commerce. She is as beautiful
As those gone down in the chronicles of Jupiter,
                                        metamorphosis
And elegance, as beautiful as the classics of love and
                                        journeys,
As beautiful as any horseman from the eastern Steppes
Who nursed an arrow to a thong and raped the Empires.
Clocks, clocks, one era replaces another, and we are dressed
In history and shaped, shaped in days, peace and war,
In the circle of blood, in the races entwined like fingers.

David Harsent, 1942–

David Harsent was born in Devon. His early work aligned him with the minimalist dramatic lyrics of the group of poets (including Ian Hamilton and Hugo Williams) associated with the magazine *The Review*. Sex, violence and dreams illuminated his brief, arresting poems, which gradually expanded, through the Mr Punch sequence, into complex partial narratives. *Selected Poems* was published in 1989, *News from the Front* in 1993 and *A Bird's Idea of Flight* in 1998. Harsent wrote the libretto for Harrison Birtwistle's opera *Gawain* and, as Jack Curtis, has written several successful thrillers.

Endurance

The orchard is lit
on one side by the evening sun.
Its yellows glow.
An odour of leaves and rind pours in.

Hillsides are dealing with last year's scars –
endurance of the just-visible.
Twin children, hair ablaze,
number the lunatic eyes of moon daisies.

It is the true magic.
In the pause between mind and movement
history claims its own.

Hugo Williams, 1942–

Hugo Williams was born in Windsor and educated at Eton. He worked for Alan Ross's *London Magazine* and Ian Hamilton's *The New Review* before establishing himself as the definitive freelance, via a famous column in the *Times Literary Supplement*. *Symptoms of Loss* (1965) and *Sugar Daddy* (1967) saw Williams moving from the influence of Thom Gunn towards a *Review*-style minimalism, and beginning to stake out his territory as the melancholy clown of married and erotic life. *Writing Home* (1985) is a poignant collection concerning the poet's father, the actor Hugh Williams. *Selected Poems* (1989) was followed by *Self-Portrait with a Slide* (1990) and *Dock Leaves* (1994). The poet's American travels are recorded in *No Particular Place to Go* (1981) and *Freelance* (1995) selects from his columns.

Bachelors

What do they know of love
These men who have never been married?
What do they know
About living face to face with happiness
These amateurs of passion?
Do they imagine it's like home used to be,
Having a family of one's own,
Watching the little bones grow lethal,
The eyes turned on you –
And realizing suddenly that it's all
Your own fault the way things are,
Because it's you now
Not your parents who're in charge?
Can they understand what it means,
These suntanned single men? Or are they into cars?

And what do they know about the bedside lamp,
These denimed Romeos,
Its sphere of influence as night descends.
Familiar switch to hand:
On-off, off-on, the thousand little clicks
Half in, half out of the dark,
As the row gets going on time, or nothing does,
Or the bulb just sings to itself
On your side of the bed?
Pride in anger. That's your happiness.
A poisonous seed washed up with you
On a desert island of your own making,
Your impotence in flower like a hothouse rose.
And they talk about love
These men who have never been married.

Vicki Feaver, 1943–

Vicki Feaver was born in Nottingham and read English at London University. She leads the MA Writing course at Chichester Institute. Her collections are *Close Relatives* (1981) and *The Handless Maiden* (1994) and there is a selection in *Penguin Modern Poets 2* (1995). The often quiet and uninsistent surfaces of Feaver's work reveal a poised and a slightly alarming power of concentration in which love and family life disclose a mythic terrain of eroticism and violence, while retaining a strong sense of physical actuality. Feaver's rendering of varieties of female experience has, like the work of Carol Ann Duffy, struck a powerful chord with her audience.

Ironing

I used to iron everything:
my iron flying over sheets and towels
like a sledge chased by wolves over snow,

the flex twisting and crinking
until the sheath frayed, exposing
wires like nerves. I stood like a horse

with a smoking hoof
inviting anyone who dared
to lie on my silver-padded board,

to be pressed to the thinness
of dolls cut from paper.
I'd have commandeered a crane

if I could, got the welders at Jarrow
to heat me an iron the size of a tug
to flatten the house.

Then for years I ironed nothing.
I put the iron in a high cupboard.
I converted to crumpledness.

And now I iron again: shaking
dark spots of water onto wrinkled
silk, nosing into sleeves, round

buttons, breathing the sweet heated smell
hot metal draws from newly washed
cloth, until my blouse dries

to a shining, creaseless blue,
an airy shape with room to push
my arms, breasts, lungs, heart into.

Judith

Wondering how a good woman can murder
I enter the tent of Holofernes,
holding in one hand his long oiled hair
and in the other, raised above
his sleeping, wine-flushed face,
his falchion with its unsheathed
curved blade. And I feel a rush
of tenderness, a longing
to put down my weapon, to lie
sheltered and safe in a warrior's
fumy sweat, under the emerald stars
of his purple and gold canopy,
to melt like a sweet on his tongue
to nothing. And I remember the glare
of the barley field; my husband
pushing away the sponge I pressed
to his burning head; the stubble
puncturing my feet as I ran,
flinging myself on a body
that was already cooling
and stiffening; and the nights
when I lay on the roof – my emptiness
like the emptiness of a temple
with the doors kicked in; and the mornings
when I rolled in the ash of the fire
just to be touched and dirtied
by something. And I bring my blade
down on his neck – and it's easy
like slicing through fish.
And I bring it down again,
cleaving the bone.

Eavan Boland, 1944–

Eavan Boland was born in Dublin to the family of a diplomat and grew up in London and New York. She studied and later taught at Trinity College, Dublin. Probably the best-known Irish woman poet outside Ireland, Boland has done much to focus attention on the meaning of the phrase 'woman poet' in Ireland. Her poems of Irish history are likewise powerful (see 'The Flight of the Earls' and 'That the Science of Cartography is Limited'). She has also written evocatively about domestic life. Some readers are troubled by Boland's sense of her role, but, equally, this seems part of her obligation as a poet. *Collected Poems* was published in 1995.

The Black Lace Fan My Mother Gave Me

It was the first gift he ever gave her,
buying it for five francs in the Galeries
in prewar Paris. It was stifling.
A starless drought made the nights stormy.

They stayed in the city for the summer.
They met in cafés. She was always early.
He was late. That evening he was later.
They wrapped the fan. He looked at his watch.

She looked down the Boulevard des Capucines.
She ordered more coffee. She stood up.
The streets were emptying. The heat was killing.
She thought the distance smelled of rain and lightning.

These are wild roses, appliquéd on silk by hand,
darkly picked, stitched boldly, quickly.
The rest is tortoiseshell and has the reticent,
clear patience of its element. It is

a worn-out underwater bullion and it keeps,
even now, an inference of its violation.
The lace is overcast as if the weather
it opened for and offset had entered it.

The past is an empty café terrace.
An airless dusk before thunder. A man running.
And no way now to know what happened then –
none at all – unless, of course, you improvise:

the blackbird on this first sultry morning,
in summer, finding buds, worms, fruit,
feels the heat. Suddenly she puts out her wing –
the whole, full, flirtatious span of it.

That the Science of Cartography is Limited

– and not simply by the fact that this shading of
forest cannot show the fragrance of balsam,
the gloom of cypress,
is what I wish to prove.

When you and I were first in love we drove
to the borders of Connacht
and entered a wood there.

Look down you said: this was once a famine road.

I looked down at ivy and the scutch grass
rough-cast stone had
disappeared into as you told me
in the second winter of their ordeal, in

1847, when the crop had failed twice,
Relief Committees gave
the starving Irish such roads to build.

Where they died, there the road ended

and ends still and when I take down
the map of this island, it is never so
I can say here is
the masterful, the apt rendering of

the spherical as flat, nor
an ingenious design which persuades a curve
into a plane,
but to tell myself again that

the line which says woodland and cries hunger
and gives out among sweet pine and cypress,
and finds no horizon

will not be there.

David Constantine, 1944–

David Constantine was born in Salford. He lectures in German at Oxford. With his early work, *A Brightness to Cast Shadows* (1980), *Watching for Dolphins* (1983) and *Madder* (1987), Constantine established himself as a poet of fine control and intense feeling, tender, desperate and sometimes uncanny, with a religious regard for the world – a romantic with a classical training. Constantine has translated *Selected Poems* from Holderlin (1996). His most recent collection is *The Pelt of Wasps* (1997). See also his *Selected Poems* (1991).

'All wraiths in Hell are single'

All wraiths in Hell are single though they keep
Company together and go in troops like sheep.
None meets a lover from the former world,
No souls go hand in hand, round each is curled
The river Acheron. They suffer most
Who violently joined the myriad host,
Who angrily to spite love in the face
Before their time intruded on that place,
Putting themselves by pride beyond recovery,
Beyond sight, beyond calling. They seem to be
Alive among the dead wishing the thing undone
By which they put themselves beyond Acheron.
Divested of anger, cold, without reprieve
Sine die along the riverbanks they grieve.
They hear one calling after love into the black
But cannot answer and cannot come back.

Watching for Dolphins

In the summer months on every crossing to Piraeus
One noticed that certain passengers soon rose
From seats in the packed saloon and with serious
Looks and no acknowledgement of a common purpose
Passed forward through the small door into the bows
To watch for dolphins. One saw them lose

Every other wish. Even the lovers
Turned their desires on the sea, and a fat man
Hung with equipment to photograph the occasion
Stared like a saint, through sad bi-focals; others,
Hopeless themselves, looked to the children for they
Would see dolphins if anyone would. Day after day

Or on their last opportunity all gazed
Undecided whether a flat calm were favourable
Or a sea the sun and the wind between them raised
To a likeness of dolphins. Were gulls a sign, that fell
Screeching from the sky or over an unremarkable place
Sat in a silent school? Every face

After its character implored the sea.
All, unaccustomed, wanted epiphany,
Praying the sky would clang and the abused Aegean
Reverberate with cymbal, gong and drum.
We could not imagine more prayer, and had they then
On the waves, on the climax of our longing come

Smiling, snub-nosed, domed like satyrs, oh
We should have laughed and lifted the children up
Stranger to stranger, pointing how with a leap
They left their element, three or four times, centred
On grace, and heavily and warm re-entered,
Looping the keel. We should have felt them go

Further and further into the deep parts. But soon
We were among the great tankers, under their chains
In black water. We had not seen the dolphins
But woke, blinking. Eyes cast down
With no admission of disappointment the company
Dispersed and prepared to land in the city.

Paul Durcan, 1944–

Paul Durcan was born in Dublin. He studied archaeology and medieval history at University College, Cork. An acclaimed performer of his work, Durcan has published prolifically since *O Westport in the Light of Asia Minor* (1975). The most accessible aspect of Durcan's work is its hilarious satirical attack on the narrowness of Irish life, whether attributable to the Church, to sexism or political prejudice. Durcan is also an eloquent love poet. His approach is often to import an irrational, even visionary element to a given situation and write as if it made the plainest sense, whether charting problematic relationships or the utopian revision of the world at which the poems often gesture. See *A Snail in My Prime: New and Selected Poems* (Collins Harvill, 1993) and *Christmas Day* (1996).

Irish Hierarchy Bans Colour Photography

After a spring meeting in their nineteenth-century
                                 fastness at Maynooth
The Irish Hierarchy has issued a total ban on the practice
                                 of colour photography:
A spokesman added that while in accordance with tradition
No logical explanation would be provided
There were a number of illogical explanations which he
                                 would discuss;
He stated that it was not true that the ban was the result
Of the Hierarchy's tacit endorsement of racial
                                 discrimination;
(And, here, the spokesman, Fr Marksman, smiled to
                                 himself
But when asked to elaborate on his smile, he would not
                                 elaborate
Except to growl some categorical expletives which
                               included the word 'liberal')
He stated that if the press corps would countenance an
                               unhappy pun
He would say that negative thinking lay at the root of the
                               ban;
Colour pictures produced in the minds of people,
Especially in the minds (if any) of young people,
A serious distortion of reality;
Colour pictures showed reality to be rich and various
Whereas reality in point of fact was the opposite;
The innate black-and-white nature of reality would have
                               to be safeguarded
At all costs and, talking of costs, said Fr Marksman,
It ought to be borne in mind, as indeed the Hierarchy had
                               borne in its collective, mind
That colour photography was far costlier than black-
                             and-white photography

And, as a consequence, more immoral;
The Hierarchy, stated Fr Marksman, was once again
                          smiting two birds with one boulder;
And the joint hegemony of Morality and Economics was
                          being upheld.

The total ban came as a total surprise to the accumulated
                          press corps
And Irish Roman Catholic pressmen and presswomen
                          present
Had to be helped away as they wept copiously in their
                          cups:
'No more oranges and lemons in Maynooth,' sobbed one
                          camera boy.
The general public, however, is expected to pay no heed
                          to the ban;
Only politicians and time-servers are likely to pay the
                          required lip service;
But the operative noun is lip: there will be no hand or
                          foot service.
And next year Ireland is expected to become
The EEC's largest moneyspender in colour photography.

This is Claudia Conway, RTE News (Colour), Maynooth.

The Pietà's Over

The Pietà's over – and, now, my dear, droll husband,
As middle age tolls its bell along the via dolorosa of life,
It is time for you to get down off my knees
And learn to walk on your own two feet.
I will admit it is difficult for a man of forty
Who has spent all his life reclining in his wife's lap,
Being given birth to by her again and again, year in, year
                                                    out,
To stand on his own two feet, but it has to be done –
Even if at the end of the day he commits hari-kari.
A man cannot be a messiah for ever,
Messiahing about in his wife's lap,
Suffering fluently in her arms,
Flowing up and down in the lee of her bosom,
Forever being mourned for by the eternal feminine,
Being keened over every night of the week for sixty
                                                mortal years.

The Pietà's over – it is Easter over all our lives:
The revelation of our broken marriage, and its
        resurrection;
The breaking open of the tomb, and the setting free.
Painful as it was for me, I put you down off my knee
And I showed you the door.
Although you pleaded with me to keep you on my knee
And to mollycoddle you, humour you, within the family
                                                circle
('Don't put me out into the cold world,' you cried),
I did not take the easy way out and yield to you.
Instead I took down the door off its hinges
So that the sunlight shone all the more squarely
Upon the pure, original brokenness of our marriage;
I whispered to you, quietly, yet audibly,

For all the diaspora of your soul to hear:
The Pietà's over.

Yet even now, one year later, you keep looking back
From one side of Europe to the other,
Gaping at my knees as if my knees
Were the source of all that you have been, are, or will be.
By all means look around you, but stop looking back.
I would not give you shelter if you were homeless in the
    streets
For you must make your home in yourself, not in a
    woman.
Keep going out the road for it is only out there –
Out there where the river achieves its riverlessness –
That you and I can become at last strangers to one
    another,
Ready to join up again on Resurrection Day.
Therefore, I must keep whispering to you, over and over:
My dear loved one, I have to tell you,
You have run the gamut of piety –
The Pietà's over.

The Mayo Accent

Have you ever tuned in to the voice of a Mayoman?
In his mouth the English language is sphagnum moss
Under the bare braceleted feet of a pirate queen:
Syllables are blooms of tentativeness in bog cotton;
Words are bog oak sunk in understatement;
Phrases are bog water in which syllables float
Or in which speakers themselves are found floating face
    upwards
Or downwards;
Conversations are smudges of bogland under cloudy skies.
Speech in Mayo is a turbary function
To be exercised as a turbary right
With turbary responsibilities
And turbary irresponsibilities.
Peat smoke of silence unfurls over turf fires of language.

A man with a Mayo accent is a stag at bay
Upon a bog rock with rabbits round its hooves.
Why then, Daddy, did you shed
The pricey antlers of your Mayo accent
For the tree-felling voice of a harsh judiciary
Whose secret headquarters were in the Home Counties or
    High Germany?
Your son has gone back to Mayo to sleep with the island
    woman
Who talks so much she does not talk at all.
If he does not sleep with her, she will kill him – the pirate
    queen.

Tom Leonard, 1944–

Tom Leonard was born in Glasgow and studied at Glasgow University. Language itself, power, class and politics are his central concerns. Much of his poetry is written in Glaswegian – accurately reproducing accent, tone and gesture, in austere but compelling and often very funny poems. The status of 'thi lang-/wij a thi/ guhtr' is examined, and that language employed as a weapon in such a way as to preserve the living quality of speech against the claims of respectability and institutionalized culture both within and beyond Scotland. He has written appreciatively of the American poet William Carlos Williams's (1883–1963) 'presentation of voice as fact'. There are parallels to be drawn with Tony Harrison and W. N. Herbert. Leonard is the most unyielding of the three. See *Intimate Voices: Selected Work 1965–83* (1995).

from Unrelated Incidents

(1)

its thi lang-
wij a thi
guhtr thaht hi
said its thi
langwij a
thi guhtr

awright fur
funny stuff
ur
Stanley Bax-
ter ur but
luv n science
n thaht naw

thi langwij
a thi
intillect hi
said thi lang-
wij a thi intill-
ects Inglish

then whin thi
doors slid
oapn hi raised
his hat geen
mi a fare-
well nod flung
oot his right

fit boldly n
fell eight

storeys
doon thi
empty
lift-shaft

(3)

this is thi
six a clock
news thi
man said n
thi reason
a talk wia
BBC accent
iz coz yi
widny wahnt
mi ti talk
aboot thi
trooth wia
voice lik
wanna yoo
scruff. if
a toktaboot
thi trooth
lik wanna yoo
scruff yi
widny thingk
it wuz troo.
jist wanna yoo
scruff tokn.
thirza right
way ti spell
ana right way
ti tok it. this
is me tokn yir
right way a
spellin. this
is ma trooth.
yooz doant no
thi trooth
yirsellz cawz

yi canny talk
right. this is
the six a clock
nyooz. belt up.

Jist ti Let Yi No

(from the American of Carlos Williams)

ahv drank
thi speshlz
that wurrin
thi frij

n thit
yiwurr probbli
hodn back
furthi pahrti

awright
they wur great
thaht stroang
thaht cawld

Craig Raine, 1944–

Born in Shildon, Co. Durham, Raine read English at Oxford, where he then taught. He has worked as an editor, a publisher and latterly once more as a university teacher. With *The Onion, Memory* (1977) and *A Martian Sends a Postcard Home* (1978) he established himself among the most popular younger poets, and figured prominently in Blake Morrison and Andrew Motion's *Penguin Book of Contemporary British Poetry* (1982). The progenitor of Martianism (as it was christened by James Fenton), Raine wrote an ingeniously observed poetry, defamiliarizing the domestic world through simile and metaphor. *Rich* (1984) drove the manner into baroque elaboration. Opinion is divided between Raine's admirers and those who detect complacency in his inventiveness. Though he wrote the libretto *The Electrification of the Soviet Union* (1986) and *1953* (1990), a version of Racine's *Andromache*, and published a book of reviews, *Haydn and the Valve Trumpet* (1990), Raine devoted much of the next decade to an epic verse novel, *History: the Home Movie* (1994). *Clay. Whereabouts Unknown* (1996) is a collection of shorter poems, where Raine's gifts of comparison are tested against age and mortality. See Alan Robinson, *Instabilities in Contemporary British Poetry* (1988), for an interesting essay on Raine.

A Martian Sends a Postcard Home

Caxtons are mechanical birds with many wings
and some are treasured for their markings –

they cause the eyes to melt
or the body to shriek without pain.

I have never seen one fly, but
sometimes they perch on the hand.

Mist is when the sky is tired of flight
and rests its soft machine on ground:

then the world is dim and bookish
like engravings under tissue paper.

Rain is when the earth is television.
It has the property of making colours darker.

Model T is a room with the lock inside –
a key is turned to free the world

for movement, so quick there is a film
to watch for anything missed.

But time is tied to the wrist
or kept in a box, ticking with impatience.

In homes, a haunted apparatus sleeps,
that snores when you pick it up.

If the ghost cries, they carry it
to their lips and soothe it to sleep

with sounds. And yet, they wake it up
deliberately, by tickling with a finger.

Only the young are allowed to suffer
openly. Adults go to a punishment room

with water but nothing to eat.
They lock the door and suffer the noises

alone. No one is exempt
and everyone's pain has a different smell.

At night, when all the colours die,
they hide in pairs

and read about themselves –
in colour, with their eyelids shut.

Retirement

(*For Terry and Joanna Kilmartin*)

The world is a beautiful woman
we love but have ceased to see,

with whom we must learn to linger
all over again, to prize and to praise

all over again, while there is time,
so much time has been lost.

And so we retire, to watch
a dark-blue, touch-paper sky

spasm with trapped light
like the storm in the Xerox machine,

or, looking away, suddenly see
the golf course powder its face.

She is shy and retiring like us
as we seek to redress

the long neglect of a life,
now there is time at last

to bring her out her playful side,
her secret poetry, her deft translations:

the mudflat's manual of knots,
nœud de soldat, nœud de vache,

the spider's virtuoso harp,
the poached egg like an octopus.

The seasons send her inspiration
to the tiring house of dirt,

where she dons and doffs
her naked disguises:

a field fluffy with pompons of clover,
a strand with three strands of pearls.

Carol Rumens, 1944–

Carol Rumens was born in London and studied at London University. Rumens's work ranges widely in theme and manner, from personal lyrics to ambitious and powerful historical-political works such as the Holocaust poem 'Outside Oswiecim'. A feminist and an internationalist of the imagination, she was also among the most astute poetic readers of the Thatcher years (see *From Berlin to Heaven*, 1989). *Thinking of Skins: New and Selected Poems* (1993) draws on eight volumes. *Best China Sky* followed in 1995. Rumens edited the *Making for the Open: The Chatto Book of Post-Feminist Poetry* (new ed., 1988).

The Hebrew Class

Dark night of the year, the clinging ice
a blue pavement-Dresden,
smoking still, and in lands more deeply frozen,
the savage thaw of tanks:

but in the Hebrew class it is warm as childhood.
It is Cheder and Sunday School.
It is the golden honey of approval,
the slow, grainy tear saved for the bread

of a child newly broken
on the barbs of his Aleph-Bet,
to show him that knowledge is sweet
– and obedience, by the same token.

So we taste power and pleasing,
and the white wand of chalk lisps on the board,
milky as our first words.
We try to shine for our leader.

How almost perfectly human
this little circle of bright heads bowed before
the declaration of grammatical law.
Who could divide our nation

of study? Not even God.
We are blank pages hungry for the pen.
We are ploughed fields, soft and ripe for planting.
What music rises and falls as we softly read.

Oh smiling children, dangerously gifted ones,
take care that you learn to ask why,
for the room you are in is also history.
Consider your sweet compliance

in the light of that day when the book
is torn from your hand;
when, to answer correctly the teacher's command,
you must speak for this ice, this dark.

Jarrow

Nothing is left to dig, little to make.
Night has engulfed both firelit hall and sparrow.
Wind and car-noise pour across the Slake.
Nothing is left to dig, little to make
A stream of rust where a great ship might grow.
And where a union-man was hung for show
Nothing is left to dig, little to make.
Night has engulfed both firelit hall and sparrow.

Jeffrey Wainwright, 1944–

Born in Stoke-on-Trent, Wainwright read English at Leeds University and teaches at Manchester Metropolitan University. Wainwright's chaste and scrupulous verse scores effects seemingly disproportionate to its means. *Selected Poems* (1985) is an exemplary work, binding the private and the political in a single field of force. There is a sense in which Wainwright links poets of the Left with the more conservative perspective of Geoffrey Hill: Wainwright's 'Thomas Muntzer', a series of monologues spoken by a revolutionary leader in the German Reformation, speaks of a kind of utopian Christian Socialism, while behind it lies the counter-example of Hill's 'Funeral Music'. A further collection, *The Red-Headed Pupil*, appeared in 1994. Wainwright has also written a stage adaptation of Charles Péguy's *The Mystery of the Charity of Joan of Arc* (1986).

1815

I/ *The Mill-Girl*

Above her face
Dead roach stare vertically
Out of the canal.
Water fills her ears,
Her nose her open mouth.
Surfacing, her bloodless fingers
Nudge the drying gills.

The graves have not
A foot's width between them.
Apprentices, jiggers, spinners
Fill them straight from work,
Common as smoke.

Waterloo is all the rage;
Coal and iron and wool
Have supplied the English miracle.

II/*Another Part of the Field*

The dead on all sides –
The fallen –
The deep-chested rosy ploughboys
Swell out of their uniforms.

The apple trees,
That were dressed overall,
Lie stripped about their heads.

'The French cavalry
Came up very well my lord.'
'Yes. And they went down
Very well too.
Overturned like turtles.
Our muskets were obliged
To their white bellies.'

No flies on Wellington.
His spruce wit sits straight
In the saddle, jogging by.

III/*The Important Man*

Bothered by his wife
From a good dinner,
The lock-keeper goes down
To his ponderous water's edge
To steer in the new corpse.

A bargee, shouting to be let through,
Stumps over the bulging lengths
Of his hatches,
Cursing the slowness
Of water.

The lock-keeper bends and pulls her out
With his bare hands.
Her white eyes, rolled upwards,
Just stare.

He is an important man now.
He turns to his charge:
The water flows uphill.

IV/*Death of the Mill-Owner*

Shaking the black earth
From a root of potatoes,
The gardener walks
To the kitchen door.

The trees rattle
Their empty branches together.

Upstairs the old man
Is surprised.
His fat body clenches –
Mortified
At what is happening.

The Dead Come Back

The dead come back to us in dreams –
As we are told they do so they come.

Thus among the tablecloths and cakes,
The ham and sliced tongue and all the objects
Of this earth,
The company known and unknown at this latest funeral,
Lily, large and powdered in her flowery dress
Appears to her brothers and all of us
Like a star, a celebrity back among her own.
Nearly a sister again, nearly an aunt,
All of us parting for her, shy of touching
What we have brought to mind.

Unable as we are to die,
The dead come back to us in dreams –
As we are told they do, so they come.

John Hartley Williams, 1944–

Born in London, Williams studied at Nottingham University and has taught linguistics in Africa, former Yugoslavia and Berlin. *Bright River Yonder* (1983) is an epic postmodern western, while *Cornerless People* (1990), *Double* (1994) and *Canada* (1997) explore politics, eroticism and the workings of language, often to comic effect, in styles ranging from the relatively conventional to the wildly experimental. Williams cannot be categorized, but might be called a poetic cousin of Peter Didsbury.

A Word from Istvan Kovács

(for Ken Smith)

Adjusting the string of my hat,
chin propped on my brass-capped stick,
I survey my pigs with a windmill eye.
When the well-pole tilts, it draws thousand year old water
from the river of my race.

Potatoes this year will be red & crisp,
fleshy to the teeth like a well-planned crime.
Peppers will be yellow & heavy,
sit in the hand like a judge's mace,
weigh down yr palm with verdicts.

I came here, you understand, with Genghis Khan
to destroy Christendom. Well, well, I thought.
You can imagine my surprise when I planted
cucumbers, beans, cauliflowers,
& they came up Christian as a girlfriend.

On a three-legged stool, by a basket of geraniums,
I wear a cloak & a woven shirt. Sunday best.
The golden clasp of my cloak is hot in the sun.
It matches the glint of my buckle.
Soon, I know, the people will come.

The donkeys put on an act of hilarity.
My cart-horse, still in the shafts, rubs its back
against a tree, tipping a wheel off the ground.
The land is flat as the vowel I use
to gee them up along the tufty track.

I see them from far off. A car across the plain.
On the high banks of the river, the trees bend & hiss.
The sky is tuned to a low resonance of wind,

like a rumour of those who resisted, the ones
who were taken away, the non-returnees.

When the guests arrive, I tip the demijohn
against my shoulder. Their eyes watch
the way it floods out – greeny-gold *kövidinka*
from the last barrel. What hospitality means
is showing the plenty you'd like to have.

I raise my glass in a cracked toast, & they try,
fumbling with the language, to repeat it.
Waiting for food, I become impatient,
let out the old familial roar of my blood
that sends the women flying into the kitchen.

'Where are you from?' I ask, imagining it,
as the women serve & retreat. The new
visitors come from the west. They praise
my viticulture. Slowly, I take my hat off
& they stare at the whiteness of my brow.

Onions might be the text for a sermon.
Garlic, the hard, white giver, its tang
richer, more forceful than a young boy's jet
might scandalize our barns this Autumn.
Shallots, I murmur, are thicker-skinned than that.

My gap-toothed grin. *Erös kolbász*,
'Here,' I say, pushing smoked pork fat
across the table, 'you never tasted anything
like this.' I think of it sclerosing their insides
like rust on an ancient drum. I think of them

back in their own country, the futtering vitriol
slowing them, winding them down,
becoming a stone in their stomachs.
Low in the trees, from the banks of the river,
the sun chips at the quartz of my buckle.

Kit Wright, 1944–

Born in Kent and educated at Oxford, Wright is a supremely accomplished comic poet, an heir to Gavin Ewart's role, sharing Ewart's fascination with verse forms but not his productiveness – at any rate in his work for adults. Wright is a very popular children's poet and has long been active in poetry education. *Poems 1974–83* (1988) and *Short Afternoons* (1989) emphasize a powerful note of near-despair beneath the exuberance.

The Boys Bump-starting the Hearse

The hearse has stalled in the lane overlooking the river
Where willows are plunging their heads in the bottle-
                                        green water
         And bills of green baize drakes kazoo.
         The hearse has stalled and what shall we do?

The old don comes on, a string bag his strongbox.
He knows what is known about Horace but carries no
                                        tool box.
         Small boys shout in the Cambridge sun.
         The hearse has stalled and what's to be done?

Lime flowers drift in the lane to the baskets of bicycles,
Sticker the wall with yellow and powdery particles.
         Monosyllabic, the driver's curse.
         Everything fires. Except the hearse

Whose gastric and gastric whinnies shoot neutered tom
                                        cats
In through the kitchen flaps of back gardens where tomtits
         Wizen away from the dangling crust.
         Who shall restart the returned-to-dust?

Shrill and sudden as birds the boys have planted
Their excellent little shoulders against the lamented
         Who bumps in second. A fart of exhaust.
         On goes the don and the holocaust.

Wendy Cope, 1945–

Wendy Cope was born in Kent, read History at Oxford and was for some years a primary school teacher. *Making Cocoa for Kingsley Amis* (1986) was a hugely popular debut. Inch-perfect parodies of poets from Wordsworth to Heaney were juxtaposed with tart reflections on love, the unsatisfactoriness of men and the struggles of the imaginary poetic underdog, Jason Strugnell. *Serious Concerns* (1991) proved similarly appealing. Like Kit Wright, Cope has been seen as a successor to Gavin Ewart, and – again like Wright – she has been less prolific than her admirers may have hoped.

A Nursery Rhyme

as it might have been written by William Wordsworth

The skylark and the jay sang loud and long,
The sun was calm and bright, the air was sweet,
When all at once I heard above the throng
Of jocund birds a single plaintive bleat.

And, turning, saw, as one sees in a dream,
It was a Sheep had broke the moorland peace
With his sad cry, a creature who did seem
The blackest thing that ever wore a fleece.

I walked towards him on the stony track
And, pausing for a while between two crags,
I asked him, 'Have you wool upon your back?'
Thus he bespake, 'Enough to fill three bags.'

Most courteously, in measured tones, he told
Who would receive each bag and where they dwelt;
And oft, now years have passed and I am old,
I recollect with joy that inky pelt.

Selima Hill, 1945–

Selima Hill was born in London in 1945. She read Moral Sciences at Cambridge. Hill is an original. She is creating a world, or a series of worlds, where love, sex, and family conflict are played out in a kind of farmyard magic realism. Her poetry is erotic and anxious, funny and alarming, and infuriating to some critics in its apparent whimsicality and abrupt similes. See *A Little Book of Meat* (1993), *Trembling Hearts in the Bodies of Dogs: New and Selected Poems* (1994) and *Violet* (1997).

The Voice of Bobo

(i.m. the late Bobo, bull terrier)

Everything inside this room is mine.
And everyone inside it has to stay.

It's where I keep my horses and my men,
cooled on summer days by giant fans

whose steady rhythm
calms the anxious mind.

Nor do I want torpor, or docility.
From the very moment I arrive

I like to have each person's full attention,
until a silence is attained so deep

some of you will hear the Voice of Bobo,
when, after having queues of tiresome people

teasing her by blowing down her ear,
she suddenly can't bear it any longer

and starts to bark, as only Bobo can.
Those who hear that precious Voice go forward

to other, smaller rooms, for the Advanced.
Everybody else must stay on here –

here between the land and the sea
where long ago I built this secret palace

balanced on the cliff among the predators
to take advantage of the sweeping views.

I Know I Ought to Love You

I know I ought to love you
but it's hopeless.
Screaming is the best I can do.
I scream at you for such a long time
that even when I stop the scream goes on.
It screams between us like a frozen street
with stiff exhausted birds embedded in it.

Coition

You'll have to lie perfectly still
like a nude with a rat;

and when I have finished,
you'll have not a hair on your head,

and everyone else in the world
will have gone to sleep.

Bernard O'Donoghue, 1945–

Bernard O'Donoghue was born in Co. Cork. He is a Fellow of Magdalen College, Oxford. He is unusual in combining his role as a medievalist with criticism of contemporary poetry, and his reputation as a critic and reviewer preceded that established with the publication of his poetry collections *The Weakness* (1991) and *Gunpowder* (1995). O'Donoghue further confounds the stereotype of the scholar-poet by writing a limpid, anecdotal verse. He is the author of a fine critical book, *Seamus Heaney and the Language of Poetry* (1994).

A Nun Takes the Veil

That morning early I ran through briars
To catch the calves that were bound for market.
I stopped the once, to watch the sun
Rising over Doolin across the water.

The calves were tethered outside the house
While I had my breakfast: the last one at home
For forty years. I had what I wanted (they said
I could), so we'd loaf bread and Marie biscuits.

We strung the calves behind the boat,
Me keeping clear to protect my style:
Confirmation suit and my patent sandals.
But I trailed my fingers in the cool green water,

Watching the puffins driving homeward
To their nests on Aran. On the Galway mainland
I tiptoed clear of the cow-dunged slipway
And watched my brothers heaving the calves

As they lost their footing. We went in a trap,
Myself and my mother, and I said goodbye
To my father then. The last I saw of him
Was a hat and jacket and a salley stick,

Driving cattle to Ballyvaughan.
He died (they told me) in the country home,
Asking to see me. But that was later:
As we trotted on through the morning mist,

I saw a car for the first time ever,
Hardly seeing it before it vanished.
I couldn't believe it, and I stood up looking
to where I could hear its noise departing

But it was only a glimpse. That night in the convent
The sisters spoilt me, but I couldn't forget
The morning's vision, and I fell asleep
With the engine humming through the open window.

Duncan Bush, 1946–

Duncan Bush was born in Cardiff and educated at Warwick University and Wadham College, Oxford. After working in industry and education, he became Director of the Writing Programme at Gwent College in 1984. He has latterly divided his time between South Wales and Luxembourg, where he holds a lecturing post. *Hook* (1997) collects Bush's earlier work. His humane concern with the social and political dimensions of individual experience is imaginatively extended in *Masks* (1994). His interest in experimental forms is sustained in *The Genre of Silence* (1988), a novel in verse and prose. Bush's other works include the thriller *Glass Shot* (1991).

Pig Farmer

Like boys who throw stones off the roadside
down on his stone-weighted tin roofs and pedal,
                                    something in me flinches
at an uncouthness in this pig farmer
guarding his triangle of black-tramped
mud between 2 ragged hedges and a stapled wire fence.

18 months ago or so he pulled into this
freehold, waste-ground
landscape like a lay-by. Now he lives in
a scrapyard compound
2 alsatians prowl on slip chains.
They're half-trained, and look half-starved – like the
                                    silence they dog, perhaps
          sullen
          ingratiating
          vicious –
in 3 moves.

Beleaguered, padlocked by misanthropy, he's here
to stay –
even the yellow-and-white, second-hand caravan trailer's
now on 4 breeze-block piles
like a Portakabin classroom . . .

                              In it he must learn
infancy's difficulties every night over again, blunted
digits listed, totted, in the red
Silvine exercise-book with the moiré cover
and multiplication-tables on the back and metric measures:
11 eggs;
a refill blue steel Calor-gas bottle;

the dusty, hard hundredweight Portland cement-bags
                                        shouldered in
        still owed for . . .

Is this the sum
of all his sojourn, his
existence? –
                barely numerate
accountancy, bleak
monomania
among feed and dung, feed and dung
where only your own
labour comes free and unreckoned, you
buy always more than you can
find or sell, and you can't
get eggs from straw . . .

He put 2 youths, trespassers, in the hospital last week.

Even the silence is harsh
and suffocated in him.

Outside, the bedraggled donkey, the look
of life-long suffering on its greying
face, stands and outwaits
in its own breath
the patience of February drizzle
and a winter when every stick of timber –
the yard's sodden, inedible driftwood, the fence-posts,
        the slimy cobbled hen-house –
has turned green.

The midden of trodden mud
will never green under the trotters of his pink and filthy
                                        pigs . . .

24 hours they stink windward from their corrugated
       Nissen domes,
once daily jostling to waste
and tepid bran-mash –
                              vomit
rolled in sawdust.
Their new metal trough
is star-blue, frost patterned from the galvanizing.

But pigs, they say, find and eat
                                   anything –
weeds; truffles of broken pottery grubbed
from the dirt; the dirt . . .
They'll crunch a corpse down past the signet-ring, the
                                        severed
finger that denied them it –
                           then snuff their shit
for more . . .

There is a moment for his whole, partial
subsistence here to be imagined brutal, bare
and barbarous as that.

Then he straightens
his back –
his scarecrow coat knotted about the waist with coarse,
       white hairy string –
and watched you stip looking at him and
go past.

Peter Didsbury, 1946–

Peter Didsbury was born in Fleetwood, Lancashire, and grew up in Hull. He studied English and Hebrew at Oxford and worked as a schoolteacher. He is now an archaeological pottery analyst. A selection of his work appeared in Douglas Dunn's Hull anthology, *A Rumoured City* (1982). His first book, *The Butchers of Hull* (also 1982), confirmed that here was a highly individual voice. While Didsbury showed affinities with John Ashbery, Roy Fisher and Christopher Middleton, the scale and detail of his imagination, his range of arcane learning and his bizarre humour, as well as his religious preoccupations, set him apart. *The Classical Farm* (1987) and *That Old-Time Religion* (1994) consolidated his unique position in contemporary poetry.

The Hailstone

Standing under the greengrocer's awning
in the kind of rain we used to call a cloudburst,
getting home later with a single hailstone in my hair.
Ambition would have us die in thunderstorms
like Jung and Mahler. Five minutes now,
for all our sad and elemental loves.

A woman sheltering inside the shop
had a frightened dog,
which she didn't want us to touch.
It had something to do with class,
and the ownership of fear. Broken ceramic lightning
was ripping open the stitching in the sky.
The rain was 'siling' down,
the kind that comes bouncing back off the pavement,
heavy milk from the ancient skins
being poured through the primitive strainer.
Someone could have done us in flat colours,
formal and observant, all on one plane,
you and me outside and the grocer and the lady
behind the gunmetal glass, gazing out over our shoulders.
I can see the weave of the paper behind the smeared
                                        reflections,
some of the colour lifting as we started a sudden dash
                                            home.
We ran by the post office and I thought, 'It is all still true,
a wooden drawer is full of postal orders, it is raining,
mothers and children are standing in their windows,
I am running through the rain past a shop which sells
                                            wool,
you take home fruit and veg in bags of brown paper,
we are getting wet, it is raining.'
                        It was like being back

in the reign of George the Sixth, the kind of small town
which still lies stacked in the back of old storerooms in
                                                    schools,
where plural roof and elf expect to get very wet
and the beasts deserve their nouns of congregation
as much as the postmistress, spinster, her title.
I imagine those boroughs as intimate with rain,
their ability to call on sentient functional downpours
for any picnic or trip to the German Butcher's
one sign of a usable language getting used,
make of this what you will. The rain has moved on,
and half a moon in a darkening blue sky
silvers the shrinking puddles in the road:
moon that emptied the post office and grocer's,
moon old kettle of rain and idiolect,
the moon the sump of the aproned pluvial towns,
cut moon as half a hailstone in the hair.

Part of the Bridge

(for Robin Moore)

The enormous mentality
of the south bank abutment's
embedded concrete block
is not impassive,
though it copes with the westering sun
as remorselessly as any god with petitions.

It is not to be blamed for its size,
its faces textured with jutting tablets, grooves,
or even our dear conviction that mass,
when sheer enough, moves over into sentience.

To enter its zone on an evening in July
is to speak the word *temple*
in as emptiness-sanctioned a voice
as is used among the mountains;

to hear what it does with the fabulations of air,
that move in its precinct like spirits of ancient birds,
is to know both the paradox, and the stimulus, of its pity.

The Romance of Steam

Sound of a distant train in the midsummer night.
Other ones, though, are too far away to be heard.
Ancient locos, forgotten in sidings and sheds,
flanks glazed with moonlight,
fast asleep in the dark.
A myriad sullen phantoms. Some consumed by rust,
and some let down upon the floor of the ocean.
Those entangled by nature, roped with jungle vines;
the many secreted by artful bandits in caves;
the ones not even arrived at the drawing board yet.
How easy they are to imagine, these silent varieties:
a dreaming ironclad crawling the coast of Honduras,
a blue-grey shunter tumbling through deepest space
with its *gravitas* intact, grazing serenely
the phosphorescent pastures of the stars.

I heard of an engine once
that some Persian railwaymen
had been forced to bury in sand.
Inspecting the line for rocks and bombs
a day ahead of a train being used by the Shah
and fate decrees they derail the thing on a bend,
stumble around for a minute or so with the shock,
check themselves for broken heads and limbs,
then cease to breathe as they realize their predicament.
If I were you, I said to them,
as sheer cold terror began to undress us all,
I'd get it buried, pronto, so they did.
In a big deep hole by the side of the line,
smoothed over the desert surface afterwards,
then hid behind a bush as the tyrant rolled by.
That's all I know. I lost *track* of them after that,
and can only relate the fervour I now employ

to get them back safely to their villages in the hills,
to greet them with bread and salt and coloured scarves,
then sit them down against walls of sun-dried brick
to take no more part in any kind of history.

Peter Reading, 1946–

Born in Liverpool, a former teacher and lecturer, the prolific Reading has been called 'the laureate of junk Britain'. His world is beset by ignorance, vandalism, violence and a sense of end-of-species futility, the effect of which is both comic and appalling. An entire book, *C* (1984), consists of a hundred hundred-word poems about cancer. A disenchanted romantic, Reading writes a poetry of statement, in which depth is generated by complex cross-referencing of themes and voices and the deployment of various devices – Swiftian satire, newspaper cuttings and other found materials, classical and Old English metres, textual lacunae and the author's careful design of the appearance of individual works. One may suspect Reading of lapsing into a posture of exhausted reaction, but *Work in Regress* (1997) is perhaps the best of his many books. The two-volume *Collected Poems* appeared in 1995–96.

from **Duologues**

3

'I wish I'd knowed im as drives tractor, afore I wed Jim.
Once you marries the wrong un youm never the same
                                                    someow.'

'Same along o me, Annie, that un as I fancied first,
e never said much all them years as us was courtin,
so I thinks as e dunna like me, an breaks up with im.
Then e thinks as I dunna like im, an takes some wench
                                                    else.
Then I sid im again, one Pig Day it were in the Arms,
and e says as e loves me an would I get wed to im
(only would I answer im quick or eed af to wed er).
Well, I never says "ar" nor "no" for days, till e thinks
as it's "no" and e weds this other out Clungunford way
an they moves down Tenbury country – Glebe Farm an
                                                    summat.
An e dunna get on with er, an just now e writes me
as e loves me, an I writes back as I loves im an all.
Just now all is stock dies – that Foot and Mouth year
                                                    afore last –
and they says as e got debts an that's why e shot isself.'

from Stet

Muse!, sing the Grotty [scant alternative].

Cro-Magnon, simian, Neanderthal,
whom Mr Justice Russell sentences
to 46 years (total) for assault
on Mr Harry Tipple and his wife . . .

Charles Bradford, Terence Bradford, Edward Mitchell,
broke into Mr Tipple's corner shop.
After they had assaulted him he had
black eyes, a broken nose, bruised lacerated
torso and face and buttocks. He had his head
banged on the floor and had his feet stamped on.
He was knocked senseless with a bottle. Cans
of aerosol paint and fly-spray were fizzed up
his nose and mouth. Bradford and Mitchell next
started to cut his ear off, but then hacked
off Tipple's toe with a serrated knife.
The toe was then stuffed into Tipple's mouth
(playing *This Little Piggy* on the kid's
little pink blobs is not so much fun now).

And Mrs Tipple croodles in the box
as she explains how both her eyes were blacked,
her nose was broken, she was 'in the most
humiliating and degrading way'
indecently assaulted by the men –
one of whom 'used a knife in an obscene
bizarre vile filthy ithyphallic manner'.
Charles Bradford, Terence Bradford, Edward Mitchell,
before they left the Tipples bound and gagged,
turned, faced them, and, unzipping, each produced

his member and pissed long and copiously
into the faces of the hapless pair.

An acned trio lowers from the front page.
Cro-Magnon, simian, Neanderthal
(but the same species as Christ, Einstein, Bach).

[Trite impotent iambic journalese,
Reading Raps Raiders/Poet Pete Protests.]

Salopian

All day, the drone of a saw,
and resin across the pines
of dark Mortimer Forest.
With each completed sever
it fell by a whining octave.

By dusk, in the clearing they'd made,
all that remained was their dust,
the dottle from someone's pipe
and ranks of seasoning limbs
weeping congealing amber.

*

The heat, the fragrance of hay,
the incontrovertible end
of summer, the country halt,
boarding the single-track train,
weeds prising the platform oblique
where they waved and waved and waved.

*

Dewed cowslips, roses, the grave
under a yew in the garden
of lichened Pipe Aston church,
a dusty Visitors' Book . . .

We were once there: 17th
of June 1975.

Douglas Houston, 1947–

Houston was born in Cardiff and educated at Hull University. Like Peter Didsbury he featured in Douglas Dunn's Hull anthology, *A Rumoured City* (1982). His debut, *With the Offal Eaters* (1986), revealed a witty and inventive poet with an appetite for the surreal dimension of ordinary life. *Hunters in the Snow* (1994) contained poems of love and family alongside Houston's habitually peculiar imaginative excursions.

The Welsh Book of the Dead

After you have died,
You may find yourself in Wales.
Do not be deterred from feeling at home.
The evaluation procedures, though lengthy,
Are informally carried out,
And a century or two soon passes.

Who knows? You may have been conducted here
By a psychopomp encountered in some poem,
Passage of singing, or suddenly there
in the glint of daylight sharpened on space
Beyond one of the more dramatic mountains.
In most cases, no objections are raised.

Planning permission may be required
For ritual and incantatory practices
Extending beyond the compass of two
Standard Welsh Anagogical Units,
But, again, time is not of the essence
In the well-appointed Induction Zones.

It's surprising, really, the people who come,
For the nature mostly, the peaks, pools, and skies,
Much like the country visited that summer
You recalled with a nod at a place-name
In the *Eschatological Gazetteer*.
The new brochure is widely available.

So. Welcome. Why not start with a few decades
In the sort of warm dark place where the Language
Sits down and tells extremely long stories
About the Goneness-Of-All-That-Was
And the Hereness-Of-All-That-Is,
Of which the endings are often remarkable?

Ruth Padel, 1947–

Ruth Padel taught Classics at London University before taking up writing full-time. *Summer Snow* (1990) and *Angel* (1993) were followed by *Fusewire* (1996). Padel's work has a speedy, omnivorous relish, touching on politics and history but most notable for an aching and exactly rendered mixture of sensuality and affection. *Rembrandt Would Have Loved You* (1998) is a book of poems about a love affair, as engaging as a novel. Padel reviews for several newspapers and her other books include *Whom Gods Destroy* (1995), a study of madness.

Tinderbox

This is innocent. Teenage. Blossom
Without leaf. It's not a gun.
Not threatening anyone's conservatory,
Private school, or bank account.

Lies are being kept to a minimum
And lives are going on as they always have
And shall. We're only Noël Coward,
Lightest of light tenors, percolating

'Fate has sent me you'
Through the cherry-snow of Russell Square;
A hedgehog star of icicles lit
By the sun's last rays on the lip of a cliff.

The song will end,
The whole thing fall to pieces, when
We get to the forbidden mountain's heart.
It'll all be known. There'll be iron

With its cruel ideas. And maybe I'll stop
Saying the 'Our Father' in that narrow space
Between the bath and sweat-foxed
Mirror, hugging a towel

And thanking Someone, Anything,
For you. Morality. A trapdoor spider's
Inner web. A tinderbox. Where we are
Has no answers.

Penelope Shuttle, 1947–

Penelope Shuttle was born in Middlesex and lives in Cornwall. Shuttle has published six collections, including *Adventures with My Horse* (1988), *Taxing the Rain* (1992) and *Building a City for Jamie* (1996). *Selected Poems* appeared in 1998. Her work is mysterious, erotic, occupied with dreams and visions and something akin to the science of the spirit advocated by her husband, the poet Peter Redgrove. A parallel among her women contemporaries might be sought in Medbh McGuckian, but Shuttle's world is airier and more hopeful.

Taxing the Rain

When I wake the rain's falling
and I think, as always, it's for the best,

I remember how much I love rain,
the weakest and strongest of us all;

as I listen to its yesses and no's,
I think how many men and women

would, if they could,
against all sense and nature,

tax the rain for its privileges;

make it pay for soaking our earth
and splashing all over our leaves;

pay for muddying our grass
and amusing itself with our roots.

Let rain be taxed, they say,
for riding on our rivers
and drenching our sleeves;

for loitering in our lakes
and reservoirs. Make rain pay its way.

Make it pay for lying full length
in the long straight sedate green waters

of our city canals,
and for working its way through processes

of dreamy complexity
until this too-long untaxed rain comes indoors

and touches our lips,
bringing assuagement – for rain comes

to slake all our thirsts, spurting
brusque and thrilling in hot needles,

showering on to anyone naked;
or balming our skins in the shape of scented baths.

Yes, there are many who'd like to tax the rain;
even now they whisper, it can be done, it must be done.

John Ash, 1948–

John Ash was born in Manchester and educated at Birmingham University. He has lived in New York since 1985. Rather than in English, the sources of Ash's work are in French poetry from the mid-nineteenth century onwards. He writes a richly observed glamorously melancholic poetry of postmodern city life, full of camp humour, a poetry of the man-made rather than the natural world. He is often linked with John Ashbery, but the mood and method of Ash's work are more stable and bear some resemblance to those of Peter Didsbury. See *The Goodbyes* (1982), *The Branching Stairs* (1984) and *The Burnt Pages* (1992).

Cigarettes

Problems of translation are, perhaps, not so great
between languages as between different versions
of the same language. Why, for example, does
'fag' mean homosexual in America, when,
in England, it means cigarette? Does this imply
that those who first observed the phenomenon
of smoking in the New World were homosexual?
This would cause some consternation on Columbus Day,
and, in all likelihood, the assumption is unjustified,
since Columbus and his crew were not English-speakers.
Yet, if we dismiss the idea of happy crowds of
homosexual Spanish or Italian mariners
returning to Europe with cigarettes in hand,
eager to introduce this new pleasure to their lovers,
we should perhaps concede that there is some connection
between the two ideas. It was Oscar Wilde, after all,
who described smoking as 'the perfect pleasure, because' –
he opined – 'it always leaves one unsatisfied.'
It is clear from this that he was thinking of sexual pleasure,
of the working-class youths with whom he so recklessly
                                      dined
in fashionable restaurants of the eighteen-nineties.
A cigarette is like a passion in that it is inhaled deeply
and seems to fill all the empty spaces of the body,
until, of course, it burns down, and is put out amid
the shells of pistachio nuts, or whatever trash
may be at hand, and the passion may leave traces
that in time will grow malignant: he who has taken
                                      pleasure
may die many years after in the room of an anonymous
hotel or hospital, under the blank gaze of a washstand,
a bad painting or an empty vase, having forgotten entirely
the moment that announced the commencement

of his dying. And perhaps he will not understand:
it is another false translation, like someone stumbling over
the word for cigarette in a new and intolerable language.

Ciaran Carson, 1948–

Ciaran Carson was born in Belfast and educated at Queen's University, Belfast. He has worked for the Arts Council of Northern Ireland as Traditional Arts Officer, and is a scholar and exponent of traditional Irish music. Carson's first book, *The New Estate* (1977), was an interesting if unspectacular debut, and was followed by a decade of silence before *The Irish for No* (1987) announced the emergence of another major poet in Northern Ireland. Here Carson adopts a long, unreeling line which bears some resemblances to the work of the American poet C. K. Williams, as well as to Louis MacNeice, and – according to the author – to the movement of traditional music. It is a richly detailed anecdotal poetry, much given to (indeed at times founded on) digression and involving the recasting or translation of other poems ('Snow', for example, makes use of MacNeice's famous poem of the same name). In *Belfast Confetti* (1989) Carson concentrates on his native city, examining its history, its deformation by violence and oppression, and its power to invoke a passionate love in its inhabitants. The book contains prose poems and a mixture of long and brief, nearly documentary pieces. Carson seems able to write English as if it were Irish, and in *First Language* (1993) includes verse in Irish, alongside translations from Baudelaire and of Rimbaud's 'Le Bateau Ivre'. These symbolist connections imply an aesthetic project akin to Rimbaud's 'alchemy of the word' and in *Opera et Cetera* (1996) Carson seems set to break the frame of convention. Ordinary pleasures – bread, whisky, cigarettes, music – are brought into arresting intimacy with the forces of history in a poetry which is funny, poignant and mysterious and begs to be heard aloud. Carson has also written about Irish music, (*Last Night's Fun*, 1996) and an impressionistic history of Belfast (*The Star Factory*, 1998). *The Ballad of HMS Belfast*, a compendium of his Belfast poems, is to appear in 1999.

Dresden

Horse Boyle was called Horse Boyle because of his brother
      Mule;
Though why Mule was called Mule is anybody's guess. I
      stayed there once,
Or rather, I nearly stayed there once. But that's another
      story.
At any rate they lived in this decrepit caravan, not two
      miles out of Carrick,
Encroached upon by baroque pyramids of empty baked
      bean tins, rusts
And ochres, hints of autumn merging into twilight. Horse
      believed
They were as good as a watchdog, and to tell you the
      truth
You couldn't go near the place without something falling
      over:
A minor avalanche would ensue – more like a shop bell,
      really,

The old-fashioned ones on string, connected to the latch,
      I think,
And as you entered in, the bell would tinkle in the empty
      shop, a musk
Of soap and turf and sweets would hit you from the
      gloom. Tobacco.
Baling wire. Twine. And, of course, shelves and pyramids
      of tins.
An old woman would appear from the back – there was a
      sizzling pan in there,
Somewhere, a whiff of eggs and bacon – and ask you
      what you wanted;
Or rather, she wouldn't ask; she would talk about the
      weather. It had rained

That day, but it was looking better. They had just put in
    the spuds.
I had only come to pass the time of day, so I bought a
    token packet of Gold Leaf.

All this time the fry was frying away. Maybe she'd a
    daughter in there
Somewhere, though I hadn't heard the neighbours talk of
    it; if anybody knew,
It would be Horse. Horse kept his ears to the ground.
And he was a great man for current affairs; he owned the
    only TV in the place.
Come dusk he'd set off on his rounds, to tell the whole
    townland the latest
Situation in the Middle East, a mortar bomb attack in
    Mullaghbawn –
The damn things never worked, of course – and so he'd
    tell the story
How in his young day it was very different. Take young
    Flynn, for instance,
Who was ordered to take this bus and smuggle some
    sticks of gelignite

Across the border, into Derry, when the RUC – or was it
    the RIC? –
Got wind of it. The bus was stopped, the peeler stepped
    on. Young Flynn
Took it like a man, of course: he owned up right away.
    He opened the bag
And produced the bomb, his rank and serial number. For
    all the world
Like a pound of sausages. Of course, the thing was, the
    peeler's bike
Had got a puncture, and he didn't know young Flynn
    from Adam. All he wanted

338 – Ciaran Carson

Was to get home for his tea. Flynn was in for seven years
and learned to speak
The best of Irish. He had thirteen words for a cow in
heat;
A word for the third thwart in a boat, the wake of a boat
on the ebb tide.

He knew the extinct names of insects, flowers, why this
place was called
Whatever: *Carrick*, for example, was *a rock*. He was
damn right there –
As the man said, *When you buy meat you buy bones,
when you buy land you buy stones.*
You'd be hard put to find a square foot in the whole
bloody parish
That wasn't thick with flints and pebbles. To this day he
could hear the grate
And scrape as the spade struck home, for it reminded him
of broken bones:
Digging a graveyard, maybe – or better still, trying to dig
a reclaimed tip
Of broken delph and crockery ware – you know that
sound that sets your teeth on edge
When the chalk squeaks on the blackboard, or you shovel
ashes from the stove?

Master McGinty – he'd be on about McGinty then, and
discipline, the capitals
Of South America, Moore's *Melodies*, the Battle of
Clontarf, and
*Tell me this, an educated man like you: What goes on four
legs when it's young,*
Two legs when it's grown up, and three legs when it's old?
I'd pretend
I didn't know. McGinty's leather strap would come up
then, stuffed

With threepenny bits to give it weight and sting. Of
    course, it never did him
Any harm. *You could take a horse to water but you
    couldn't make him drink.*
He himself was nearly going on to be a priest.
*And many's the young cub left the school, as wise as
    when he came.*

Carrowkeel was where McGinty came from – *Narrow
    Quarter*, Flynn explained –
Back before the Troubles, a place that was so mean and
    crabbed,
Horse would have it, men were known to eat their dinner
    from a drawer.
Which they'd slide shut the minute you'd walk in.
He'd demonstrate this at the kitchen table, hunched and
    furtive, squinting
Out the window – past the teetering minarets of rust,
    down the hedge-dark aisle –
To where a stranger might appear, a passer-by, or what
    was maybe worse,
Someone he knew. Someone who wanted something.
    Someone who was hungry.
Of course who should come tottering up the lane that
    instant but his brother

Mule. I forgot to mention they were twins. They were as
    like two –
No, not peas in a pod, for this is not the time nor the
    place to go into
Comparisons, and this is really Horse's story, Horse who –
    now I'm getting
Round to it – flew over Dresden in the war. He'd
    emigrated first, to
Manchester. Something to do with scrap – redundant
    mill machinery,

Giant flywheels, broken looms that would, eventually, be
  ships, or aeroplanes.
He said he wore his fingers to the bone.
And so, on impulse, he had joined the RAF. He became a
  rear gunner.
Of all the missions, Dresden broke his heart. It reminded
  him of china.

As he remembered it, long afterwards, he could hear, or
  almost hear
Between the rapid desultory thunderclaps, a thousand
  tinkling echoes –
All across the map of Dresden, store-rooms full of china
  shivered, teetered
And collapsed, an avalanche of porcelain, slushing and
  cascading: cherubs,
Shepherdesses, figurines of Hope and Peace and Victory,
  delicate bone fragments.
He recalled in particular a figure from his childhood, a
  milkmaid
Standing on the mantelpiece. Each night as they knelt
  down for the rosary,
His eyes would wander up to where she seemed to beckon
  to him, smiling,
Offering him, eternally, her pitcher of milk, her mouth of
  rose and cream.

One day, reaching up to hold her yet again, his fingers
  stumbled, and she fell.
He lifted down a biscuit tin, and opened it.
It breathed an antique incense: things like pencils, snuff,
  tobacco.
His war medals. A broken rosary. And there, the
  milkmaid's creamy hand, the outstretched
Pitcher of milk, all that survived. Outside, there was a
  scraping

And a tittering; I knew Mule's step by now, his careful
    drunken weaving
Through the tin-stacks. I might have stayed the night, but
    there's no time
To go back to that now; I could hardly, at any rate, pick
    up the thread.
I wandered out through the steeples of rust, the gate that
    was a broken bed.

Slate Street School

Back again. Day one. Fingers blue with cold. I joined the
  lengthening queue.
Roll-call. Then inside: chalk-dust and iced milk, the smell
  of watered ink.
Roods, perches, acres, ounces, pounds, tons weighed
  imponderably in the darkening
Air. We had chanted the twelve-times table for the twelfth
  or thirteenth time
When it began to snow. Chalky numerals shimmered
  down; we crowded to the window –

*These are the countless souls of purgatory, whose numbers
  constantly diminish*
*And increase; each flake as it brushes to the ground is yet
  another soul released.*
And I am the avenging Archangel, stooping over mills and
  factories and barracks.
I will bury the dark city of Belfast forever under snow:
  inches, feet, yards, chains, miles.

Army

The duck patrol is waddling down the odd-numbers side of
  Raglan Street,
The bass-ackwards private at the rear trying not to think of
  a third eye
Being drilled in the back of his head. Fifty-five. They stop.
  The head
Peers round, then leaps the gap of Balaclava Street. He
  waves the body over
One by one. Forty-nine. Cape Street. A gable wall. Garnet
  Street. A gable wall.

Frere Street. Forty-seven. Forty-five-and-a-half. Milan
  Street. A grocer's shop.
They stop. They check their guns. Thirteen. Milton Street.
  An iron lamp-post.
Number one. Ormond Street. *Two ducks in front of a duck
  and two ducks*
Behind a duck, how many ducks? Five? No. *Three.* This is
  not the end.

Drunk Boat

After Rimbaud, Le Bateau Ivre

As I glided down the lazy Meuse, I felt my punters had
      gone AWOL –
In fact, Arapahoes had captured them for target practice,
      nailing them to stakes. Oh hell,

I didn't give a damn. I didn't want a crew, nor loads of
      Belgian wheat, nor English cotton.
When the whoops and hollers died away, their jobs were
      well forgotten.

Through the tug and zip of tides, more brain-deaf than an
      embryo, I bobbled;
Peninsulas, unmoored and islanded, were envious of my
      Babel-babble.

Storms presided at my maritime awakening. Like a cork I
      waltzed across the waves,
Which some call sailors' graveyards; but I despised their
      far-off, lighted enclaves.

As children think sour apples to be sweet, so the green sap
      swamped the planks
And washed away the rotgut and the puke, the rudder and
      the anchor-hanks.

I've been immersed, since then, in Sea Poetry, anthologized
      by stars,
As through the greenish Milky Way a corpse drifts down-
      wards, clutching a corrupted spar;

When suddenly, those sapphire blues are purpled by Love's
      rusty red. No lyric
Alcohol, no Harp, can combat it, this slowly-pulsing, twilit
      panegyric.

I've known lightning, spouts, and undertows, maelstrom
        evenings that merge into Aurora's
Blossoming of doves. I've seen the Real Thing; others only
        get its aura.

I've seen the sun's demise, where seas unroll like violet,
        antique
Venetian blinds; dim spotlight, slatted by the backstage
        work of Ancient Greeks.

I dreamed the green, snow-dazzled night had risen up to
        kiss the seas'
Blue-yellow gaze, the million plankton eyes of
        phosphorescent argosies.

I followed then, for many months, the mad-cow waves of
        the Antipodes,
Oblivious to the Gospel of how Jesus calmed the waters,
        walking on his tippy-toes.

I bumped, you know, into the Floridas, incredible with
        pupil-flowers
And manatees, which panther-men had reined with
        rainbows and with Special Powers.

I saw a whole Leviathan rot slowly in the seething marsh,
        till it became
All grot and whalebone. Blind cataracts lurched into
        oubliettes, and were becalmed.

Glaciers and argent seas, pearly waves and firecoal skies! A
        tangled serpent-cordage
Hauled up from the Gulf, all black-perfumed and slabbered
        with a monster's verbiage!

I would have liked the children to have seen them: goldfish,
        singing-fish, John Dorys –
My unanchored ones, I'm cradled by the tidal flowers and
        lifted near to Paradise.

Sometimes, fed-up with the Poles and Zones, the sea would
	give a briny sob and ease
Off me; show me, then, her vented shadow-flowers, and I'd
	be like a woman on her knees . . .

Peninsular, I juggled on my decks with mocking-birds and
	ostriches
And rambled on, until my frail lines caught another upside-
	down, a drowned Australian.

Now see me, snarled-up in the reefs of bladder-wrack, or
	thrown by the waterspout like craps
Into the birdless Æther, where Royal Navy men would slag
	my sea-drunk corpse –

Smoking, languorous in foggy violet, I breathed a fireglow
	patch into
The sky, whose azure trails of snot are snaffled by some
	Poets as an entrée –

Electromagnets, hoof-shaped and dynamic, drove the
	Nautilus. Black hippocampuses
Escorted it, while heat-waves drummed and blattered on
	the July campuses.

Me, I shivered: fifty leagues away, I heard the bumbling
	Behemoths and Scarabs;
Spider spinning in the emerald, I've drifted off the ancient
	parapets of Europe!

Sidereal archipelagoes I saw! Island skies, who madly
	welcomed the explorer;
O million starry birds, are these the endless nights you
	dream of for the Future?

I've whinged enough. Every dawn is desperate, every bitter
	sun. The moon's atrocious.
Let the keel split now, let me go down! For I am bloated,
	and the boat is stotious.

Had I some European water, it would be that cold, black puddle
    puddle
Where a child once launched a paper boat – frail
    butterfly – into the dusk; and huddled

There, I am no more. O waves, you've bathed and cradled me and shaped
    me and shaped
Me. I'll gaze no more at Blue Ensigns, nor merchant- men,
    nor the drawn blinds of prison-ships.

Liz Lochhead, 1948–

Liz Lochhead was born in Motherwell. She studied at Glasgow School of Art. A successful playwright, she is a popular performer of her poems (describing some of her writing as 'recitations'), which are close to speech and rich in dramatic gesture, showing the influence of her work for the stage. Love, politics, comedy and memory figure largely among her subjects. See *Dreaming Frankenstein and Collected Poems* (1982) and *Bagpipe Muzak* (1991).

After the War

(For Susanne Ehrhardt)

After the war
was the dull country I was born in.
The night of Stafford Cripps's budget
My dad inhaled the blue haze of one last Capstan
then packed it in.
'*You were just months old . . .*'
The Berlin airlift.
ATS and REME badges
rattled in our button box.

Were they surprised that everything was different now?
Did it cheese them off that it was just the same
stuck in one room upstairs at my grandma's
jammed against the bars of my cot
with one mended featherstitch jumper drying
among the nappies on the winterdykes,
the puffed and married maroon counterpane
reflected in the swinging mirror of the wardrobe.
Radio plays. Them loving one another
biting pillows
in the dark while I was sleeping.
All the unmarried uncles were restless,
champing at the bit for New Zealand, The Black
                                    Country, Corby.
My aunties saved up for the New Look.

By International Refugee Year
we had a square green lawn and a twelve-inch tele.

George Szirtes, 1948–

George Szirtes was born in Hungary. His parents fled after the defeat of the 1956 Uprising. He grew up in England and was educated at Leeds Art School, where he received encouragement from Martin Bell. Szirtes's highly individual blend of hard-edged realism and surreal complication has added richness to the poetic diet in England. Hungarian life – as in the sequence 'The Court-yards' – has become central to his work, introducing themes of loss and suffering. A fine *Selected Poems 1976–1996* appeared in 1996 and *Portrait of My Father in an English Garden* in 1998. Szirtes has also translated the Hungarian poet Zsusza Rakovsky (*New Life*, 1994) and edited, with George Gomöri, *The Colonnade of Teeth: Modern Hungarian Poetry* (1996).

Ghost Train

Is it an illusion? It must be. Cesare
Pavese, sitting on a train, in a third-class
Carriage, alone with a woman who smokes.
He is too embarrassed to smile or make a pass
Among those empty seats that other women
Have at times vacated. It is history,
And the long train croaks
And shudders, smelling of upholstery,
Remaining empty, no place for encounters.

Public transport has been stitching together
The unfinished business of old Europe.
Believing in ghost buses that fail to stop
When requested, that appear only in foul weather,
Inhabitants of inner cities glamorize
Familiar places where the traffic chunters
Like some vigilant but dull
Official, an Argus with myopic eyes
Who cannot watch over his human cattle.
The ghost buses are empty, driverless.
They come upon one suddenly, with a noise
Of thunder and faint bells, their progress
Unsteady, vast overgrown toys
That have run away, and found this special route,
These special streets. Now someone tells a story
Of those who have managed the trick of boarding
By somehow leaping on, getting a foot
On the platform and grasping the ghost bar. According
To him their fate is terrible, a gory
Compound of brown wire, a cross between
A prison and a farmyard, shitty, poisonous.

Such buses and such trains keep rolling on.
Infected landscapes watch them, half asleep

And, perversely amorous,
They listen for flirtations in the spin
Of the wheel or the hiss of the smoke.
Now Cesare Pavese will not keep
Appointments, nor at this time of night
Is it possible to stay awake
And see the stations sweeping out of sight.

Gillian Allnutt, 1949–

Gillian Allnutt was born in London in 1949 and studied at Oxford. Formerly the poetry editor of *Time Out*, she was joint editor of the anthology *The New British Poetry* (1988). She lives in Co. Durham. With her third collection, *Blackthorn* (1994), Allnutt unleashed a combination of rhythmic dexterity and sheer imaginative oddity which compelled wider attention. *Nantucket and the Angel* (1997) brought a further intensification. A religious sensibility lit with strange humour and pathos recalls but stands independently of the work of Stevie Smith.

The Garden in Esh Winning

Go then into the unfabricated dark
With your four bare crooked tines, fork,
And get my grandmother out of that muddle of dock and
                                        dandelion root
And put an end to neglect
While the wind says only *Esh Esh*
In the late apple blossom, in the ash
And all the hills rush down to Durham
Where the petulant prince bishops dream
In purple vaults.
It's not the earth's fault,
Fork, but mine, that I for forty years of days and nights
                                        invented dragons
To guard my grandmother's bare arthritic bones
From my own finding. Now of all things I imagine a
                                        garden
Laid over, and dumb as, a disused coalmine.
In the north there are no salley gardens, no, nor bits of
                                        willow pattern
Plate to plead for me, no, only bones
Unmourned, the memory of the memory of a plane shot
                                        down
And its discolouration.
Who now humbly brings me my grandmother in pieces
Like Osiris,
Fork? Who eases out old sorrel gone to seed, old scallions?
Who pulls the purple columbines
Out of the not quite dark midsummer midnight? In the
                                        north the sky is green,
The long grass, partly shorn, lies down like a lion
And *something's happened to John*
And in this valley of discoloured bones
Ezekiel lies open to the wind, the fork-work done.

The Bible propped like an elbow on the ironing-board

                                            within

The house is full of visions, Gran,
Of what we are, were, always might have been.

My grandmother's son John was an RAF navigator, shot down
over France in 1943. The night it happened, she woke and sat up
in bed saying 'Something's happened to John'.

356 – Gillian Allnutt

James Fenton, 1949–

James Fenton was born in Lincoln and studied psychology and philosophy at Oxford. He has worked as a foreign correspondent and drama critic and was elected Oxford Professor of Poetry in 1993. Fenton has published comparatively little, and his career has been marked by dramatic developments. *Terminal Moraine* (1972) was an extremely accomplished book, ranging from satirical letters to ambitious historical work, from found poems to the complex meditation 'The Pitt-Rivers Museum, Oxford'. The poems eventually gathered in *The Memory of War and Children in Exile: Poems 1968–83* (1983) include some of the most important of the period – the war-amnesia piece 'A German Requiem'; the country house poems 'Nest of Vampires' and 'A Vacant Possession'; 'A Staffordshire Murderer'; and poems derived from Fenton's first-hand knowledge of the latter days of the Vietnam War. Fenton has written some of the period's plainest and some of its most tantalizingly postmodern poetry. *Out of Danger* (1993) showed him shifting ground again, into elegies, light verse and horror-poems such as 'Ballad of the Shrieking Man'. To date Fenton has at times exhibited a definitive power comparable to that of W. H. Auden. If he seems unlikely to match Auden for scale, developments in Fenton's work are none the less awaited with the keenest interest.

The Pitt-Rivers Museum, Oxford

Is shut
22 hours a day and all day Sunday
And should not be confused
With its academic brother, full of fossils
And skeletons of bearded seals. Take
Your heart in your hand and go; it does not sport
Any of Ruskin's hothouse Venetian
And resembles rather, with its dusty girders,
A vast gymnasium or barracks – though
The resemblance ends where

Entering
You will find yourself in a climate of nut castanets,
A musical whip
From the Torres Straits, from Mirzapur a sistrum
Called Jumka, 'used by aboriginal
Tribes to attract small game
On dark nights', a mute violin,
Whistling arrows, coolie cigarettes
And a mask of Saagga, the Devil Doctor,
The eyelids worked by strings.

Outside,
All around you, there are students researching
With a soft electronic
Hum, but here, where heels clang
On iron grates, voices are at best
Disrespectful: 'Please sir, where's the withered
Hand?' For teachers the thesis is salutary
And simple, a hierarchy of progress culminating
In the Entrance Hall, but children are naturally
Unaware of and unimpressed by this.

358 – James Fenton

Encountering
'A jay's feather worn as a charm
In Buckinghamshire, Stone',
We cannot either feel that we have come
Far or in any particular direction.
Item. A dowser's twig, used by Webb
For locating the spring, 'an excellent one',
For Lord Pembroke's waterworks at Dinton
Village. 'The violent twisting is shown
On both limbs of the fork.'

Yes
You have come upon the fabled lands where myths
Go when they die,
But some, especially the Brummagem capitalist
Juju, have arrived prematurely. Idols
Cast there and sold to tribes for a huge
Price for human sacrifice do
(Though slightly hidden) actually exist
And we do well to bring large parties
Of schoolchildren here to find them.

Outdated
Though the cultural anthropological system be
The lonely and unpopular
Might find the landscapes of their childhood marked out
Here, in the chaotic piles of souvenirs.
The claw of a condor, the jaw-bone of a dolphin,
These cleave the sky and the waves but they
Would trace from their windowseats the storm petrel's
                                                    path
From Lindness or Naze to the North Cape,
Sheltered in the trough of the wave.

For the solitary,
The velveted only child who wrestled

With eagles for their feathers
And the young girl on the hill, who heard
The din on the causeway and saw the large
Hound with the strange pretercanine eyes
Herald the approach of her turbulent lover,
This boxroom of the forgotten or hardly possible
Is laid with the snares of privacy and fiction
And the dangerous third wish.

Beware.
You are entering the climate of a foreign logic
And are cursed by the hair
Of a witch, earth from the grave of a man
Killed by a tiger and a woman who died
in childbirth, 2 leaves from the tree
Azumü, which withers quickly, a nettle-leaf,
A leaf from the swiftly deciduous 'Flame of the
Forest' and a piece of a giant taro,
A strong irritant if eaten.

Go
As a historian of ideas or a sex-offender,
For the primitive art,
As a dusty semiologist, equipped to unravel
The seven components of that witch's curse
Or the syntax of the mutilated teeth. Go
In groups to giggle at curious finds.
But do not step into the kingdom of your promises
To yourself, like a child entering the forbidden
Woods of his lonely playtime:

All day,
Watching the groundsman breaking the ice
From the stone trough,
The sun slanting across the lawns, the grass
Thawing, the stable-boy blowing on his fingers,
He had known what tortures the savages had prepared

For him there, as he calmly pushed open the gate
And entered the wood near the placard: 'TAKE NOTICE
MEN-TRAPS AND SPRING-GUNS ARE SET ON THESE
                                      PREMISES.'
For his father had protected his good estate.

A Staffordshire Murderer

Every fear is a desire. Every desire is fear.
The cigarettes are burning under the trees
Where the Staffordshire murderers wait for their
                                    accomplices
And victims. Every victim is an accomplice.

It takes a lifetime to stroll to the carpark
Stopping at the footbridge for reassurance,
Looking down at the stream, observing
(With one eye) the mallard's diagonal progress backwards.

You could cut and run, now. It is not too late.
But your fear is like a long-case clock
In the last whirring second before the hour,
The hammer drawn back, the heart ready to chime.

Fear turns the ignition. The van is unlocked.
You may learn now what you ought to know:
That every journey begins with a death,
That the suicide travels alone, that the murderer needs
                                    company.

And the Staffordshire murderers, nervous though they are,
Are masters of the conciliatory smile.
A cigarette? A tablet in a tin?
Would you care for a boiled sweet from the famous
                                    poisoner

Of Rugeley? These are his own brand.
He has never had any complaints.
He speaks of his victims as a sexual braggart
With a tradesman's emphasis on the word 'satisfaction'.

You are flattered as never before. He appreciates
So much, the little things – your willingness for instance

To bequeath your body at once to his experiments.
He sees the point of you as no one else does.

Large parts of Staffordshire have been undermined.
The trees are in it up to their necks. Fish
Nest in their branches. In one of the Five Towns
An ornamental pond disappeared overnight

Dragging the ducks down with it, down to the old seams
With a sound as of a gigantic bath running out,
Which is in turn the sound of ducks in distress.
Thus History murders mallards, while we hear nothing

Or what we hear we do not understand.
It is heard as the tramp's rage in the crowded precinct:
'Woe to the bloody city of Lichfield.'
It is lost in the enthusiasm of the windows

From which we are offered on the easiest terms
Five times over in colour and once in monochrome
The first reprisals after the drill-sergeant's coup.
How speedily the murder detail makes its way

Along the green beach, past the pink breakers,
And binds the whole cabinet to the oil-drums,
Where death is a preoccupied tossing of the head,
Where no decorative cloud lingers at the gun's mouth.

At the Dame's School dust gathers on the highwayman,
On Sankey and Moody, Wesley and Fox,
On the snoring churchwarden, on Palmer the Poisoner
And Palmer's house and Stanfield Hall.

The brilliant moss has been chipped from the Red Barn.
They say that Cromwell played ping-pong with the
                                              cathedral.
We train roses over the arches. In the Minster Pool
Crayfish live under carved stones. Every spring

The rats pick off the young mallards and
The good weather brings out the murderers
By the Floral Clock, by the footbridge,
The pottery murderers in jackets of prussian blue.

'Alack, George, where are thy shoes?'
He lifted up his head and espied the three
Steeple-house spires, and they struck at his life.
And he went by his eye over hedge and ditch

And no one laid hands on him, and he went
Thus crying through the streets, where there seemed
To be a channel of blood running through the streets,
And the market-place appeared like a pool of blood.

For this field of corpses was Lichfield
Where a thousand Christian Britons fell
In Diocletian's day, and 'much could I write
Of the sense that I had of the blood – '

That winter Friday. Today it is hot.
The cowparsley is so high that the van cannot be seen
From the road. The bubbles rise in the warm canal.
Below the lock-gates you can hear mallards.

A coot hurries along the tow-path, like a Queen's
                                        Messenger.
On the heli-pad, an arrival in blue livery
Sends the water-boatmen off on urgent business.
News of a defeat. Keep calm. The cathedral chimes.

The house by the bridge is the house in your dream.
It stares through new frames, unwonted spectacles,
And the paint, you can tell, has been weeping.
In the yard, five striped oildrums. Flowers in a tyre.

This is where the murderer works. But it is Sunday.
Tomorrow's bank holiday will allow the bricks to set.

You see? he has thought of everything. He shows you
The snug little cavity he calls 'your future home'.

And 'Do you know,' he remarks, 'I have been counting
                                        my victims.
Nine hundred and ninety nine, the Number of the Beast!
That makes you. . .' But he sees he has overstepped the
                                        mark:
'I'm sorry, but you cannot seriously have thought you
                                        were the first?'

A thousand preachers, a thousand poisoners,
A thousand martyrs, a thousand murderers –
Surely these preachers are poisoners, these martyrs
                                        murderers?
Surely this is all a gigantic mistake?

But there has been no mistake. God and the weather are
                                        glorious.
You have come as an anchorite to kneel at your funeral.
Kneel then and pray. The blade flashes a smile.
This is your new life. This murder is yours.

Tom Paulin, 1949–

Born in Leeds, Paulin grew up in Belfast and was educated at Hull and Oxford. The most explicitly political of the leading Northern Irish poets, he has applied a highly individual blend of nonsectarian socialist republicanism to Ulster, the British empire and modern European history. His style has moved dramatically from an early realist mode coloured by Auden and Douglas Dunn towards a quirky, jagged, speech-based 'writing to the moment', incorporating Ulster dialect and a wide range of learning in some of the most interesting, if forbidding, work of the period. A tireless controversialist, he writes essays of great urgency and force which serve to re-politicize the characteristically rather neutral discussion of poetry in England (see *Writing to the Moment: Selected Critical Essays 1980–1996* (1996). *Selected Poems 1972–1990* (1993) was followed by *Walking a Line* (1994). Paul has edited *The Faber Book of Political Verse* (1986) and his plays include *Antigone* (1986).

Desertmartin

At noon, in the dead centre of a faith,
Between Draperstown and Magherafelt,
This bitter village shows the flag
In a baked absolute September light.
Here the Word has withered to a few
Parched certainties, and the charred stubble
Tightens like a black belt, a crop of Bibles.

Because this is the territory of the Law
I drive across it with a powerless knowledge –
The owl of Minerva in a hired car.
A Jock squaddy glances down the street
And grins, happy and expendable,
Like a brass cartridge. He is a useful thing,
Almost at home, and yet not quite, not quite.

It's a limed nest, this place. I see a plain
Presbyterian grace sour, then harden,
As a free strenuous spirit changes
To a servile defiance that whines and shrieks
For the bondage of the letter: it shouts
For the Big Man to lead his wee people
To a clean white prison, their scorched tomorrow.

Masculine Islam, the rule of the Just,
Egyptian sand dunes and geometry,
A theology of rifle-butts and executions:
These are the places where the spirit dies.
And now, in Desertmartin's sandy light,
I see a culture of twigs and bird-shit
Waving a gaudy flag it loves and curses.

Hegel and the War Criminals

The föhn was blowing
– a soft flimflam
as Hegel dug in the roots
of a liberty tree
– it was *populus alba*
the white or silver poplar
not the aspen
the trembling poplar
Hegel was nineteen
the Bastille had just been broken up
into doorstops paperweights and keyrings
and already Stalin's greatuncles
were busy digging pits

*

When Himmler visited Auschwitz
he noted that the crematorium
had been badly positioned
– foursquare and obvious
it needed concealing
so a screen of quickgrowing poplars
began to shoot up like rhubarb
– in summer sunlight the drizzly
almost tinselly light of the poplar leaves
flickered like chaff in a radar beam

*

During denazification
the Allies banned a cunning brownshirt
from giving classes and lectures
so Heidegger's fans
gathered in Freiburg
to hear a voice drone and spit

behind a net curtain
– half-pope half-fortuneteller
almost a popular figure
he rambled on about oaktrees
– you can still watch his acquittal
behind this text and that text

Christopher Reid, 1949–

Christopher Reid was born in Hong Kong and educated at Oxford. There he was briefly taught by Craig Raine, the other significant figure in Martian poetry. Reid is a more light-hearted, teasing poet than Raine, as his two 'Martian' volumes, *Arcadia* (1979) and *Pea Soup* (1982), demonstrate. With *Katerina Brac* (1985) Reid undertook a book-length collection in the persona of a woman poet from Eastern Europe. As readers might have expected, the political dimension of all this seemed to Reid the least interesting: it is the workings of the vernacular which excite him. His subsequent books are *In the Echoey Tunnel* (1991), which contains the ambitious 'found' poem 'Memres of Alfred Stoker', and the charming *Expanded Universes* (1996).

A Whole School of Bourgeois Primitives

Our lawn in stripes, the cat's pyjamas,
rain on a sultry afternoon

and the drenching, mnemonic smell this brings us
surging out of the heart of the garden:

these are the sacraments and luxuries
we could not do without.

Welcome to our peaceable kingdom,
where baby lies down with the tiger-rug

and bumblebees roll over like puppies
inside foxglove-bells . . .

Here is a sofa, hung by chains
from a gaudy awning.

Two puddles take the sun
in ribbon-patterned canvas chairs.

Our television buzzes like a fancy tie,
before the picture appears –

and jockeys in art-deco caps and blouses
caress their anxious horses,

looking as smart as the jacks on playing-cards
and as clever as circus monkeys.

Douanier Rousseau had no need to travel
to paint the jungles of his paradise.

One of his tigers, frightened by a thunder-storm,
waves a tail like a loose dressing-gown cord:

it does not seem to match the coat at all,
but is ringed and might prove dangerous.

Medbh McGuckian, 1950–

Medbh McGuckian was born in Belfast and studied at Queen's University, Belfast. The leading woman poet to emerge in Northern Ireland, McGuckian has staked out a territory quite different from any of her male peers. It involves an inward, deeply encoded treatment of love, gender and language, using lavishly detailed and dream-lit versions of domesticity. *The Flower Master* (1982), *Venus and the Rain* (1984) and *On Ballycastle Beach* (1988) were followed by *Marconi's Cottage* (1992). McGuckian's work is discussed by Clair Wills in *Improprieties: Politics and Sexuality in Northern Irish Poetry* (1993). *Selected Poems* appeared in 1998.

The Dowry Murder

The danger of biscuit-coloured silk
Is how it just reveals you, the chill
Of the balloon material swaying
In the wind that is not there – the part
Of my body that deals with it needs churching,
Where I keep secret house, a room within
A room, or an organic, touch-dry garden
Where I sit upon my hair. From deep-set
Windows I contemplate the immature moon
Upon the louvered roof of the orangery,
The snow-well thatched with straw, my
Moorish fabrics sapient with
My love of heavy clothing.
Though my railway novel ends
With the bride's sari catching fire
While cooking succotash, something about
The light that is just there musters
A last kiss, your clutch on my ordinary stem,
Then your head falling off into a drawer.

From the Dressing Room

Left to itself, they say, every foetus
Would turn female, staring in, nature
Siding then with the enemy that
Delicately mixes up genders. This
Is an absence I have passionately sought,
Brightening nevertheless my poet's attic
With my steady hands, calling him my blue
Lizard till his moans might be heard
At the far end of the garden. For I like
His ways, he's light on his feet and does
Not break anything, puts his entire soul
Into bringing me a glass of water.

I can take anything now, even his being
Away, for it always seems to me his
Writing is for me, as I walk springless
From the dressing-room in a sisterly
Length of flesh-coloured silk. Oh there
Are moments when you think you can
Give notice in a jolly, wifely tone,
Tossing off a very last and sunsetty
Letter of farewell, with strict injunctions
To be careful to procure his own lodgings,
That my good little room is lockable.
But shivery, I recover at the mere
Sight of him propping up my pillow.

Grace Nichols, 1950–

Grace Nichols was born in Guyana and came to Britain in 1977, working first as a journalist then as a poet and children's writer. Her books *I is a Long Memoried Woman* (1983), *The Fat Black Woman's Poems* (1984), *Lazy Thoughts of a Lazy Woman* (1989) and *Sunris* (1996) have won a large audience, and she is a popular performer of her work. Nichols combines salty humour with pithy observations on love and life in England, while incorporating a mythic-historical dimension in her treatment of blackness and womanhood.

Blackout

Blackout is endemic to the land.
People have grown sixthsense
and sonic ways, like bats,
emerging out of the shadows
into the light of their own flesh.

But the car headlamps coming towards us
make it seem we're in some thirdworld movie,
throwing up potholes and houses exaggeratedly,
the fresh white painted and grey ramshackle
blending into snug relief.

And inside, the children are still hovering,
hopeful moths around – the flickerless Box,
immune to the cloying stench of toilets
that can't be flushed. The children,
all waiting on electric-spell to come
and trigger a movie, the one featuring America,
played out endlessly in their heads.

While back outside, coconut vendors decapitate
the night, husky heads cutlassed off
in the medieval glow of bottle lamps.

And everywhere there are flittings
and things coming into being,
in a night where footfall is an act of faith –
A group of young girls huddled in a questionable doorway;
The sudden dim horizontal of an alleyway;
And the occasional generator-lit big house,
obscenely bright –
hurting the soft iris of darkness
in this worn-out movie, slow reeling

Under the endless cinema of the skies.

Charles Boyle, 1951–

Charles Boyle was born in Leeds and educated at St John's College, Cambridge. He has worked as a schoolteacher and a publisher's editor. Boyle writes a nervy, amusing, alienated and at times alarming poetry of the failure of places (North Africa, London) and life to add up or reveal themselves. His work has affinities with both Paul Muldoon and Michael Hofmann. Boyle's sixth book, *Paleface*, appeared in 1996.

Sheds

The way weeds and stiff grasses have reclaimed the yard,
the way the tracks lead frankly nowhere;
the dry rust, the continuous mockery
of insects, of birds; the way the toolsheds
could still be nothing but toolsheds
even without their tools, with their corners smelling of
                                                    shame

and their little piles of filth . . .

Exhaustion, waste, relief
at being one again with nature –
and still a kind of reckless belief
that just one more day, another hour of light
would have seen it through.

Paul Muldoon, 1951–

Paul Muldoon was born in County Armagh and educated at Queen's University, Belfast. For some years he worked as a producer for BBC radio, since then he has divided his time between writing and teaching, currently at Princeton University. Since the appearance of his fourth book, *Quoof* (1983), Muldoon has become one of the most influential poets of the period. His appeal lies partly in his enormous technical facility and inventive use of varieties of rhyme, and in his deployment and deformation of the sonnet. Furthermore, his cast of mind – sidelong, at times hallucinatory, driven by long-distance association of ideas, puns and resemblances, and with a prominent narrative element – has seemed the very definition of postmodernist poetry for the mainstream. His handling of themes of identity, violence, love and belonging has placed him in the forefront of an intimidatingly talented group of poets from Northern Ireland, and his work contains a critique of the artistic and political stance of his leading predecessor, Seamus Heaney. Muldoon's whole body of work indicates a distrust of 'public' poetry. His hugely ambitious book *Madoc* (1990) 'reads' western philosophy in the light of what might have happened had Coleridge and Southey ever attempted to set up their Pantisocratic republic in the United States. The vertiginous 'Yarrow' from *The Annals of Chile* (1994) examines the poet's family background. Muldoon is often at his most distinctive and effective in briefer poems. *New Selected Poems 1968–94* (1996) is a good introduction, and Tim Kendall's *Paul Muldoon* (1996) is the first full-length study of his work. *Hay* appeared in 1998.

Cuba

My eldest sister arrived home that morning
In her white muslin evening dress.
'Who the hell do you think you are,
Running out to dances in next to nothing?
As though we hadn't enough bother
With the world at war, if not at an end.'
My father was pounding the breakfast-table.

'Those Yankees were touch and go as it was –
If you'd heard Patton in Armagh –
But this Kennedy's nearly an Irishman
So he's not much better than ourselves.
And him with only to say the word.
If you've got anything on your mind
Maybe you should make your peace with God.'

I could hear May from beyond the curtain.
'Bless me, Father, for I have sinned.
I told a lie once, I was disobedient once.
And, Father, a boy touched me once.'
'Tell me, child. Was this touch immodest?
Did he touch your breast, for example?'
'He brushed against me, Father. Very gently.'

The Right Arm

I was three-ish
when I plunged my arm into the sweet-jar
for the last bit of clove-rock.

We kept a shop in Eglish
that sold bread, milk, butter, cheese,
bacon and eggs,
Andrews Liver Salts,
and, until now, clove-rock.

I would give my right arm to have known then
how Eglish was itself wedged between
ecclesia and *église*.

The Eglish sky was its own stained-glass vault
and my right arm was sleeved in glass
that has yet to shatter.

The Frog

Comes to mind as another small upheaval
amongst the rubble.
His eye matches exactly the bubble
in my spirit-level.
I set aside hammer and chisel
and take him on the trowel.

The entire population of Ireland
springs from a pair left to stand
overnight in a pond
in the gardens of Trinity College,
two bottles of wine left there to chill
after the Act of Union.

There is, surely, in this story
a moral. A moral for our times.
What if I put him to my head
and squeezed it out of him,
like the juice of freshly squeezed limes,
or a lemon sorbet?

Gathering Mushrooms

The rain comes flapping through the yard
like a tablecloth that she hand-embroidered.
My mother has left it on the line.
It is sodden with rain.
The mushroom shed is windowless, wide,
its high-stacked wooden trays
hosed down with formaldehyde.
And my father has opened the Gates of Troy
to that first load of horse manure.
Barley straw. Gypsum. Dried blood. Ammonia.
Wagon after wagon
blusters in, a self-renewing gold-black dragon
we push to the back of the mind.
We have taken our pitchforks to the wind.

All brought back to me that September evening
fifteen years on. The pair of us
tripping through Barnett's fair demesne
like girls in long dresses
after a hail-storm.
We might have been thinking of the fire-bomb
that sent Malone House sky-high
and its priceless collection of linen
sky-high.
We might have wept with Elizabeth McCrum.
We were thinking only of psilocybin.
You sang of the maid you met on the dewy grass –
And she stooped so low gave me to know
it was mushrooms she was gathering O.

He'll be wearing that same old donkey-jacket
and the sawn-off waders.
He carries a knife, two punnets, a bucket.
He reaches far into his own shadow.

We'll have taken him unawares
and stand behind him, slightly to one side.
He is one of those ancient warriors
before the rising tide.
He'll glance back from under his peaked cap
without breaking rhythm:
his coaxing a mushroom – a flat or a cup –
the nick against his right thumb;
the bucket then, the punnet to left or right,
and so on and so forth till kingdom come.

We followed the overgrown towpath by the Lagan.
The sunset would deepen through cinnamon
to aubergine,
the wood-pigeon's concerto for oboe and strings,
allegro, blowing your mind.
And you were suddenly out of my ken, hurtling
towards the ever-receding ground,
into the maw
of a shimmering green-gold dragon.
You discovered yourself in some outbuilding
with your long-lost companion, me,
though my head had grown into the head of a horse
that shook its dirty-fair mane
and spoke this verse:

*Come back to us. However cold and raw, your feet
were always meant
to negotiate terms with bare cement.
Beyond this concrete wall is a wall of concrete
and barbed wire. Your only hope
is to come back. If sing you must, let your song
tell of treading your own dung,
let straw and dung give a spring to your step.
If we never live to see the day we leap
into our true domain,*

lie down with us now and wrap
yourself in the soiled grey blanket of Irish rain
that will, one day, bleach itself white.
Lie down with us and wait.

Something Else

When your lobster was lifted out of the tank
to be weighed
I thought of woad,
of madders, of fugitive, indigo inks,

of how Nerval
was given to promenade
a lobster on a gossamer thread,
how, when a decent interval

had passed
(*son front rouge encor du baiser de la reine*)
and his hopes of Adrienne

proved false,
he hanged himself from a lamp-post
with a length of chain, which made me think

of something else, then something else again.

Nuala Ní Dhomhnaill, 1952–

Nuala Ní Dhomhnaill was born in Lancashire and grew up in the Irish Gaeltacht. She studied at University College, Cork. Her books are *Selected Poems*, translated by Michael Hartnett (1996), *Pharaoh's Daughter*, translated by several hands (1990), and *The Astrakhan Cloak*, translated by Paul Muldoon (1992). The calibre of Ní Dhomhnaill's translators – they also include Ciaran Carson, Seamus Heaney, Derek Mahon and Medbh McGuckian – indicates the esteem in which she is held in Ireland.

Gan do Chuid Éadaigh

Is fearr liom tú
gan do chuid éadaigh ort –
do léine shíoda
is do charabhat,
do scáth fearthainne faoi t'ascaill
is do chulaith
trí phíosa faiseanta
le barr feabhais táilliúrachta,

do bhróga ar a mbíonn
i gcónaí snas,
do lámhainní craiceann eilite
ar do bhois,
do hata *crombie*
feircthe ar fhaobhar na cluaise –
ní chuireann siad aon ruainne
le do thuairisc,

mar thíos fúthu
i ngan fhios don slua
tá corp gan mhaisle, mháchail
nó míbhua
lúfaireacht ainmhí allta,
cat mór a bhíonn amuigh
san oíche
is a fhágann sceimhle ina mharbhshruth.

Do ghuailne leathan fairsing
is do thaobh
chomh slim le sneachta séidte
ar an sliabh;

Nude

The long and short
of it is I'd far rather see you nude –
your silk shirt
and natty

tie, the brolly under your oxter
in case of a rainy day,
the three-piece seersucker
suit that's so incredibly trendy,

your snazzy loafers
and, la-di-da,
a pair of gloves
made from the skin of a doe,

then, to top it all, a crombie hat
set at a rak-
ish angle – none of these add
up to more than the icing on the cake.

For, unbeknownst to the rest
of the world, behind the outward
show lies a body unsurpassed
for beauty, without so much as a wart

or blemish, but the brill-
iant slink of a wild animal, a dream-
cat, say, on the prowl,
leaving murder and mayhem

in its wake. Your broad, sinewy
shoulders and your flank
smooth as the snow
on a snow-bank.

do dhrom, do bhásta singil
is i do ghabhal
an rúta
go bhfuil barr pléisiúrtha ann.

Do chraiceann atá chomh dorcha
is slim
le síoda go mbeadh tiús veilbhite
ina shníomh
is é ar chumhracht airgid luachra
nó meadhg na habhann
go ndeirtear faoi
go bhfuil suathadh fear is ban ann.

Mar sin is dá bhrí sin
is tú ag rince liom anocht
cé go mb'fhearr liom tú
gan do chuid éadaigh ort,
b'fhéidir nárbh aon díobháil duit
gléasadh anois ar an dtoirt
in ionad leath ban Éireann
a mhilleadh is a lot.

Your back, your slender waist,
and, of course,
the root that is the very seat
of pleasure, the pleasure-source.

Your skin so dark, my beloved,
and soft
as silk with a hint of velvet
in its weft,

smelling as it does of meadowsweet
or 'watermead'
that has the power, or so it's said,
to drive men and women mad.

For that reason alone, if for no other,
when you come with me to the dance tonight
(though, as you know, I'd much prefer
to see you nude)

it would probably be best
for you to pull on your pants and vest
rather than send
half the women of Ireland totally round the bend.

(*Translated by Paul Muldoon*)

Aubade

Is cuma leis an mhaidin cad air a ngealann sí –
ar na cáganna ag bruíon is ag achrann ins na crainn
dhuilleogacha; ar an mbardal glas ag snámh go tóstalach
i measc na ngiolcach ins na curraithe; ar thóinín bán
an chircín uisce ag gobadh aníos as an bpoll portaigh;
ar roilleoga ag siúl go cúramach ar thránna móra.

Is cuma leis an ghrian cad air a n-éiríonn sí –
ar na tithe bríce, ar fhuinneoga de ghloine snoite
is gearrtha i gcearnóga Seoirseacha: ar na saithí beach
ag ullmhú chun creach a dhéanamh ar ghairdíní
                                    bruachbhailte;
ar lánúine óga fós ag méanfach i gcomhthiúin is fonn
a gcúplála ag éirí aníos iontu; ar dhrúcht ag glioscarnach
ina dheora móra ar lilí is ar róiseanna; ar do ghuaille.

Ach ní cuma linn go bhfuil an oíche aréir
thart, is go gcaithfear glacadh le pé rud a sheolfaidh
an lá inniu an tslí; go gcaithfear imeacht is cromadh síos
arís is píosaí beaga brealsúnta ár saoil a dhlúthú
le chéile ar chuma éigin, chun gur féidir
lenár leanaí uisce a ól as babhlaí briste
in ionad as a mbosa, ní cuma linne é.

Aubade

It's all the same to morning what it dawns on –
On the bickering of jackdaws in leafy trees;
On that dandy from the wetlands, the green mallard's
Stylish glissando among reeds; on the moorhen
Whose white petticoat flickers around the boghole;
On the oystercatcher on tiptoe at low tide.

It's all the same to the sun what it rises on –
On the windows in houses in Georgian squares;
On bees swarming to blitz suburban gardens;
On young couples yawning in unison before
They do it again; on dew like sweat or tears
On lilies and roses; on your bare shoulders.

But it isn't all the same to us that night-time
Runs out; that we must make do with today's
Happenings, and stoop and somehow glue together
The silly little shards of our lives, so that
Our children can drink water from broken bowls,
Not from cupped hands. It isn't the same at all.

(*Translated by Michael Longley*)

Helen Dunmore, 1952–

Helen Dunmore was born in Beverley, East Yorkshire, and read English at York University. She taught for some time in Finland and now lives in Bristol. Dunmore is a prolific poet, whose work ranges over love, gender, *realpolitik* and parenthood. She juxtaposes novelistic episodes against brief epiphanies and lyrics, usually in ear-perfect free verse. See *Short Days, Long Nights: New and Selected Poems* (1991), *Recovering a Body* (1994), *Bestiary* (1997) and *Penguin Modern Poets 12* (1997). She is also a highly successful novelist (see *Talking to the Dead*, 1996).

Those Shady Girls

Those shady girls on the green side of the street,
those far-from-green girls who keep to the shade,
those shady girls in mysterious suits
with their labels half-showing
as the cream flap of the jacket swings open,
those girls kicking aside the front-panelled pleats
of their cream suits with cerise lapels,

those on-coming girls,
those girls swinging pearly umbrellas
as tightly-sheathed as tulips in bud
from an unscrupulous street-seller,
those girls in cream and cerise suits
which mark if you touch them,
those girls with their one-name appointments
who walk out of the sunshine.

At the Emporium

He is the one you can count on
for yesterday's bread, rolling tobacco
and the staccato
tick of the blinds
on leathery Wednesday afternoons.
He has hand-chalked boards with the prices
of Anchor butter and British wine.
He doesn't hold with half-day closing.

He's the king of long afternoons
lounging vested in his doorway.
He watches the children dwindle
and dawdle, licking icepops
that drip on the steps.
His would be the last face that saw them
before an abduction. Come in,
he is always open.

John Glenday, 1952–

John Glenday was born in Monifieth near Dundee. He has worked as a printer's devil, a van driver and a psychiatric nurse. At present he is drug counsellor in Dundee. His collections are *The Apple Ghost* (1989) and *Undark* (1995). Glenday's is a delicately but powerfully atmospheric poetry, in some ways akin to his fellow Scot John Burnside's in reaching for a dimension of the mystical within and beyond the everyday. It is his strong grasp of the particular that grants him access to the mysterious zones of consciousness which seem to interest him most.

The Empire of Lights

After Magritte: L'Empire des Lumieres 1954

The past is the antithesis of burglary. Imagine
a house in darkness. Or to be more precise,
imagine darkness in a house. Something akin

to that Magritte where the light is held
at tree's length by a clutch of tungsten bulbs.
The looming woods proofed with shadow thicker than tar.

In the House of the Past we move backwards
from room to room, forever closing doors
on ourselves, always closing doors.

In each room, we leave some of those little trinkets
we love most, that the house is stealing from us.
Because we cherish them, we abandon them

to the furniture of strangers. Whenever we go
the doors swing shut behind us without a sound,
and the dust drifts up into the ceiling like smoke.

Oh there is so much we would love to hold on to,
but so little room. If only we could come back,
if only we could come back in the morning,

things would be so much better. But on we must go,
creeping backwards through silent bedrooms,
closing doors quietly for fear of waking ourselves.

Emptying our pockets, emptying our hands. Heavy
with emptiness, we crouch down at last in the lee
of a shattered window, where we dream of those

ancient burdens, long resolved. And the fragments
of glass fidget like broken insects on the rug,
eager to heal where our fists will gently touch.

Linton Kwesi Johnson, 1952–

Linton Kwesi Johnson was born in Jamaica and grew up in London. He studied Sociology at London University. Poetry, music and politics form a unity in Kwesi Johnson's work: the poems – 'dub' poetry, meant for declamation – voice the discontents and at times the fury of young blacks; the music, reggae, lends a brooding or celebratory power to the poetry; and the politics are those of radical protest, never far from taking to the streets, as in 'The Great Insoreckshan'. Kwesi Johnson is an enormously popular performer of his work, both by himself and with a band. *Tings and Times* (1991) is his Selected Poems, also available on CD.

Reggae Sounds

Shock-black bubble-doun-beat bouncing
rock-wise tumble-doun sound music;
foot-drop find drum, blood story,
bass history is a moving
        is a hurting black story.

Thunda from a bass drum sounding
lightening from a trumpet and a organ,
bass and rhythm and trumpet double-up,
team up with drums for a deep doun searching.

Rhythm of a tropical electrical storm
(cooled doun to the pace of the struggle),
flame-rhythm of historically yearning
flame-rhythm of the time of turning,
measuring the time for bombs and for burning.

Slow drop. make stop. move forward.
dig doun to the root of the pain;
shape it into violence for the people,
they will know what to do, they will do it.

Shock-black bubble-doun-beat bouncing
rock-wise tumble-doun sound music;
foot-drop find drum, blood story,
bass history is a moving
        is a hurting black story.

Robert Minhinnick, 1952–

Robert Minhinnick was born in Neath, Glamorgan, and educated at the University Colleges of Aberystwyth and Cardiff. After working as a postman, salvage worker and schoolteacher, he has managed numerous ecological projects. Minhinnick's collections of poetry include *Native Ground* (1979), *Life Sentences* (1983), *The Dinosaur Park* (1985), *The Looters* (1989) and *Hey Fatman* (1994). Much of his poetry conveys a disquieting sense of dispossession and cultural impoverishment in a contemporary social context. *Watching the Fire Eater* (1992) and *Badlands* (1996) are collections of essays drawing on his travels in America and elsewhere.

Sunday Morning

I choose back lanes for the pace they will impose,
    An old perspective half forgotten
Surprising me now as the world slows
With these things the broad road lacked:
    Carboys of vitriol stacked in a garage,
Orange hooks of honeysuckle gripping a wall.

Here a church window becomes an arch of light
    And the pitching of a hymn a brief
Infusion of the air. Voices, and low
Indistinguishable words, the organ's bass
    The foundation for a ritual
I trespass in, that suddenly

Intensifies the day. On the other side
    I picture them: the ranked devout
Pulling the ribbons from the black prayerbooks
And each with his or her accustomed doubt
    Submitting to a poetry
Triumphant as the church's muscular brass.

Thus Sunday morning: a gleaning
    Of its strange wisdoms. The certainty
Of hymns comes with me through a different town
Of derelict courts and gardens, a stable
    Where a vizored man beats sparks from a wheel,
An old man splitting marble in a mason's yard,

The creamy splinters falling into my mind
    Like the heavy fragments of hymns,
Then walking on, much further, this morning being
                           Sunday.

Andrew Motion, 1952–

Andrew Motion was born in London and read English at Oxford. He is Professor of Creative Writing at the University of East Anglia. *The Pleasure Steamers* (1978) introduced a poet capable of elegiac lyricism and ambitious dramatic effects. The latter came to the fore in *Independence* (1981) and *Secret Narratives* (1983), in poems of novelistic complexity, often with a late-imperial cast. The early work is selected in *Dangerous Play: Poems 1974–1984* (1985), since when Motion has been prolific (and various) in his poetry – *Natural Causes* (1987), *Love in a Life* (1991), *The Price of Everything* (1994) and *Salt Water* (1997). Motion's combination of 'traditional' (i.e. romantic lyric) virtues with the concerns (if by no means all the mannerisms) of the postmodern era illustrate both the durability and the dilemmas of the English poet in the age of Muldoon. With Blake Morrison he edited *The Penguin Book of Contemporary British Poetry* (1982), whose contents and introduction set the terms for the discussion of poetry in the 1980s and after. Motion is also a biographer, author of the controversial *Philip Larkin: A Writer's Life* (1993) and *Keats* (1997). A new edition of *Selected Poems* appeared in 1998.

The Letter

If I remember right, his first letter.
Found where? My side-plate perhaps,
or propped on our heavy brown tea-pot.
One thing is clear – my brother leaning
across asking *Who is he?* half angry
as always that summer before enlistment.

Then alone in the sunlit yard, mother
unlocking a door to call *Up so early?*
– waving her yellow duster goodbye
in a small sinking cloud. The gate creaks
shut and there in the lane I am running
uphill, vanishing where the woodland starts.

The Ashground. A solid contour swept
through ripening wheat, and fringe
of stippled green shading the furrow.
Now I am hardly breathing, gripping
the thin paper and reading *Write to me.*
Write to me please. I miss you. My angel.

Almost shocked, but repeating him line
by line, and watching the words jitter
under the pale spidery shadows of leaves.
How else did I leave the plane unheard
so long? But suddenly there it was –
a Messerschmitt low at the wood's edge.

What I see today is the window open,
the pilot's unguarded face somehow
closer than possible. Goggles pushed up,
a stripe of ginger moustache, and his eyes
fixed on my own while I stand
with the letter held out, my frock blowing,

before I am lost in cover again,
heading for home. He must have banked
at once, climbing steeply until his jump
and watching our simple village below –
the Downs swelling and flattening, speckled
with farms and bushy chalk-pits. By lunch

they found where he lay, the parachute
tight in its pack, and both hands spread
as if they could break the fall. I still
imagine him there exactly. His face pressed
close to the sweet-smelling grass. His legs
splayed wide in a candid unshamable V.

The Lines

November, and the Sunday twilight fallen
dark at four – its hard unbroken rain
battering the garden. Vacantly I fill
this first week-end alone with anything –

the radio, a paperback you never read:
In 1845 200,000 navvies, 3,000 miles of line.
Lost faces lift – *a mania, a human alligator,*
shovels clinking under high midsummer sun.

The heat-haze dances meadowsweet and may,
whole cliffs collapse, and line by line
I bring your death to lonely hidden villages,
red-tiled farms, *helpless women and timid men.*

Matthew Sweeney, 1952–

Matthew Sweeney was born in Donegal and studied at the University of Freiburg. It was with his third collection, *The Lame Waltzer* (1985), that he came into his own, establishing a realm of strange narrative episodes and enigmatic events alongside more recognizably lyric pieces. With *Blue Shoes* (1988) and *Cacti* (1991) the roots of his work in Catholic ritual were more clearly exposed. His best poems – for example, 'Where Fishermen Can't Swim' or 'The U-Boat' – achieve a haunting, baffling clarity. In *The Bridal Suite* (1997) Sweeney strips his world down to a core of alarm and black humour. He is also a popular writer of poems for children: see *The Flying Spring Onion* (1992) and *Fatso in the Red Suit* (1995). With Jo Shapcott he edited the lively and unusual anthology *Emergency Kit: Poems for Strange Times* (1996).

The U-Boat

I am floating by the wrecked U-boat,
naked as a dolphin in the August sun.
I've got away, again, from everyone.
I've moored my raft to the periscope
that stays underwater. On it I keep
my shorts and shoes, and coca-cola,
and a Bavarian girly magazine.
I've become so at-home in the ocean
that I think I must someday drown.
Miles away, on the edge of my hometown,
twin cooling towers fork the sky
where an airship phuts, selling beer.
No-one knows the U-boat is here –
no boats approach these rocks,
no swimmers advance. I don't advertise.
I dive to the conning-tower and enter.
Bubbles speed behind me, above me,
but I am fast. I slide past my friend
the skeleton, until my breath runs low,
then I hit the surface he saw long ago
but never quite saw in the end.

The Glass Coffin

The Brocagh boys
are carrying one of their number
in a glass coffin.
They are taking him
to his caravan, the best place
to wake him in.
They can see him
lying on his left side
facing the mountain.
One is pushing
his antiquated bicycle
behind the coffin.
They will go in the grave together,
first the bicycle,
then the glass coffin.
His third nervous breakdown
was his last one.
He won't ask again
how to spell three.
he won't fall in a sheugh
when he's in the grave.
The Brocagh girls
are leaving the factory
to wake him.
They are shouting
about nylons, for the legs,
for the thighs.
Some have bottles,
some have tyres
for a funeral blaze.
They follow the glass coffin
and the boys
up the steps of the caravan.

Jo Shapcott, 1953–

Jo Shapcott was born in London and educated at Trinity College, Dublin, Oxford and Harvard. *Electroplating the Baby* (1988) introduced a sophisticated poet with interests in gender, science and the nature of representation. In *Phrase Book* (1992) language becomes a central subject – as a source of authority and identity (see the title poem) and as an affirmative power. Shapcott's Mad Cow and other animals, a curiously relaxed menagerie, achieve an unexpected liberty. With Matthew Sweeney, she edited the anthology *Emergency Kit: Poems for Strange Times* (1996). *My Life Asleep* appeared in 1998.

Motherland

after Tsvetayeva

Language is impossible
in a country like this. Even
the dictionary laughs when I look up
'England', 'Motherland', 'Home'.

It insists on falling open instead
three times out of the nine I try it
at the word 'Distance' – degree
of remoteness, interval of space.

Distance. The word is ingrained like pain.
So much for England and so much
for my future to walk into the horizon
carrying distance in a broken suitcase.

The dictionary is the only one
who talks to me now, says, laughing,
'Come back HOME!' but takes me
further and further into the cold stars.

I am blue, bluer than water.
I am nothing while all I do
is waste syllables this way.

England. It hurts my lips to shape
the word. This country makes me say
too many things I can't say. Home
of me, myself, my Motherland.

Goat

Dusk, deserted road, and suddenly
I was a goat. To be truthful, it took
two minutes, though it seemed sudden,
for the horns to pop out of my skull,
for the spine to revolutionize and go
horizontal, for the fingers to glue
together and for the nails to become
important enough to upgrade to hoof.
The road was not deserted any more, but full
of goats, and I liked that, even though I hate
the rush hour on the tube, the press of bodies.
Now I loved snuffling behind his or her ear,
licking a flank or two, licking and snuffling here,
there, wherever I liked. I lived for the push
of goat muscle and goat bone, the smell of goat fur,
goat breath and goat sex. I ended up on the edge
of the crowd where the road met the high
hedgerow with the scent of earth, a thousand
kinds of grass, leaves and twigs, flower-heads
and the intoxicating tang of the odd ring-pull
or rubber to spice the mixture. I wanted
to eat everything. I could have eaten the world
and closed my eyes to nibble at the high
sweet leaves against the sunset. I tasted
that old sun and the few dark clouds
and some tall buildings far away in the next town.
I think I must have swallowed an office block
because this grinding enormous digestion tells me
it's stuck on an empty corridor which has
at the far end, I know, a tiny human figure.

Michael Donaghy, 1954–

Michael Donaghy was born in New York of an Irish background. He was educated at Fordham and the University of Chicago, where he served as poetry editor of *Chicago Review*. He has lived in England since 1985 and published two main collections, *Shibboleth* (1988) and *Errata* (1993). Highly imaginative and dextrous, Donaghy is in the best sense a learned writer. His poems of memory, love, belief and the mysteries of art recall the high formalism of Richard Wilbur but avoid academicism and supply a strong admixture of humour and the erotic. Donaghy's glittering and tragic world owes much to a Catholic upbringing. He also plays traditional Irish music.

The Tuning

If anyone asks you how I died, say this:
The angel of death came in the form of a moth
And landed on the lute I was repairing.
I closed up shop
And left the village on the quietest night of summer,
The summer of my thirtieth year,
And went with her up through the thorn forest.

Tell them I heard yarrow stalks snapping beneath my feet
And heard a dog bark far off, far off.
That's all I saw or heard,
Apart from the angel at ankle level leading me,
Until we got above the treeline and I turned
To look for the last time on the lights of home.

That's when she started singing.
It's written that the voice of the god of Israel
Was the voice of many waters.
But this was the sound of trees growing,
The noise of a pond thrown into a stone.

When I turned from the lights below to watch her sing,
I found the angel changed from moth to woman,
Singing inhuman intervals through her human throat,
The notes at impossible angles justified.

If you understand, friend, explain to them
So they pray for me. How could I go back?
How could I bear to hear the heart's old triads –
Clatter of hooves, the closed gate clanging,
A match scratched toward a pipe –
How could I bear to hear my children cry?

I found a rock that had the kind of heft
We weigh the world against

And brought it down fast against my forehead
Again, again, until blood drenched my chest
And I was safe and real forever.

Caliban's Books

Hair oil, boiled sweets, chalk dust, squid's ink . . .
Bear with me. I'm trying to conjure my father,
age fourteen, as Caliban – picked by Mr Quinn
for the role he was born to play because
'I was the handsomest boy at school'
he'll say, straight faced, at fifty.
This isn't easy. I've only half the spell,
and I won't be born for twenty years.
I'm trying for rainlight on Belfast Lough
and listening for a small, blunt accent
barking over the hiss of a stove getting louder like surf.
But how can I read when the schoolroom's gone
black as the hold of a ship? Start again.

Hair oil, boiled sweets . . .
But his paperbacks are crumbling in my hands,
seachanged bouquets, each brown page
scribbled on, underlined, memorized,
forgotten like used pornography:
The Pocket Treasury of English Verse
How to Win Friends and Influence People
Thirty Days To a More Powerful Vocabulary

Fish stink, pitch stink, seaspray, cedarwood . . .
I seem to have brought us to the port of Naples,
midnight, to a shadow below deck
dreaming of a distant island.
So many years, so many ports ago!
The moment comes. It slips from the hold
and knucklewalks across the dark piazza
sobbing *maestro! maestro!* But the duke's long dead
and all his magic books are drowned.

Ian Duhig, 1954–

Ian Duhig was born in London of Irish parents and educated at Leeds University. He was for some years a social worker. Duhig, like Michael Donaghy, represents a learned and humorous strain in contemporary poetry, with nods to Paul Muldoon but his own firm grasp of tradition, including poetry in Irish. In Duhig's work this takes the form of rococo elaboration, interrupted by belly laughs. Unapologetically difficult at times, Duhig's work is also extremely hospitable. Language, history, religion and politics are his wide terrain, explored in three collections, *The Bradford Count* (1991), *The Mersey Goldfish* (1995) and *Nominies* (1998).

Margin Prayer from an Ancient Psalter

Lord I know, and I know you know I know
this is a drudge's penance. Only dull scholars
or cowherds maddened with cow-watching
will ever read *The Grey Psalter of Antrim*.
I have copied it these thirteen years
waiting for the good bits – High King of the Roads,
are there any good bits in *The Grey Psalter of Antrim*?

(Text illegible here because of teeth-marks.)

It has the magic realism of an argumentum:
it has the narrative subtlety of the Calendar of Oengus;
it has the oblique wit of the Battle-Cathach of the
                                              O'Donnells;
it grips like the colophon to The Book of Durrow;
it deconstructs like a canon-table;
it makes St Jerome's Defence of his Vulgate look racy.
I would make a gift of it to Halfdane the Sacker
that he might use it to wipe his wide Danish arse.
Better its volumes intincted our cattle-trough
and cured poor Luke, my three-legged calf,
than sour my wit and spoil my calligraphy.
Luke! White Luke! Truer beast than Ciarán's Dun Cow!
You would rattle the abbot with your soft off-beats
butting his churns and licking salt from his armpits.
Luke, they flayed you, pumiced your skin to a wafer –
such a hide as King Tadhg might die under –
for pages I colour with ox-gall yellow . . .

(Text illegible here because of tear-stains.)

Oh Forgiving Christ of scribes and sinners
intercede for me with the jobbing abbot!
Get me re-assigned to something pagan
with sex and perhaps gratuitous violence

which I might deplore with insular majuscule
and illustrate with Mozarabic complexity
Ad maioram gloriam Dei et Hiberniae,
and lest you think I judge the book too harshly
from pride or a precious sensibility
I have arranged for a second opinion.
Tomorrow our surveyor, Ronan the Barbarian,
will read out loud as only he can read out loud
selected passages from this which I have scored
while marking out his new church in Killaney
in earshot of that well-versed man, King Suibhne . . .

(Text completely illegible from this point
because of lake-water damage and otter dung.)

Lost Boys

The day from the big burn he hooked a trout
that would pull the scales through seven pound
(to train the wee stuttering rhetorician
he'd slipped into its little mouth a stone),
when he'd turned away to tie his special fly,
in case, he said, smaller fish should snatch it;
the day he'd cut back to watch out for by the jetty

osmundroyal, marsh pennywort, water bedstraw,
the asphodel and the bog-myrtle – which was itself,
men leant back to quote, 'a beautiful emblem of the
Christian: who needs be pounded in affliction's mortar
before the odour of his grace will flow out in words',
the words flowing from the most unpounded of them,
their eyes still shining with that familiar old light;

the day, to try to get back to the beginning,
he got back to wailing, a short coffin on big As,
trestles shining with their blackwash coats still wet
and Davy, cold as pence. This is the beginning. He
climbed to the dark room where his mother cried his name,
O vain tabernacle, his mother cried the name of her Davy.
After her breath ran out he breathed 'it's no him, only me'.

He wrote 'the pretty boy glides like a ray of black
                                        sunshine'.
He put away egg-cap, put away even the capey-dykey.
His wife asked him to stop kissing her goodnight
as a gift for their Tin Wedding Anniversary.
He's the one we call The Boy Who Couldn't Get Up.
He knew too much dead babies will not teach us,
and the words. But don't worry. It's no him, only me.

Anne Rouse, 1954–

Anne Rouse grew up in Virginia and read History at London
University. She worked as a nurse and was a NUPE shop steward.
Sharp-eyed and frequently sharp-tongued, Rouse is a wry commen-
tator on the warring sexes, and her tersely comic poems also take
in a street-level sense of contemporary politics and the lives of the
dispossessed. Hard to place in any grouping, she has published
two impressive collections, *Sunset Grill* (1993) and *Timing* (1997).

The Hen Night Club's Last Supper

Take this bread roll and this
Sangria cup in remembrance that we
are one another's blood,
and come from women's body.

Drink, and eat tonight, my chucks,
in solidarity,
for dawn affrays with bloody men
in their obstinate beauty.

Go bravely into the world of snooker halls,
Downing Street and the packet of three.
Nil carborundum, bless the Marks,
and bless this company.

John Burnside, 1955–

John Burnside was born in Dunfermline and read English and European Studies at Cambridgeshire College of Technology. He worked in the computer industry before taking up writing full-time. Burnside has written prolifically from a sense of the vestigially miraculous – the suggestions carried by half-rural settings, memories and dreams. His free verse is delicately precise in tracing mood and feeling and a religious dimension presses in on what is clearly a romantic sensibility. Geoffrey Hill is an informing but not deafening presence. *The hoop* (1989) was followed by *Common Knowledge* (1991), *Feast Days* (1993), *The Myth of the Twin* (1994), *Swimming in the Flood* (1995) and *A Normal Skin* (1996). A novel, *The Dumb House*, was published in 1997.

Source Code

The same life happens again:
a city of clocks and leaves
delivered through fog,
bakeries, print rooms, the famille verte
of municipal gardens
continued, the way a memory runs on
from somewhere unrecollected
and vast,
how you always imagine the suburbs
busy with bonfires and hymns
at Halloween,
when every house is lit, a déjà-vu,
leading through street names and churchyards
from nothing to nothing.

The Old Gods

Now they are condemned
to live in cracks,
in bubbles of plaster and rust,
and spiders' webs
behind the furniture:

speaking a derelict language
to empty space,
sealed with the vapour
in bottles, closed in the blown
robins' eggs
in some abandoned loft.

Each has its given power.
Each has its hearth, its secret,
its local name,
and each has its way of learning
the skill of return,
the science of bleeding through, when anger or fear
is fuzzing the surface,
making us dizzy and whole.

David Dabydeen, 1955–

David Dabydeen was born in Guyana and studied at the universities of Cambridge and London. He teaches at Warwick University.
The ferocious and painful *Slave Song* (1984), about the lives of
cane-cutters, is written in Guyanese creole, while *Coolie Odyssey*
(1988) deals with East Indian experience in the Caribbean and
Britain. The title poem notes ironically what the author considers
a fashion in England and Ireland for peasant and working-class
linguistic roots before turning to a characteristically bitter and
sombre elegy. *Turner* (1994) selects from earlier work and is
named for the ambitious title poem, which animates J. M. W.
Turner's painting *The Slave Ship* in a series of powerful dramatic
meditations on slavery.

The Old Map

Empty treasure chests dumped from departed ships
And jettisoned slaves washed
Into an arc from Jamaica to Guiana.
Islands aborted from the belly of sea
Forever unborn in rock and swamp.
Other fragments rot in the sun
Like cane chewed and spat
From coolie mouth.
Haiti is a crab with broken claw.
Cuba droops in fear at the foot of America.
Blue is deep and everywhere of European eye,
Green of seamen's hopes and gangrene,
Yellow of the palm of dead Amerindian
Unyielding gold.

Carol Ann Duffy, 1955–

Carol Ann Duffy was born in Glasgow of Irish parents, grew up in Stafford and read Philosophy at Liverpool University. *Standing Female Nude* (1985), *Selling Manhattan* (1987), *The Other Country* (1990) and *Mean Time* (1993) have established her as one of the most popular poets of the time. Duffy is perhaps best known for her use of dramatic monologue, often employing the voices of the powerless or the mad ('Warming Her Pearls', 'Psychopath'), at times playing to great effect on the tension between the formality of poetry and vernacular speech. In poems of childhood and education (see 'In Mrs Tilscher's Class') she makes a kind of history-from-within of the flowering and death of the post-war political consensus, while her love poems have a universal appeal in her sensual rendering of lesbian experience. In *The World's Wife* (1999) she is rewriting some familiar ancient and modern stories from a female viewpoint ('Mrs Midas', 'Queen Kong') in a richly humorous way. Perhaps Duffy's primary importance lies in her use of a sophisticated imagination and technique in ways accessible to readers far beyond the usual poetry audience. See also *Selected Poems* (1994).

Warming Her Pearls

(*for Judith Radstone*)

Next to my own skin, her pearls. My mistress
bids me wear them, warm then, until evening
when I'll brush her hair. At six, I place them
round her cool, white throat. All day I think of her,

resting in the Yellow Room, contemplating silk
or taffeta, which gown tonight? She fans herself
whilst I work willingly, my slow heat entering
each pearl. Slack on my neck, her rope.

She's beautiful. I dream about her
in my attic bed; picture her dancing
with tall men, puzzled by my faint, persistent scent
beneath her French perfume, her milky stones.

I dust her shoulders with a rabbit's foot,
watch the soft blush seep through her skin
like an indolent sigh. In her looking-glass
my red lips part as though I want to speak.

Full moon. Her carriage brings her home. I see
her every movement in my head . . . Undressing,
taking off her jewels, her slim hand reaching
for the case, slipping naked into bed, the way

she always does . . . And I lie here awake,
knowing the pearls are cooling even now
in the room where my mistress sleeps. All night
I feel their absence and I burn.

In Mrs Tilscher's Class

You could travel up the Blue Nile
with your finger, tracing the route
while Mrs Tilscher chanted the scenery.
Tana. Ethiopia. Khartoum. Aswân.
That for a hour, then a skittle of milk
and the chalky Pyramids rubbed into dust.
A window opened with a long pole.
The laugh of a bell swung by a running child.

This was better than home. Enthralling books.
The classroom glowed like a sweetshop.
Sugar paper. Coloured shapes. Brady and Hindley
faded, like the faint, uneasy smudge of a mistake.
Mrs Tilscher loved you. Some mornings, you found
she'd left a good gold star by your name.
The scent of a pencil slowly, carefully, shaved.
A xylophone's nonsense heard from another form.

Over the Easter term the inky tadoles changed
from commas into exclamation marks. Three frogs
hopped in the playground, freed by a dunce,
followed by a line of kids, jumping and croaking
away from the lunch queue. A rough boy
told you how you were born. You kicked him, but stared
at your parents, appalled, when you got back home.

That feverish July, the air tasted of electricity.
A tangible alarm made you always untidy, hot,
fractious under the heavy, sexy sky. You asked her
how you were born and Mrs Tilscher smiled,
then turned away. Reports were handed out.
You ran through the gates, impatient to be grown,
as the sky split open into a thunderstorm.

Litany

The soundtrack then was a litany – *candlewick
bedspread three piece suite display cabinet* –
and stiff-haired wives balanced their red smiles,
passing the catalogue. *Pyrex*. A tiny ladder
ran up Mrs Barr's American Tan leg, sly
like a rumour. Language embarrassed them.

The terrible marriages crackled, cellophane
round polyester shirts, and then The Lounge
would seem to bristle with eyes, hard
as the bright stones in engagement rings,
and sharp hands poised over biscuits as a word
was spelled out. An embarrassing word, broken

to bits, which tensed the air like an accident.
This was the code I learnt at my mother's knee, pretending
to read, where no one had cancer, or sex, or debts,
and certainly not leukaemia, which no one could spell.
The year a mass grave of wasps bobbed in a jam-jar;
a butterfly stammered itself in my curious hands.

A boy in the playground, I said, *told me
to fuck off*; and a thrilled, malicious pause
salted my tongue like an imminent storm. Then
uproar. *I'm sorry, Mrs Barr, Mrs Hunt, Mrs Emery,
sorry, Mrs Raine*. Yes, I can summon their names.
My mother's mute shame. The taste of soap.

Prayer

Some days, although we cannot pray, a prayer
utters itself. So, a woman will lift
her head from the sieve of her hands and stare
at the minims sung by a tree, a sudden gift.

Some nights, although we are faithless, the truth
enters our hearts, that small familiar pain;
then a man will stand stock-still, hearing his youth
in the distant Latin chanting of a train.

Pray for us now. Grade I piano scales
console the lodger looking out across
a Midlands town. Then dusk, and someone calls
a child's name as though they named their loss.

Darkness outside. Inside, the radio's prayer –
Rockall. Malin. Dogger. Finisterre.

Alan Jenkins, 1955–

Alan Jenkins was born in London and read Modern Languages at Sussex University. He is deputy editor of the *Times Literary Supplement*. *In the Hothouse* (1988) contains poems of the erotic life, focused on the ambitious and alarming AIDS story 'Or Would You Rather Not Be Saved?', which shows the influence of Paul Muldoon. The title poem of *Greenheart* (1990), a narrative *tour de force* of postmodern Gothic horror, is juxtaposed with more elegiac work. *Harm* (1994), which concentrates on love poems, seems to mark a new assurance.

Visiting

He visited, the man who takes your life
and turns it upside-down, from floor
to ceiling; and he saw I had no wife,
and saw the things that I had worked hard for
and smiled, as if he knew what went on *here*.

He visited the corner of my flat
where daily I had spooned out food
for my dainty-footed, air-sniffing cat
and through the summer, chunks left half-chewed
had poured rich smells into the atmosphere.

Flies visited the smells. They hung in heat
like helicopters seen from a distance,
they drooled and fed on rotting processed meat,
they laid their eggs. The buzzing small insistence
should have warned me, the cat not going near.

Friends visited, but no-one noticed anything.
And when he tore my carpet up, the man –
No lie, I nearly puked my ring.
I saw yellow-white seethe in a silver can
full of dank sawdust, a towpath by a weir –

I visited my father on the bank
where he and I went fishing each week-end;
the shrubs, the weir, the lock and river shrank,
our bicycles had vanished round a bend
and a high tide taken all our gear.

I visited my father in the pubs
where I had watched him drink away the hours
of talk or silence, piling up the stubs
in ashtrays, but the cigarettes were sour
and the bitter had an aftertaste of fear.

I visited my father by the sea
where he had scrubbed me with a gritty towel
and held me till I squirmed and struggled free;
I heard the gulls scream and the sea-wind howl,
the freezing water writhed and flung me clear.

I visited my father in his grave
and grubbed until I found all that was left –
a matchbook of maggots. *Grieve, grieve*
they whispered when I held it aloft.
Grieve, grieve when I put it to my ear.

Jamie McKendrick, 1955-

Jamie McKendrick was born in Liverpool in 1955. He taught for some years at the University of Salerno. McKendrick's three books – *The Sirocco Room* (1991), *The Kiosk on the Brink* (1993) and *The Marble Fly* (1997) – draw heavily on his experience in Mediterranean countries, and of that ancient and modern Mediterranean of the mind that lights dreams against 'the black north crouching in my bones'. McKendrick is both funny and chilling. Amid the superbly observed decay and Protestant-pagan ardour for experience is a warning of Apocalypse.

Ancient History

The year began with baleful auguries:
comets, eclipses, tremors, forest fires,
the waves lethargic under a coat of pitch
the length of the coastline. And a cow spoke,
which happened last year too, although last year
no one believed cows spoke. Worse was to come.
There was a bloody rain of lumps of meat
which flocks of gulls snatched in mid-air
while what they missed fell to the ground
where it lay for days without festering.
Then a wind tore up a forest of holm-oaks
and jackdaws pecked the eyes from sheep.
Officials construing the Sibylline books
told of helmeted aliens occupying
the crossroads, and high places of the city.
Blood might be shed. Avoid, they warned,
factions and in-fights. The tribunes claimed
this was the usual con-trick
trumped up to stonewall the new law
about to be passed. Violence was only curbed
by belief in a rumour that the tribes
to the east had joined forces and forged
weapons deadlier than the world has seen
and that even then the hooves of their scouts
had been heard in the southern hills.
The year ended fraught with the fear of war.
Next year began with baleful auguries.

The Spleen Factory

(after Carlos Drummond de Andrade)

I want to make a sonnet that's not a sonnet
according to any civilized notion of what
that is. I want it ugly as concrete,
and just about impossible to read.

And I'd like my sonnet in the future
to give no living soul an ounce of pleasure,
not by being merely foulmouthed and perverse
but also (why not?) by being both and worse

if it feels the urge. Plus I want the whole thing caustic
and obstrusive – with intent to pierce and hurt
like stitches done without anaesthetic

somewhere tender. So it won't be learnt by heart.
So it's a wall with a hole pissed through – in the hole a star
transmitting incomprehensible clarity.

Sujata Bhatt, 1956–

Sujata Bhatt was born in Ahmedabad and grew up in the United States. She now lives in Germany. In *Brunizem* (1988), *Monkey Shadows* (1991) and *The Stinking Rose* (1994) Bhatt can be heard negotiating between Gujarati and English, lending her second language a new tone and angle. Hers is a wide-ranging poetry, crossing several cultures and strongly drawn to myth.

Muliebrity

I have thought so much about the girl
who gathered cow-dung in a wide, round basket
along the main road passing by our house
and the Radhavallabh temple in Maninagar.
I have thought so much about the way she
moved her hands and her waist
and the smell of cow-dung and road-dust and wet canna
lilies,
the smell of monkey breath and freshly washed clothes
and the dust from crows' wings which smells different –
and again the smell of cow-dung as the girl scoops
it up, all these smells surrounding me separately
and simultaneously – I have thought so much
but have been unwilling to use her for a metaphor,
for a nice image – but most of all unwilling
to forget her or to explain to anyone the greatness
and the power glistening through her cheekbones
each time she found a particularly promising
mound of dung –

Peter Armstrong, 1957–

Peter Armstrong was born in Blaydon on Tyneside and educated at Sunderland Polytechnic. He works as a cognitive therapist in the NHS. Armstrong's first collection, *Risings* (1988), was studious, strongly religious in cast and clearly influenced by Geoffrey Hill. Its successor, *The Red-Funnelled Boat* (1998), is observant and imaginative and more confidently unbuttoned, ranging over northern life and landscape, politics, madness and music.

The Red-Funnelled Boat

Comrades, since it's evident
that the voices teasing us at nightfall
with their inklings of another island
where Jerusalem might be builded,
are at best of shady origin,
and more likely beg the question
of the demon in the synapse,

let's go line up at the jetty
for the red-funnelled boat to take us
by black-watered sea-lochs
to its approximate asylum
– *aliéné, égalité, fraternité*
inscribed on the gateposts
and the inside of the inmates' foreheads –

where we might hope to be permitted,
under the benevolent dictatorship
of the monthly needle,
to establish our republic
of tweeds and decorum:
one last collective indulgence
in the dreams of the mind politic.

Between the ashlar ward-blocks
and the rusticated boundary,
the light will be democratic
on the backs of garden details
and the chronically second-sighted,
the electrodes reserved only
for those weeping over their Isaiah.

Tell those who come after
how we boarded in one body,
feeling, but not flinching at
the bow's one long incision
down the firth's dark mirror:
the red stump of its funnel lifted
as high as it was ploughing under.

Maura Dooley, 1957–

Maura Dooley, who is of Irish descent, was born in Truro, Cornwall, and grew up in Bristol. She studied at York University. She has worked as Centre Director of the Arvon Foundation at Lumb Bank in Yorkshire and as Literature Officer at the South Bank Centre in London. Dooley has played an important role in the encouragement of poetry and the development of its audience in recent years, both as an administrator and as an editor – see *Making for Planet Alice: New Women Poets* (1997). Her poems are lyrically intense and minutely particular, ranging widely over love, family, history and the political dimension of everyday life. Her main collections to date are *Turbulence* (1988), *Explaining Magnetism* (1991) and *Kissing a Bone* (1996).

St Brendan Explains to the Angel

You cannot understand this bog
how it seeps under the rock and broods,

how this hillside's green
forces me on from here, silent, fearful.

Nor how this hand of stone simmers
in a cool sea, great slabs of it to tear

a leather boat or barb an angel,
slapping at the waves, beaching the frail fish,

and the sun a crack in a stormy sky
where Lucifer always falls, is falling now.

Michael Hofmann, 1957–

Michael Hofmann was born in Freiburg and grew up in England and the United States. He studied English at Cambridge. Since 1983 he has worked as a reviewer and translator from German. *Nights in the Iron Hotel* (1983) presented an assured voice – endemically ironic, flatly detailed, sombre and unsurprisable. *Acrimony* (1986) moved between urban life under 'late capitalism' (see 'Nighthawks') and an account of the poet's complex relationship with his father, the novelist Gert Hofmann – the latter poems bringing reminders of Robert Lowell. *Corona, Corona* (1993) ranged further afield. Hofmann exemplifies the means by which some of the conditions of postmodernism make their presence known in English. With James Lasdun, he edited the widely admired anthology *After Ovid: New Metamorphoses* (1994).

The Machine that Cried

'Il n'y a pas de détail' – Paul Valéry

When I learned that my parents were returning
to Germany, and that I was to be jettisoned,
I gave a sudden lurch into infancy and Englishness.
Carpets again loomed large in my world: I sought out
their fabric and warmth, where there was nowhere to
fall . . .

I took up jigsaw puzzles, read mystical cricket thrillers
passing all understanding, even collected toy soldiers
and killed them with matchsticks fired from the World
War One
field-guns I bought from Peter Oborn down the road
– he must have had something German, with that name –

who lived alone with his mother, like a man . . .
My classmates were equipped with sexual insults
for the foaming lace of the English women playing
Wimbledon,
but I watched them blandly on our rented set
behind drawn curtains, without ever getting the point.

My building-projects were as ambitious as the Tower of
Babel.
Something automotive of my construction limped across
the floor
to no purpose, only lugging its heavy battery.
Was there perhaps some future for Christiaan Barnard,
or the electric car, a milk-float groaning like a sacred
heart?

I imagined Moog as von Moog, a mad German scientist.
His synthesizer was supposed to be the last word in
versatility,

Michael Hofmann – 447

but when I first heard it on Chicory Tip's
Son of my Father, it was just a unisono metallic drone,
five notes, as inhibited and pleonastic as the title.

My father bought a gramophone, a black box,
and played late Beethoven on it, which my mother was
                                                      always
to associate with her miscarriage of that year.
I was forever carrying it up to my room,
and quietly playing through my infant collection of singles,

Led Zeppelin, The Tremoloes, *My Sweet Lord* . . .
The drums cut like a scalpel across the other instruments.
Sometimes the turntable rotated slowly, then everything
went flat, and I thought how with a little more care
it could have been all right. There again, so many things

were undependable . . . My first-ever British accent
                                              wavered
between Pakistani and Welsh. I called *Bruce's* record shop
just for someone to talk to. He said, 'Certainly, Madam.'
Weeks later, it was 'Yes sir, you can bring your children.'
It seemed I had engineered my own birth in the new
                                                      country.

Lament for Crassus

Who grows old in fifty pages of Plutarch:
mores, omens, campaigns, Marius at sixty,
fighting fit, working out on the Campus Martius?

It surely isn't me, pushing thirty, taking a life a night,
my head on a bookshelf, five shelves of books overhead,
the bed either a classic or remaindered?

– I read about Crassus, who owned most of Rome.
Crassus, the third man, the third triumvir,
the second term in any calculation.

Crassus, the pioneer of insuranburn,
with his architect slaves and firefighter slaves,
big in silver, big in real estate, big in personnel.

Crassus, who had his name linked with a Vestal Virgin,
but was only after her house in the suburbs.
Crassus of bread and suburbs and circuses,

made Consul for his circuses, Crassus
impresario, not Crassus *imperator*, Crassus
who tried to break the military-political nexus.

Crassus, the inventor of the demi-pension holiday,
holed up in a cave on the coast of Spain for a month,
getting his dinner put out for him, and a couple of slave-
                                                        girls.

Crassus, whose standards wouldn't rise on the final day,
who came out of his corner in careless black,
whose head was severed a day later than his son's.

Ian McMillan, 1957–

Ian McMillan grew up and still lives in Darfield, near Barnsley, South Yorkshire. He was educated at Crewe and Alsager College. McMillan's roles as performer/comedian and poet for the page are deliberately hard to separate. Trained in working men's clubs, he is immensely entertaining – and much in demand – in performance. His work runs the gamut from stand-up jokes to elaborate surrealist narratives, in which politics (e.g. the 1984–5 miners' strike) shares the stage with rewritings of the life of Elvis Presley. See *Selected Poems* (1987) and *Dad, the Donkey's on Fire* (1994).

Poem Occasioned by the High Incidence of Suicide amongst the Unemployed

Now then, fatha, how's your Fred?
They found him in the kitchen
with a bullet in his head.

Now then, fatha, how's your John?
They found him in the river
with his donkey jacket on.

Now then, fatha, how's your Bill?
He jumped under a bus
on Spital Hill.

Now then, fatha, how's your Tom?
He blew hissen to pieces
with a home made bomb.

Now then, fatha, how's your Pete?
He's hanging off a lamp post
on Market Street.

Now then, fatha, how's your Rex?
He strangled hissen
wi' his wedding kex.

Now then, fatha, how's your Stan?
He brayed hissen to death
wi' a watterin can.

Now then, fatha, wheers the wives?
They're cutting their sens
wi' carving knives.

Sarah Maguire, 1957–

Sarah Maguire was born in West London and studied at the University of East Anglia and Cambridge. She is a trained gardener. *Spilt Milk* (1991) was a bold debut. Intimate, even confessional in tone, her poems have been characterized as showing 'matter penetrated by desire'. *The Invisible Mender* (1997) contains poems about travel and horticulture, as well as love and the body under the gaze of time.

What is Transparent

The liquidity of glass: aeons from now
These panes will be a puddle on the floor.
Tonight I gaze through tricks and flaws
Which make the houses billow, the police van
On the corner monstrous – or a flick of black.

I hold the failed bulb to my ear and shake
Its filaments: still warm, it hardens in my palm.
In the winter of 'seventy-four we made love
By candle-light. After the strike the shops were
Glutted with candles: relics of fingers, sweating.

The miners are on strike again. I find two candles,
Turn out all the lights and watch the news:
The bluish screen tricking the faces of these men
Who work with darkness, underground.

Linda France, 1958–

Linda France was born on Tyneside and lives in Northumberland. She has published three collections, *Red* (1992), *The Gentleness of the Very Tall* (1994) and *Storyville* (1997). Sensual, accessible, often concerned with gender and identity, France's poetry has found a wide appeal. She has also edited a very successful anthology, *Sixty Women Poets* (1993).

Zoology Is Destiny

You won't let me be ostrich, armadillo,
invertebrate. Although for you I'm zoo,
a new creature, prowling behind bars, howling
at the moon, the way you can stroke the hairs
riding the roaring switchback of my spine –
a terrible gesture of tenderness.

If I can't come out, you'll come in – pick
the lock on the door of my cage with your teeth.
We dine on watermelon and figs, milk
and almonds, our tongues cunning as Eden snakes.
Our hands build an ark, two by two, for fur,
feathers flying, hoof, breastbone, muzzle, wing.

This is not a parable wishing itself
would happen, like weather in a fable
by Aesop, a date in *The Fox and Grapes*.
It's simply the vatic utterance
of a white rhinoceros who knows
the difference between rocks and crocodiles.

Robert Crawford, 1959–

Born in Bellshill, Crawford studied at Glasgow and Oxford. He is a Professor of Modern Scottish Literature at St Andrews University. As a poet, critic and a founding editor of the magazine *Verse*, Crawford has been an important advocate for twentieth-century Scottish poetry, including poetry in Scots (see his collaboration with W. N. Herbert, *Sharawaggi*, 1990). His work in English, influenced by Edwin Morgan, has a strange inventive plainness and a frequent note of celebration. His most recent collection is *Masculinity* (1996). A selection of his work appears in *Penguin Modern Poets 9* (1996). See also his critical books, *Devolving English Literature* (1992), *Identifying Poets: Self and Territory in Twentieth-Century Poetry* (1993) and *The Scottish Invention of English Literature* (1998).

Scotland

Semiconductor country, land crammed with intimate
                                                    expanses,
Your cities are superlattices, heterojunctive
Graphed from the air, your cropmarked farmlands
Are epitaxies of tweed.

All night motorways carry your signal, swept
To East Kilbride or Dunfermline. A brightness off low
                                                    headlands
Beams-in the dawn to Fife's interstices,
Optoelectronics of hay.

Micro-nation. So small you cannot be forgotten,
Bible inscribed on a ricegrain, hi-tech's key
Locked into the earth, your televised Glasgows
Are broadcast in Rio. Among circuitboard crowsteps

To be miniaturized is not small-minded.
To love you needs more details than the Book of Kells –
Your harbours, your photography, your democratic
                                                    intellect
Still boundless, chip of a nation.

La Mer

Is that a bathing cap or a seal's head
Surfacing in the 1930s?

This morning the sea does a huge baking
Of scones and fresh apple tart,

Mixed up with herring, cod and shrimps,
Cuttlefish, fruits de mer.

The sea clears everything away
To set a fresh place. It repeats itself

Like Alzheimer's Disease.
Its moony rollers cast me ashore –

A creel, a fishbox from Crail or Vilnius,
A piece of boat, old but ready

To be put to some startling re-use.
Voices, phonelines, everything flows:

Dad in his landing-craft, beached
At Normandy, us cruising the Small Isles

In the Seventies, Eigg, Rhum, Muck, Canna
Bobbing up one by one, dark collies

Chasing their tails, retrieving sticks from the breakers,
Mr McConnochie's painting of Aphrodite

Breezing to the Arisaig beach on a clamshell.
When I was wee I knew the music

Was about the sea, but I thought its title
Was a French phrase meaning 'My Mother'.

Gwyneth Lewis, 1959–

Gwyneth Lewis was born in Cardiff, read English at Cambridge, and works as a documentary film maker. She has written in both Welsh *(Sonedau Redsa*, 1990) and English (the acclaimed *Parables and Faxes*, 1995). Witty and formally assured, she looks likely to lead a revival in the fortunes of Anglo-Welsh poetry. *Zero Gravity* appeared in 1998.

Going Primitive

Who can resist a didgeridoo
in the middle of Queen St – not one, but three
from the Northern Territory,
each one more deeply, eucalyptically rude?

For the builders have lost the passers-by
who are drawn like water to the swirl and squelch,
the monstrous plumbing of his breath,
sucked in and further, and then atomized,

breathed out in stiff shirts and office skirts
but feeling looser . . .
A wasp photographer
hassles the man for something sweet

and the women, who sweat at his embouchure,
grow broad as rivers to his narrow lips,
dirty as deltas, with silting hips
and alluvial bosoms. The men, unsure,

cower behind their totem wives,
puny and trouty; now chimpanzees
swing through the scaffolding with ease
and screech with the newly arrived macaws;

cranes buck and bow and the wooden thrum
makes men recall a biography
of sludge and savannah, how it was when the sky
arched its blue back and started to come.

Fred D'Aguiar, 1960–

Born in London and educated at the University of Kent, D'Aguiar grew up in Guyana – the setting of many poems in *Mama Dot* (1985) and *Airy Hall* (1989). D'Aguiar's work contrasts a matriarchal rural childhood with the sombre political realities of modern Britain and the Caribbean. He has harnessed his evocative power to ambitious narrative poems such as 'The Kitchen Bitch', and is much influenced by the experimental modernism of the novelist Wilson Harris's *Guyana Quartet*. Following *British Subjects* (1993), D'Aguiar has published a series of novels, including the acclaimed *Dear Future* (1996) and *Feeding the Ghosts* (1997). A new book of poems, *Bill of Rights*, appeared in 1998.

Home

These days whenever I stay away too long,
anything I happen to clap eyes on,
(that red telephone box) somehow makes me
miss here more than anything I can name.

My heart performs a jazzy drum solo
when the crow's feet on the 747
scrape down at Heathrow. H.M. Customs . . .
I resign to the usual inquisition,

telling me with Surrey loam caked
on the tongue, home is always elsewhere.
I take it like an English middleweight
with a questionable chin, knowing

my passport photo's too open-faced,
haircut wrong (an afro) for the decade;
the stamp, British Citizen not bold enough
for my liking and too much for theirs.

The cockney cab driver begins chirpily
but can't or won't steer clear of race,
so rounds on Asians. I lock eyes with him
in the rearview when I say I live with one.

He settles at the wheel grudgingly,
in a huffed silence. Cha! Drive man!
I have legal tender burning in my pocket
to move on, like a cross in Transylvania.

At my front door, why doesn't the lock
recognize me and budge? I give an extra
twist and fall forward over the threshold
piled with the felicitations of junk mail,

into a cool reception in the hall.
Grey light and close skies I love you.
chokey streets, roundabouts and streetlamps
with tyres chucked round them, I love you.

Police officer, your boots need re-heeling.
Robin Redbreast, special request – a burst
of song so the worm can wind to the surface.
We must all sing for our suppers or else.

Eva Salzman, 1960–

Born in New York, Eva Salzman studied at Bennington and Columbia and worked as a choreographer. She has lived in Britain since 1985. Salzman's poems range widely from satire ('With Steve Ovett in Preston Park') and family reminiscence in her debut, *The English Earthquake* (1992), to reports from the sex war which produce an intense, rather baffled eroticism – this last being much to the fore in the impressive *Bargain with the Watchman* (1997).

The Refinery

You cannot look at narrow-brush moustaches.
You cannot think about gas-cookers, their ovens
flame-rimmed, the diadem of fire, or hear the bell
when it's done. Or think of teeth, lamp-shades, soap,
the refinery chimney-stacks, puffing cheerfully.

You cannot raise your hand in history class
to ask a simple question; your arm freezes
in a parody of salute. You cannot write 'horror'
because horror is a good film for anyone
with a strong stomach and a taste for gore.

Anyway, the antique photographs are grainy,
have blurred into art – that vaseline trick with the lens.

At dinner you sip the rot-gut wine
and listen to the table-talk – an operation botched
or an ache in the joints the doctor couldn't diagnose.
You choke with rage at the meal, gibbering,
while the devil samples your soul like buttered croissant.

W. N. Herbert, 1961-

W. N. Herbert was born in Dundee and read English at Oxford. He writes both in Scots and English. The former he makes from a mixture of common parlance, dictionary-language and imagination. He resembles a postmodernist Hugh McDiarmid, with the same scope and ambitions. Scots, he proposes, can criticize and extend English – not a popular view in some quarters. His work ranges from elaborate fantasias like 'The Landfish' and 'The Dundee Doldrums' to ballads, comic improvisations ('Cabaret McGonagall'), love poems and literary manifestos. *Sharawaggi*, co-written with Robert Crawford, appeared in 1990. Other works include *The Testament of the Reverend Thomas Dick* (1994), *Forked Tongue* (1994) and *Cabaret McGonagall* (1996). *The Laurelude* appeared in 1998. He is the editor of the magazine *Gairfish*.

Mappamundi

Eh've wurkt oot a poetic map o thi warld.

Vass tracts o land ur penntit reid tae shaw
Englan kens naethin aboot um. Ireland's
bin shuftit tae London, whaur
oafficis o thi Poetry Sock occupeh fehv
squerr mile. Seamus Heaney occupehs three
o thon. Th'anerly ithir bits in Britain
ur Oaxfurd an Hull. Scoatlan, Thi Pool,
an Huddersfield, ur cut ti cuttilbanes in
America, which issa grecht big burdcage wi
a tartan rug owre ut, tae shaw
Roabirt Lowell. Chile disnae exist.
Argentina's bin beat. Hungary and Russia
haena visas. Africa's editid doon ti
a column in *Poetry Verruca*,
whaur Okigbo's gote thi ghaist
o Roy Campbill hingin owre um. Thi Faur East's
faan aff – aa but China: thon's renemmed
Ezra Poond an pit i thi croncit cage.
France disna get a luke-in:
accoardin tae Geoffrey Hill, plucky wee
Charles Péguy is wrasslin wi
this big deid parrot caad 'Surrealism' fur
thi throne o Absinthe Sorbet.

In this scenario Eh'm a bittern stoarm aff Ulm.

from Featherhood

5

Sae licht thi lives that laive us
oor griefs maun growe insteed;
thi anely wean
a man can cairry's
absence inniz heid.

But leese me oan thi lea-laik-gair
that spelt me oot this speech,
thi sma hills o thi Stewartry
sae saftly preach
Eh nearly nivir heard yir nemm
i thi burr o ilka bee;

but ken noo that ut is your breist
Eh'm liggin oan tae listen.
Ut is your braith
that blaws thi feathirs o thi wurds
by me and awa.

leese me oan – an expression of preference; *lea-laik-gair* – the place where two hills join together and form a kind of bosom; *burr* – a whirring noise as made in the throat in pronouncing the letter 'r'; *liggin* – lying.

Ode to Scotty

We kent ut wiz yir accent that
they couldna tak much mair o –
thae engines – foarmed somewhaur atween
Belfast and Ontario.

O Mister Scott, weel may ye talk
aboot WARP Factor Seven:
you tuke thi clash o Brigadoon –
transpoartit ut tae Heaven.

But still we luve ye tho ye werr
a Canuck in disguise:
tho Spock an Banes baith fanciet Kirk
you luved thi Enterprise.

Noo that we aa could undirstaund
fur ilka Scoatsman dotes
oan engines – see hoo Clydesiders
still bigg thir wee toy boats.

An syne therr wiz yir pash fur booze
fae Argyle tae Arcturus;
ye ootdrank Klingons grecht an smaa –
anither trait no spurious.

We kent dilithium crystals werr
(tho in thir future foarm)
thi semm gems that ye find gin you
crack stanes aroond Cairngorm.

An whit a bony fechtir, eh?
Sae martial a revure,

---

clash – conversation, local speech; *ilka* – each; *bigg* – build; *syne* – then; *gin* – if; *revure* – a look of calm scorn or contempt.

while Kirk left you in oarbit fur
three-quaartirs o an oor

while he an Spock an Banes plunked aff
tae some furbidden planit –
ye kent they werr oan lusty splores
but still ye birled lyk granite.

But maist o aa we luve ye coz
ye saved oor naishun's fiss:
ye nivir whinged aboot Englan but –
ye beat thum intae Space!

plunked aff – played truant; *splores* – jaunts, antics; *birled* – spun.

Jackie Kay, 1961–

Jackie Kay was born in Edinburgh and studied at Stirling University. Her first book, *The Adoption Papers* (1991), was originally a radio drama. Its powerful and poignant blending of the voices of child, birth-mother and adoptive mother, and its treatment of racism, had an immediate impact. Kay's ability to render complex feelings with clarity and precision, and to relate private events to their political context, has made her popular as a performer of her work as well as a writer. *Other Lovers* followed in 1993. Her plays include *The Twilight Shift* (1994). She has also written poetry for children (*Two's Company*, 1992 and *Three Has Gone*, 1994) and a biography of the blues singer Bessie Smith. A new book of poems, *Off Colour*, and a novel, *Trumpet*, appeared in 1998.

Teeth

This is X who has all her own teeth.
Her mother is horrified by this.

Look into her mouth. She still has them.
Perfect pearls. Milk stones. Pure ivory.

Not a filling, no receding gums.
X was a woman with a lively

smile. Since she was a girl. No dark holes.
Her mother wore, still does, false teeth. Tusks,

badly fitted, left something unsaid
– a tiny gap between tooth and gum.

Her mum's teeth, in a glass tumbler, swam
at night: a shark's grin; a wolf's slow smirk.

What upsets her mother now, oddly,
is this: X had such beautiful lips.

This morning the men broke in – 8 a.m.
X was wearing her dressing gown, white

towelling. They came wearing her number
on their arms. *Did you know*, her mother says,

*they taped my daughter's mouth to choke her
screams. They covered her mouth in white tape.*

The small boy pulled at the sharp trousers.
He was soundless. The big men flung him

into that grey corner. His voice burst.
He will stand there, that height, forever, see

those minutes grab and snatch and repeat
themselves. The men in plain clothes have claws;

they attack his mother like dogs, gagging her,
binding her, changing her into someone

else. He will watch her hands smash and thrash.
His hands making a church, then a tall

steeple. He crosses his fingers. Squeezes them.
His hands wet themselves. He is five years old.

He knows his address. He knows his name.
He has ten fingers. He counts them again.

This is X who has all her own teeth.
Came to this country with her own teeth.

Soundbites will follow. Lies will roll
tomorrow. The man with the abscess

will say she had a weak heart. High blood.
Illegal. Only doing his job.

Fill it in. Write it down. Bridge the gap.
Give him a stamp of approval: silver

or gold or NHS, she resisted arrest;
there's your cause of death. On a plate.

She was wrong. Give her a number. Think
of a number. Take away the son.

Kathleen Jamie, 1962–

Kathleen Jamie grew up in Midlothian and read philosophy at Edinburgh University. Her first book, *Black Spiders*, appeared in her twentieth year. *The Way We Live* (1987) revealed Jamie's uncluttered power of evocation, and her ambitious condition-of-Scotland volume *The Queen of Sheba* (1994) showed her to be capable of sustained imaginative flights, funny, grave and mysterious by turns. Jamie has also published a collaborative work, *The Autonomous Region*, with the photographer Sean Mayne Smith (1993) and a travel book, *The Golden Peak* (1992).

Skeins o Geese

Skeins o geese write a word
across the sky. A word
struck lik a gong
afore I wis born.
The sky moves like cattle, lowin.

I'm as empty as stane, as fields
ploo'd but not sown, naked
an blin as a stane. Blin
tae the word, blin
tae a' soon but geese ca'ing,

Wire twists lik archaic script
roon a gate. The barbs
sign tae the wind as though
it was deef. The word whustles
ower high for ma senses. Awa.

No lik the past which lies
strewn aroun. Nor sudden death.
No like a lover we'll ken
an connect wi forever.
The hem of its goin drags across the sky.

Whit dae birds write on the dusk?
A word niver spoken or read.
The skeins turn hame,
on the wind's dumb moan, a soun,
maybe human, bereft.

Mr and Mrs Scotland are Dead

On the civic amenity landfill site,
the coup, the dump beyond the cemetery
and the 30-mile-an-hour sign, her stiff
old ladies' bags, open mouthed, spew
postcards sent from small Scots towns
in 1960: Peebles, Largs, the rock-gardens
of Carnoustie, tinted in the dirt.
Mr and Mrs Scotland, here is the hand you were dealt:
fair but cool, showery but nevertheless,
Jean asks kindly; the lovely scenery;
in careful school-room script –
The Beltane Queen was crowned today.
But Mr and Mrs Scotland are dead.

Couldn't he have burned them? Released
in a grey curl of smoke
this pattern for a cable knit? Or this:
tossed between a toppled fridge
and sweet-stinking anorak: *Dictionary for Mothers*
M: – Milk, *the woman who worries . . . ;*
And here, Mr Scotland's John Bull Puncture Repair Kit;
those days when he knew intimately
the thin roads of his country, hedgerows
hanged with small black brambles' hearts;
and here, for God's sake his last few joiners' tools,
SCOTLAND, SCOTLAND, stamped on their tired handles.

Do we take them? Before the bulldozer comes
to make more room, to shove aside
his shaving brush, her button tin.
Do we save this toolbox, these old-fashioned views
addressed, after all, to Mr and Mrs Scotland?
Should we reach and take them? And then?
Forget them, till that person enters

our silent house, begins to open
to the light our kitchen drawers,
and performs for us this perfunctory rite:
the sweeping up, the turning out.

Forget It

History in a new scheme. I strain
through hip, ribs, oxter, bursting
the cuff of my school-shirt, because
this, Mr Hannay, is me. *Sir!*
Sir!   Sir!
– he turns and I deflate and claim
just one of these stories,
razed places,
important as castles
as our own. *Mum!*

We done the slums today!
I bawled from the glass
front door she'd long desired.
What for? bangs the oven shut.
Some history's better forgot.
         So how come
we remember the years
before we were born? Gutters
still pocked with 50s rain,
trams cruised dim
streetlit afternoon; war
at our backs. The black door
of the close wheezed
till you turned the third stair
then resounded like cannon.
A tower of banisters. Nana
and me toiled past windows
smeared in black-out, condemned
empty stone. The neighbours had flit
to council-schemes, or disappeared . . .
Who were the disappeared? Whose
the cut-throat

razor on the mantelpiece, what man's
coat hung thick with town-gas,
coal, in the lobby press?
                              And I mind
being stood, washed like a dog
with kettle and one cold tap
in a sink plumbed sheer
from the window
to the back midden
as multi-storeys rose
across the goods-yard,
and shunters clanked
through nights shared
in the kitchen recess bed.

I dreamed about my sister in America,
I doot she's dead. What rural
feyness this? Another sibling
lost in Atlantic cloud,
a hint of sea in the rain –
the married in England,
the drunken and the mad,
a couple of notes postmarked Canada,
then mist: but this is a past
not yet done; else how come
our parents slam shut; deny
like criminals: *I can't remember, cannae*
mind, then turn at bay: *Why?*

what wants to know? stories
spoken through the mouths
of closes; who cares
who trudged those worn stairs,
or daily ran down the very helix
of her genes, to play
in now rubbled back greens?
What happened about my grandad? Why

did Agnes go? How come
you don't know

that stories are balm,
ease their own pain, contain
a beginning, a middle –
and ours is a long driech
now demolished street. *Forget it!*
Forget them that vanished,
voted with their feet,
away for good
or ill through the black door
even before the great clearance came,
turning tenements outside-in,
exposing gas-pipes, hearths
in damaged gables, wallpaper
hanging limp and stained
in the shaming rain.

History, Mr Hannay.
The garden shrank for winter
and Mum stirred our spaghetti hoops
not long before she started back
part-time at Debenham's
to save for Christmas,
the odd wee
luxury, our first
foreign
holiday.

Glyn Maxwell, 1962–

Glyn Maxwell has a Welsh background and grew up in Welwyn Garden City. He read English at Oxford and studied poetry at Boston University under Derek Walcott. His style has alternately excited and infuriated readers: syntactically elaborate and evasive, it incorporates love, politics and comedy and at times reaches for an Audenesque authority. *Tales of the Mayor's Son* (1990), *Out of the Rain* (1992) and *Rest for the Wicked* (1995) have established him as a leading younger poet. Maxwell has written verse plays, *Gnyss the Magnificent and Other Plays* (1993) and *Wolfpit* (1996), and a novel, *Blue Burneau* (1994). *The Breakage* appeared in 1998.

The Uninvited

We did not care muchly who, in the murder,
we turned out to be, providing whoever
used to inhabit the white chalk figure
frozenly pawing the blood-stained sofa
was not one of us but a different dier.

Dazzled colonel, distracted lover,
meddling couple of the library whisper,
cook unpoisoned or ponderous super,
sleuth, inheritor, innocent, actual
killer detected or undetected – it

didn't matter, but not that ended
individual manning the hour
he died in, as we would all one *dies*
man one hour, one mo, one jiffy.
Let us be Anybody other than Body!

But then we'd go on with the game all summer:
the three allowed queries on the hot verandah,
the fib in the gazebo, the starlit rumour,
the twitching curtain and the dim unhelpful
gardener's boy: it would all be explicable

soon in the lounge, and we didn't mind waiting.
No, what we minded was the hairless stranger
who wasn't invited and wouldn't answer
and had no secrets or skeletons either,
and got up later than us, then later

than even the bodies, and never turned in,
or blamed or suspected or guessed the outcome
but always was exiting, vanishing, going,
seen on the lawn – then there were more of them
massing, unarmed, parting when followed,

combing the country but not for a weapon
or corpse or clue, then halting and singing
unknown thunderous hymns to a leader
new on us all at our country party he'd
caught in the act of an act of murder.

The Eater

Top of the morning, Dogfood Family!
How's the chicken? How's the chicken?
Haven't you grown? Or have you grown,
here in the average kitchen all noontime
      down in the home, at all?

Bang outside, the bank officials
are conga-dancing and in their pinstripe
this is the life! But it isn't your life
out in the swarming city at crushhour
      dodging humans, is it?

Vacant city – where did they find it?
Blossom of litter as the only car
for a man goes by. When the man goes by
His girl will sulkily catch your eye:
      will you catch hers?

Snow-white shop – how do they do that?
Lamb-white medical knowing and gentle
man, advise her, assure and ask her:
do you desire the best for your children
      and theirs? Well do you?

Take that journey, delight in chocolate,
you won't find anyone else in the world,
lady, only the man, the sweet man
opening doors and suggesting later
      something – what thing?

Short time no see, Dogfood Family!
How's the chicken? How's the chicken?
How have you done it? Have you done it
with love, regardless of time and income
      and me? Who am I?

I am the eater and I am the eater.
These are my seconds and these are my seconds.
Do you understand that? Do you get that,
you out there where the good things grow
            and rot? Or not?

The Sentence

Lied to like a judge I stepped down.
My court cleared to the shrieks of the set free.
I know the truth, I know its level sound.
It didn't speak, or didn't speak to me.

The jury caught the tan of her bright look,
The ushers smoothed her path and bowed aside,
The lawyers watched her fingers as she took
Three solemn vows, her lipstick as she lied.

She vowed and lied to me and won her case.
I'm glad she won. I wouldn't have had her led
However gently into the shrunken space
I'd opened for her. There. There now it's said,

Said in this chamber where I sleep of old,
Alone with books and sprawling robes and scent.
With all I have, I have no power to hold
The innocent or the found innocent.

Simon Armitage, 1963–

Born in Huddersfield, Simon Armitage studied Geography at Portsmouth Polytechnic and worked for several years as a probation officer. With the publication of *Zoom!* (1989) Armitage became perhaps the most popular young poet to emerge since the Liverpool Poets in the 1960s – though Armitage is a far more complex and sophisticated writer than such a comparison might suggest. He combines 'ordinary' language (filtered through a study of the New York poet Frank O'Hara), comic patter, sinister monologues, astute social observation and ingenious formal improvisations which are somewhat indebted to Paul Muldoon. Authoritative and memorable at his best, he has been prolific in his first decade in print, producing *Zoom* (1989), *Kid* (1992), *Book of Matches* (1993), *The Dead Sea Poems* (1995), *Cloudcuckooland* (1997) and a collaborative book about Iceland with Glyn Maxwell, *Moon Country* (1996). A prose book about northern life, *All Points North*, appeared in 1998.

On Miles Platting Station

the stitchwort has done well for itself, clinging
as it must to the most difficult corners
of near-derelict buildings. In the breeze
a broken cable mediates between the stanchions
and below the bridge a lorry has jack-knifed

attempting to articulate an impossible junction. This,
after all, is only a beginning. After the long
chicanery of the express train picking its way
across the fishplates we will rattle backwards
through the satellite towns. From Greenfield we will

fail to hold our breath the length of the tunnel
then chase the sixpence of the entrance and burst
the surface of light just over the border.
It will be the hour after rain. The streets will shine
and the trees bend, letting their soft load.

Until then, the platform holds us out against the townscape
high enough to see how Ancoats meshes with Beswick,
how Gorton gives onto Hattersley and Hyde, to where
Saddleworth declines the angle of the moor.
Somewhere beyond that the water in Shiny Brook

spills like a broken necklace into our village.
The police are there again; boxhauling the traffic,
adjusting the arc-lights. They have new evidence tonight
and they lift it from behind the windbreak, cradle it
along their human chain and lower it carefully down

into Manchester.

Lines Thought to have been Written on the Eve of the Execution of a Warrant for His Arrest

Boys, I have a feeling in my water,
in my bones, that should we lose our houses
and our homes, our jobs, or just in general
come unstuck, she will not lend one button
from her blouse, and from her kitchen garden
not one bean. But through farmyards and dust bowls
we will lay down out topcoats, or steel ourselves
and bare our backs over streams and manholes.

Down Birdcage Walk in riots or wartime
we will not hear of her hitching her skirt
or see for ourselves that frantic footwork,
busy like a swan's beneath the surface.
But quickly our tank will stop in its tracks;
they'll turn the turret lid back like a stone;
inside, our faces set like flint, her name
cross-threaded in the barrels of our throats.

I have this from reliable sources:
boys, with our letters, our first-class honours
and diplomas we are tenfold brighter
than her sons and daughters put together.
But someone hangs on every word they speak,
and let me mention here the hummingbird
that seems suspended at the orchid's lips,
or else the bird that picks the hippo's teeth.

Boys, if we burn, she will not pass one drop
of water over us, and if we drown
she will not let a belt or bootlace down,
or lend a hand. She'll turn instead and show
a leg, a stocking, sheer and ladderless.
And even then we will not lose our heads

Simon Armitage – 489

by mouthing an air bubble out of turn
or spouting a smoke ring against her name.

But worse than this, in handouts and speeches
she will care for us, and cannot mean it.
Picture the stroke of the hour that takes her:
our faces will freeze as if the wind had changed,
we shall hear in our hearts a note, a murmur,
and talk in terms of where we stood, how struck,
how still we were the moment this happened,
in good faith, as if it really mattered.

To Poverty

After Laycock

You are near again, and have been there
or thereabouts for years. Pull up a chair.
I'd know that shadow anywhere, that silhouette
without a face, that shape. Well, be my guest.
We'll live like sidekicks – hip to hip,
like Siamese twins, joined at the pocket.

I've tried too long to see the back of you.
Last winter when you came down with the flu
I should have split, cut loose, but
let you pass the buck, the bug. Bad blood.
It's cold again; come closer to the fire, the light,
and let me make you out.

How have you hurt me, let me count the ways:
the months of Sundays
when you left me in the damp, the dark,
the red, or down and out, or out of work.
The weeks on end of bread without butter,
bed without supper.

That time I fell through Schofield's shed
and broke both legs,
and Schofield couldn't spare to split
one stick of furniture to make a splint.
Thirteen weeks I sat there till they set.
What can the poor do but wait? And wait.

How come you're struck with me? Go see the Queen,
lean on the doctor or the dean,
breathe on the major,
squeeze the mason or the manager,

go down to London, find a novelist at least
to bother with, to bleed, to leech.

On second thoughts, stay put.
A person needs to get a person close enough
to stab him in the back.
Robert Frost said that. Besides,
I'd rather keep you in the corner of my eye
than wait for you to join me side by side
at every turn, on every street, in every town.
Sit down. I said sit down.

Lavinia Greenlaw, 1963–

Lavinia Greenlaw was born in London and has worked in publishing and arts administration. Greenlaw is one of the few contemporary poets to take an active interest in science – astronomy, global warming, fertility treatment, plastic surgery, all variously suggestive of the fragility and malleability of the human form. Given the scale of Greenlaw's interests, what is also striking is the sense of emotional restraint carried by her poems. Her books are *Night Photograph* (1993) and *A World Where News Travelled Slowly* (1997).

The Innocence of Radium

With a head full of Swiss clockmakers,
she took a job at a New Jersey factory
painting luminous numbers, copying the style
believed to be found in the candlelit backrooms
of snowbound alpine villages.

Holding each clockface to the light,
she would catch a glimpse of the chemist
as he measured and checked. He was old enough,
had a kind face and a foreign name
she never dared to pronounce: Sochocky.

For a joke she painted her teeth and nails,
jumped out on the other girls walking home.
In bed that night she laughed out loud
and stroked herself with ten green fingertips.
Unable to sleep, the chemist traced each number

on the face he had stolen from the factory floor.
He liked the curve of her eights;
the way she raised the wet brush to her lips
and, with a delicate purse of her mouth,
smoothed the bristle to a perfect tip.

Over the years he watched her grow dull.
The doctors gave up, removed half her jaw,
and blamed syphilis when her thighbone snapped
as she struggled up a flight of steps.
Diagnosing infidelity, the chemist pronounced

the innocence of radium, a kind of radiance
that could not be held by the body of a woman,
only caught between her teeth. He was proud
of his paint and made public speeches
on how it could be used by artists to convey

the quality of moonlight. Sochocky displayed
these shining landscapes on his walls;
his faith sustained alone in a room
full of warm skies that broke up the dark
and drained his blood of its colour.

His dangerous bones could not keep their secret.
Laid out for X-ray, before a single button was pressed,
they exposed the plate and pictured themselves
as a ghost, not a skeleton, a photograph
he was unable to stop being developed and fixed.

Don Paterson, 1963 –

Don Paterson was born in Dundee. On leaving school he worked as a sub-editor on D. C. Thomson comics before beginning a career as a guitarist. He co-leads the jazz-folk ensemble Lammas. Paterson's work is complex and musical, with themes including the imagination, belief, love and sex. He is both a postmodernist and a formalist – a combination which indicates an early debt to Paul Muldoon, though Paterson's terrain is now clearly his own. See *Nil Nil* (1993) and *God's Gift to Women* (1997). *The Eyes*, translations from Antonio Machado, will appear in 1999.

The Lover

after Propertius

Poor mortals, with your horoscopes and blood-tests –
what hope is there for you? Even if the plane
lands you safely, why should you not return
to your home in flames or ruins, your wife absconded,
the children blind and dying in their cots?
Even sitting quiet in a locked room
the perils are infinite and unforeseeable.
Only the lover walks upon the earth
careless of what the fates prepare for him:

so you step out at the lights, almost as if
you half-know that today you are the special one.
The woman in the windshield lifting away
her frozen cry, a white mask on a stick,
reveals herself as grey-eyed Atropos;
the sun leaves like a rocket; the sky goes out;
the road floods and widens; on the distant kerb
the lost souls groan and mew like sad trombones;
the ambulance glides up with its black sail –

when somewhere in the other world, she fills
your name full of her breath again, and at once
you float to your feet: the dark rose on your shirt
folds itself away, and you slip back
into the crowd, who, being merely human,
must remember nothing of this incident.
Just one flea-ridden dog chained to the railings,
who might be Cerberus, or patient Argos,
looks on, knowing the great law you have flouted.

11:00: Baldovan

Base Camp. Horizontal sleet. Two small boys
have raised the steel flag of the 20 terminus:

me and Ross Mudie are going up the Hilltown
for the first time ever on our own.

I'm weighing up my spending power: the shillings,
tanners, black pennies, florins with bald kings,

the cold blazonry of a half-crown, threepenny bits
like thick cogs, making them chank together in my pockets.

I plan to buy comics,
sweeties, and magic tricks.

However, I am obscurely worried, as usual,
over matters of procedure, the protocol of travel,

and keep asking Ross the same questions:
where we should sit, when to pull the bell, even

if we have enough money for the fare,
whispering, *Are ye sure? Are ye sure?*

I cannot know the little good it will do me;
the bus will let us down in another country

with the wrong streets and streets that suddenly forget
their names at crossroads or in building-sites

and where no one will have heard of the sweets we ask for
and the man will shake the coins from our fists onto the
                                                    counter

and call for his wife to come through, come through and
                                                    see this

and if we ever make it home again, the bus

will draw into the charred wreck of itself
and we will enter the land at the point we left off

only our voices sound funny and all the houses are gone
and the rain tastes like kelly and black waves fold in

very slowly at the foot of Macalpine Road
and our sisters and mothers are fifty years dead.

Index of Poets

O'Donoghue, Bernard – 308

Padel, Ruth – 328
Paterson, Don – 496
Paulin, Tom – 366
Plath, Sylvia – 161
Porter, Peter – 124

Raine, Craig – 282
Reading, Peter – 321
Redgrove, Peter – 166
Redpath, Frank – 103
Reid, Christopher – 370
Rouse, Anne – 421
Rumens, Carol – 287

Salzman, Eva – 464
Scammell, William – 231
Shapcott, Jo – 410
Shuttle, Penelope – 330
Simmons, James – 173
Sisson, C. H. – 34
Smith, Ian Crichton – 111
Smith, Ken – 207
Smith, Sidney Goodsir – 36

Stevenson, Anne – 175
Sweeney, Matthew – 407
Szirtes, George – 351

Thomas, R. S. – 26
Thwaite, Anthony – 142
Tomlinson, Charles – 106
Tonks, Rosemary – 170

Index of Titles

Index of First Lines

Acknowledgements

Dannie Abse: 'Epithalamion' and 'Case History', from *Selected Poems* copyright © Penguin 1994, are reprinted by permission of the Peters, Fraser and Dunlop Group on behalf of Dannie Abse.

Fleur Adcock: for 'The Ex-Queen among the Astronomers' and 'Street Song' from *Selected Poems* copyright © Oxford University Press 1983.

Gillian Allnutt: for 'The Garden in Esh Winning' from *Nantucket and the Angel* copyright © Bloodaxe Books Ltd 1997.

Simon Armitage: for 'On Miles Platting Station' from *Zoom* copyright © Bloodaxe Books Ltd 1989; for 'Lines Thought to have been Written on the Eve of the Execution of a Warrant for His Arrest' from *Kid* copyright © Faber and Faber Ltd 1992; for 'To Poverty' from *Book of Matches* copyright © Faber and Faber Ltd 1993.

Peter Armstrong: for 'The Red-Funnelled Boat' from *The Red-Funnelled Boat* copyright © Macmillan Publishers Ltd 1998.

John Ash: for 'Cigarettes' from *Selected Poems* copyright © Carcanet Press 1996.

Martin Bell: for 'Winter Coming On' from *Collected Poems* copyright © Bloodaxe Books Ltd 1988.

James Berry: for 'On an Afternoon Train from Purley to Victoria, 1955' from *Hot Earth Cold Earth* copyright © Bloodaxe Books Ltd 1995.

Sujata Bhatt: for 'Muliebrity' from *Brunizem* copyright © Carcanet Press 1988.

Eavan Boland: for 'The Black Lace Fan My Mother Gave Me' and 'That the Science of Cartography is Limited' from *Collected Poems* copyright © Carcanet Press 1995.

Charles Boyle: for 'Sheds' from *Paleface* copyright © Faber and Faber Ltd 1996.

George Mackay Brown: for 'Hamnavoe Market' from *The Year of the Whale* copyright © John Murray Publishers Ltd 1965, and for 'Seven Translations of a Lost Poem' from *Winterfold* copyright © John Murray Publishers Ltd 1976.

Alan Brownjohn: for 'An Elegy on Mademoiselle Claudette' and 'The Ship of Death' from *Collected Poems*, Hutchinson, copyright © Alan Brownjohn 1988.

Basil Bunting: *Briggflatts*, I, from *The Complete Poems of Basil Bunting* copyright © Oxford University Press 1994.

John Burnside: for 'Source Code' from *Common Knowledge* copyright © Secker and Warburg 1991, and 'The Old Gods' from *Swimming in the Flood* copyright © Jonathan Cape 1995.

Duncan Bush: for 'Pig Farmer' from *The Hook* copyright © Seren Books 1987.

Norman Cameron: for 'Green Green is El Aghir' from *Selected Poems and Translations*, edited by Warren Hope and Jonathan Barker, copyright © Anvil Press 1990.

Ciaran Carson: for 'Dresden', 'Slate Street School' and 'Army' from *The Irish for No* copyright © The Gallery Press 1987, and for 'Drunk Boat' from *First Language* copyright © The Gallery Press 1993.

Charles Causley: for 'Armistice Day' and 'My Young Man's a Cornishman' from *Collected Poems* copyright © Macmillan Publishers Ltd 1997.

Eiléan Ní Chuilleanáin: for 'Letter to Pearse Hutchinson' and 'The Second Voyage' from *The Second Voyage* copyright © The Gallery Press 1986.

Gillian Clarke: for 'Llŷr', from *Collected Poems* copyright © Carcanet Press 1997.

Tony Conran: for 'Elegy for the Welsh Dead in the Falkland Islands, 1982' from *Blodeuwedd* copyright © Poetry Wales Press 1983.

David Constantine: for ' "All wraiths in Hell are single" ' and 'Watching for Dolphins' from *Selected Poems* copyright © Bloodaxe Books Ltd 1991.

Wendy Cope: for 'A Nursery Rhyme' from *Making Cocoa for Kingsley Amis* copyright © Faber and Faber Ltd 1986.

Robert Crawford: for 'Scotland' from *A Scottish Assembly* copyright © Chatto and Windus 1990, and for 'La Mer' from *Masculinity* copyright © Jonathan Cape 1996.

Fred D'Aguiar: for 'Home' from *British Subjects* copyright © Bloodaxe Books Ltd 1993.

David Dabydeen: for 'The Old Map' from *Turner* copyright © Jonathan Cape 1994.

Donald Davie: for 'Remembering the Thirties' and 'Time Passing, Beloved' from *Selected Poems* copyright © Carcanet Books 1985.

Nuala Ní Dhomhnaill: for 'Nude' and 'Aubade', translated by Paul Muldoon, from *Pharaoh's Daughter* copyright © The Gallery Press 1990.

Peter Didsbury: for 'The Hailstone' from *The Classical Farm* © Bloodaxe Books Ltd 1987; for 'Part of the Bridge' from *That Old Time Religion* copyright © Bloodaxe Books Ltd 1994; for 'The Romance of Steam' copyright © Peter Didsbury 1998.

Michael Donaghy: for 'The Tuning' from *Shibboleth* copyright © Oxford University Press 1988, and for 'Caliban's Books' copyright © Michael Donaghy 1996.

Maura Dooley: for 'St Brendan Explains to the Angel' from *Explaining Magnetism* copyright © Bloodaxe Books Ltd 1991.

Keith Douglas: for 'Vergissmeinicht' and 'How to Kill', from *The*

Complete Poems of Keith Douglas copyright © Oxford University Press 1978.

Carol Ann Duffy: for 'Warming Her Pearls' from *Selling Manhattan* copyright © Anvil Press 1987; for 'In Mrs Tilscher's Class' from *The Other Country* copyright © Anvil Press 1990; for 'Litany' and 'Prayer' from *Mean Time* copyright © Anvil Press 1993.

Ian Duhig: for 'Margin Prayer from an Ancient Psalter' from *The Bradford Count* copyright © Bloodaxe Books Ltd 1991, and for 'Lost Boys' from *The Mersey Goldfish* copyright © Bloodaxe Books Ltd 1995.

Helen Dunmore: for 'Those Shady Girls' from *Short Days, Long Nights: New and Selected Poems* copyright © Bloodaxe Books Ltd 1991, and for 'At the Emporium' from *Bestiary* copyright © Bloodaxe Books Ltd 1997.

Douglas Dunn: for 'From the Night-Window', 'The River Through the City', 'Empires', 'Loch Music' and 'Europa's Lover', vi, from *Selected Poems 1964–83* copyright © Faber and Faber Ltd 1986.

Paul Durcan: for 'Irish Hierarchy Bans Colour Photography', 'The Pietà's Over' and 'The Mayo Accent' from *A Snail in My Prime*, first published by the Harvill Press in 1993. Copyright © Paul Durcan 1993. Reproduced by permission of the Harvill Press.

Gavin Ewart: for 'Fiction: A Message', from *Be My Guest*, Trigram Press, copyright © Margot Ewart 1975.

U. A. Fanthorpe: 'Rising Damp' from *Standing To* copyright © U. A. Fanthorpe 1982. Reproduced by permission of Peterloo Poets.

Vicki Feaver: for 'Ironing' and 'Judith' from *The Handless Maiden* copyright © Jonathan Cape 1994.

James Fenton: for 'The Pitt-Rivers Museum, Oxford' and 'A Staffordshire Murderer' from *The Memory of War and Children in Exile: Poems 1968–83* copyright © Salamander Press/Penguin 1983. Reproduced by kind permission of Peters, Fraser and Dunlop.

Roy Fisher: for an extract from *City*, 'For Realism' and 'It is Writing' from *The Dow Low Drop: New and Selected Poems* copyright © Bloodaxe Books Ltd 1996.

Linda France: for 'Zoology is Destiny' from *The Gentleness of the Very Tall* copyright © Bloodaxe Books Ltd 1994.

John Fuller: for 'England' from *Collected Poems* copyright © Chatto and Windus 1996.

Roy Fuller: for 'Poem Out of Character' from *New and Collected Poems* copyright © Secker and Warburg 1985. Reproduced by kind permission of the estate of Roy Fuller.

Robert Garioch: for 'Elegy' from *Complete Poetical Works* copyright © Ian D. Sutherland. Reproduced by kind permission of the estate of Robert Garioch.

John Glenday: for 'The Empire of Lights' from *Undark* copyright © Peterloo Poets 1995.

W. S. Graham: for 'Loch Thom', 'Lines on Roger Hilton's Watch' and 'Johann Joachim Quantz's Five Lessons' from *Collected Poems* copyright © Faber and Faber Ltd 1979. Reproduced by kind permission of the estate of W. S. Graham.

Lavinia Greenlaw: for 'The Innocence of Radium' from *Night Photograph* copyright © Faber and Faber Ltd 1993.

Thom Gunn: for 'On the Move' and 'My Sad Captains' from *Collected Poems* copyright © Faber and Faber Ltd 1993.

Tony Harrison: for 'The Nuptial Torches', 'Them & [uz]', 'Continuous', 'The Rhubarbarians' and 'A Kumquat for John Keats' from *Selected Poems* copyright © Penguin 1987. Reproduced by kind permission of Gordon Dickerson.

David Harsent: for 'Endurance' from *Selected Poems* copyright © Oxford University Press 1989.

Seamus Heaney: for 'Punishment' and 'Exposure' from *North* copyright © Faber and Faber Ltd 1975; for 'The Underground' from *Station Island* copyright © Faber and Faber Ltd 1984; for 'Alphabets' and 'Clearances', iii, from *The Haw Lantern* copyright © Faber and Faber Ltd 1987; for 'Lightenings', viii, from *Seeing Things* copyright © Faber and Faber Ltd 1991.

W. N. Herbert: for 'Mappamundi' from *Forked Tongue* copyright © Bloodaxe Books Ltd 1994, and for 'Featherhood', v, and 'Ode to Scotty' from *Cabaret McGonagall* copyright © Bloodaxe Books Ltd 1996.

John Hewitt: for 'Because I Paced My Thought' from *Collected Poems* copyright © Blackstaff Press 1991.

Geoffrey Hill: for 'Funeral Music', iii, 'A Song from Armenia' and *Mercian Hymns* i and xxvii, from *Collected Poems* copyright © Penguin 1985.

Selima Hill: for 'Coition' from *A Little Book of Meat* copyright © Bloodaxe Books Ltd 1993; for 'The Voice of Bobo' from *Trembling Hearts in the Bodies of Dogs: New and Selected Poems* copyright © Bloodaxe Books Ltd 1994; for 'I Know I Ought to Love You' from *Violet* copyright © Bloodaxe Books Ltd 1997.

Michael Hofmann: for 'The Machine that Cried' from *Acrimony* copyright © Faber and Faber Ltd 1986, and for 'Lament for Crassus' from *Corona Corona* copyright © Faber and Faber Ltd 1993.

Douglas Houston: for 'The Welsh Book of the Dead' copyright © Douglas Houston 1998.

Ted Hughes: for 'Pike' from *Lupercal* copyright © Faber and Faber Ltd 1960; for 'Thistles' from *Wodwo* copyright © Faber and Faber Ltd 1967; for 'Sunstruck' from *Remains of Elmet* copyright © Faber and Faber Ltd 1979; for 'Tiger' from *A March Calf* copyright © Faber and Faber Ltd 1995.

Kathleen Jamie: for 'Skeins o Geese' and 'Mr and Mrs Scotland are Dead' from *The Queen of Sheba* copyright © Bloodaxe Books Ltd 1994; for 'Forget It', copyright © Kathleen Jamie 1996.

Alan Jenkins: for 'Visiting' from *Harm* copyright © Chatto and Windus 1994.

Elizabeth Jennings: for 'One Flesh' from *Collected Poems* copyright © Carcanet 1987. Reproduced by kind permission of David Higham Associates.

Patrick Kavanagh: for 'The Great Hunger', III from *Selected Poems* copyright © Penguin, 1996. Reproduced by kind permission of Peter Fallon.

Jackie Kay: for 'Teeth' from *Off Colour*, Bloodaxe Books Ltd, copyright © Jackie Kay 1998.

Brendan Kennelly: for 'Oliver to His Brother' from *Cromwell* copyright © Bloodaxe Books Ltd 1987.

Thomas Kinsella: for 'In the Ringwood' from *Another September* copyright © Dolmen Press 1958. Reproduced by kind permission of the author.

Linton Kwesi Johnson: 'Reggae Sounds' from *Tings and Times: Selected Poems* copyright © Bloodaxe Books 1991.

Philip Larkin: for 'Ambulances', 'The Whitsun Weddings', 'Livings' and 'Money' from *Collected Poems* copyright © Faber and Faber Ltd 1988.

Tom Leonard: 'Unrelated Incidents' 1 and 2 and 'Just ti Let Yi No' from *Intimate Voices: Selected Work 1965–83*, copyright © Tom Leonard 1993. Reproduced by kind permission of Vintage Press.

Gwyneth Lewis: for 'Going Primitive' from *Parables and Faxes* copyright © Bloodaxe Books Ltd 1995.

Liz Lochhead: for 'After the War' from *Bagpipe Music* copyright © Penguin 1991.

Michael Longley: for 'Wounds', 'Arrest' and 'Peace' from *Collected Poems* copyright © Jonathan Cape 1998.

George MacBeth: for 'The God of Love' from *Collected Poems 1958–82* copyright © Hutchinson 1990.

Norman MacCaig: for 'Summer Farm', 'The Shore Road' and 'Notations of Ten Summer Minutes' from *Collected Poems* copyright © Chatto and Windus 1990.

Roger McGough: 'Ex Patria' from *Defying Gravity* copyright © Penguin 1992. Reprinted by permission of the Peters, Fraser, Dunlop Group on behalf of Roger McGough.

Medbh McGuckian: for 'The Dowry Murder' from *The Flower Master and Other Poems* copyright © Oxford University Press 1993, and for 'From the Dressing Room' from *Venus and the Rain* copyright © The Gallery Press 1994.

Jamie McKendrick: for 'Ancient History' and 'The Spleen Factory' from *The Marble Fly* copyright © Oxford University Press 1997.

Sorley MacLean: for 'Hallaig' from *From Wood to Ridge* copyright © Carcanet Press 1989.

Ian McMillan: for 'Poem Occasioned by the High Incidence of Suicide amongst the Unemployed' from *Dad, the Donkey's on Fire* copyright © Carcanet Press 1994.

Sarah Maguire: for 'What is Transparent' from *Spilt Milk* copyright © Secker and Warburg 1991. Reproduced by kind permission of the author.

Derek Mahon: for 'A Disused Shed in Co. Wexford', 'Last of the Fire Kings' and 'Leaves' from *Poems 1962–78* copyright © Oxford University Press 1979; for 'Courtyards in Delft' from *The Hunt by Night* copyright © Oxford University Press 1982; for 'Death and the Sun' from *Antarctica* copyright © The Gallery Press 1985.

Glyn Maxwell: for 'The Uninvited' and 'The Eater' from *Out of the Rain* copyright © Bloodaxe Books Ltd 1992, and for 'The Sentence' from *Rest for the Wicked* copyright © Bloodaxe Books Ltd 1995.

Christopher Middleton: for 'Briefcase History' from *111 Poems* copyright © Carcanet Press 1983.

Robert Minhinnick: for 'Sunday Morning' from *Life Sentences* copyright © Poetry Wales Press 1983.

Elma Mitchell: 'Thoughts After Ruskin' from *People Et Cetera* copyright © Peterloo Poets 1987. Reproduced by kind permission of Elma Mitchell.

John Montague: for 'A Lost Tradition' from *Collected Poems* copyright © The Gallery Press 1995.

Edwin Morgan: for 'Stanzas of the Jeopardy', 'The Video Box', 25, from *Stobhill*: 'The Porter', 'On John Maclean' and 'The Sheaf' from *Collected Poems* copyright © Carcanet Press 1990.

Andrew Motion: 'The Letter' and 'The Lines', from *Dangerous Play: Poems 1974–84* copyright © Penguin 1985. Reprinted by kind permission of the Peters, Fraser, Dunlop Group Ltd.

Paul Muldoon: for 'Cuba', 'The Right Arm', 'The Frog' and 'Gathering Mushrooms' from *New Selected Poems 1968–1994* copyright © Faber and Faber Ltd 1996; for 'Something Else' from *Meeting the British* copyright © Faber and Faber Ltd 1987.

Grace Nichols: 'Blackout' from *Sunris* copyright © Virago 1996. Reproduced by kind permission of Curtis Brown Ltd., London, on behalf of Grace Nichols.

Norman Nicholson: for 'To the Memory of a Millom Musician' from *Collected Poems* copyright © Faber and Faber Ltd 1994. Reproduced by kind permission of David Higham Associates.

Bernard O'Donoghue: for 'A Nun Takes the Veil' from *The Weakness* copyright © Chatto and Windus 1991.

Ruth Padel: for 'Tinderbox' from *Rembrandt Would Have Loved You* copyright © Chatto and Windus 1998.

Don Paterson: for 'The Lover' and '11.00: Baldovan' from *God's Gift to Women* copyright © Faber and Faber Ltd 1997.

Tom Paulin: for 'Desertmartin' from *Liberty Tree* copyright © Faber and Faber Ltd 1983, and for 'Hegel and the War Criminals' from *Walking a Line* copyright © Faber and Faber Ltd 1994.

Sylvia Plath: for 'Poppies in October', 'The Moon and the Yew Tree', 'Sheep in Fog' and 'Edge', from *Collected Poems* copyright © Faber and Faber Ltd 1981.

Peter Porter: for 'Soliloquy at Potsdam', 'The Last of England' and 'The Future', from *Collected Poems* copyright © Oxford University Presss 1983, and for 'And No Help Came' from *The Automatic Oracle* copyright © Oxford University Press 1987.

Craig Raine: for 'A Martian Sends a Postcard Home' from *A Martian Sends a Postcard Home* copyright © Oxford University Press 1979, and for 'Retirement' from *Clay. Whereabouts Unknown* copyright © Penguin 1996.

Peter Reading: for 'Duologues', 3, from *Collected Poems 1: Poems 1970–84* copyright © Bloodaxe Books Ltd 1995; for an extract from *Stet* (*Collected Poems 2: Poems 1985–96*) copyright © Bloodaxe Books Ltd 1996; for 'Salopian' from *Work in Regress* copyright © Bloodaxe Books Ltd 1997.

Peter Redgrove: for 'Under the Reservoir', from *Under the Reservoir* copyright © Secker and Warburg 1992, reproduced by kind permission of David Higham Associates; for 'The Big Sleep' from *Poems 1954–1987* copyright © Secker and Warburg 1987.

Frank Redpath: for 'Transit Camp' from *How It Turned Out* copyright © The Rialto 1996. Reproduced by kind permission of the estate of Frank Redpath.

Christopher Reid: for 'A Whole School of Bourgeois Primitives' from *Arcadia* copyright © Oxford University Press 1979.

Anne Rouse: for 'The Hen Night Club's Last Supper' from *Timing* copyright © Bloodaxe Books Ltd 1997.

Carol Rumens: for 'The Hebrew Class' and 'Jarrow' from *Thinking of Skins: New and Selected Poems* copyright © Bloodaxe Books Ltd 1993.

Eva Salzman: for 'The Refinery' from *The English Earthquake* copyright © Bloodaxe Books Ltd 1992.

William Scammell: 'Bleeding Heart Yard' from *Bleeding Heart Yard* copyright © Peterloo Poets 1992.

Jo Shapcott: for 'Goat' from *Phrase Book* copyright © Oxford University Press 1992, and for 'Motherland' copyright © Jo Shapcott 1996.

Penelope Shuttle: for 'Taxing the Rain' from *Taxing the Rain* copyright © Oxford University Press 1992. Reproduced by kind permission of David Higham Associates.

James Simmons: for 'Censorship' from *Poems 1956–86* copyright © The Gallery Press 1986.

C. H. Sisson: for 'Eastville Park' from *Poems: Selected* copyright © Carcanet Press 1995.

Ian Crichton Smith: for 'The White Air of March' and 'How Often I Feel Like You' from *Collected Poems* copyright © Carcanet Press 1992.

Ken Smith: for 'Colden Valley' from *Terra* copyright © Bloodaxe Books Ltd 1986; for 'Writing in Prison' from *The heart, the border* copyright © Bloodaxe Books Ltd 1990; for 'The Man Who Ran Away from the Circus' from *Tender to the Queen of Spain* copyright © Bloodaxe Books Ltd 1993.

Sidney Goodsir Smith: for 'Slugabed', from *Under the Eildon Tree*, from *Collected Poems* copyright © Calder Publications Ltd 1975. Reproduced by kind permission of the estate of Sydney Goodsir Smith and the Calder Educational Trust.

Anne Stevenson: for 'North Sea off Carnoustie' from *The Collected Poems 1955–1995* copyright © Oxford University Press 1996.

Matthew Sweeney: for 'The Glass Coffin' from *The Bridal Suite* copyright © Jonathan Cape 1997, and for 'The U-Boat', from *Blue Shoes* copyright © Secker and Warburg 1989. Reproduced by kind permission of the author.

George Szirtes: for 'Ghost Train' from *Selected Poems 1976–1996* copyright © Oxford University Press 1996.

R. S. Thomas: for 'Welsh Landscape', 'Evans', 'On the Farm' and Reservoirs' from *Collected Poems* copyright © Macmillan Publishers Ltd 1993.

Anthony Thwaite: for 'Imagine a City' from *Selected Poems 1956–1996* copyright © Enitharmon Press 1997. Reproduced by kind permission of Anthony Thwaite.

Charles Tomlinson: for 'The Weathercocks' from *Collected Poems* copyright © Oxford University Press 1985.

Jeffrey Wainwright: for '1815' and 'The Dead Come Back' from *Selected Poems* copyright © Carcanet Press 1985.

Hugo Williams: for 'Bachelors' from *Selected Poems* copyright © Oxford University Press 1989.

John Hartley Williams: for 'A Word from Istvan Kovács' from *Canada* copyright © Bloodaxe Books Ltd 1997.

Kit Wright: for 'The Boys Bump-starting the Hearse' from *Poems 1974–83* copyright © 1988 Hutchinson. Reproduced by kind permission of the author.